CHINA AND OURSELVES

"China, for all its remoteness, is neither a collection of oddities, nor a field for our experiments, nor some Martian entity to be observed with detachment. We must understand China and ourselves at the same time; there is no other way. In the words of the medieval poem:

> . . . si est de nos:
> ne vos sans moi, ne moi sans vos!

(That's how it is with us: neither you without me, nor me without you)."

Francois Geoffroy-Dechaume, *China Looks at the World* (1967)

CHINA
AND OURSELVES

*EXPLORATIONS
AND REVISIONS
BY A
NEW GENERATION*

*EDITED BY
BRUCE DOUGLASS
AND ROSS TERRILL*

Preface by Edgar Snow

*Beacon Press
Boston*

Contents

Preface

EDGAR SNOW

This refreshing collective effort by young scholars and teachers is notably free of ideological prejudice and of preoccupation with the punditry of Cold Warriors who sometimes dominate China studies in the West. The book is awake and modern. It expresses a determination to "begin anew" with China, to use the words of an unkept promise of President Kennedy. It advocates the examination of our common dilemmas prospectively much more than retrospectively and reciprocally. It asserts an urgent need to utilize the present time to prepare for grave future problems of coexistence with a China respected as a peer.

All that is to be expected in thoughtful writers still in their twenties and thirties. They are citizens of the world—three Australians, one Canadian, one Filipino, one Japanese, and four Americans—who share a radical or Christian background as well as the special interests of Asian scholars. Of course each generation has the desire to begin all over again, as if the past were only a rough draft, as Chekhov said, so that "we could throw it all away and start on a clean sheet." And each generation is doomed to learn for itself that the new print cannot altogether obscure the underlying "old misunderstandings"—the heritage of myths or issues already decided by ancient wars. Aware of that, our authors nevertheless would free their own minds from vestigial error by discovering China as it looks to the Chinese. In that faith they project a new sense of mutuality and fellowship.

The People's Republic is, they say, the only China they have known; in accepting it as the great reality they have no guilt feelings about a "lost" China they never knew. Despite their youth these authors possess firsthand knowledge of their subject. A majority of them have visited the People's Republic and two have worked there as teachers. It is as children of the Vietnam experience that they feel purged of false assumptions of the Dullesian creed of encirclement and strangulation of China.

In common with other concerned Asian scholars, they proclaim themselves humanists who seek to bypass the old priorities given to policy questions of "national interest"—a flag-waving term too often used to obscure Pentagon–C.I.A. schemes, bureaucratic pressure groups, and their tie-ins with minority interests or war industry, special lobbies, and febrile propagandists of the Alsopian school of old-time religion known as chauvinism. These young scholars recognize instead the priority of the common interests of the Chinese people as their neighbors. In their search to identify those interests their approach is would-be scientific and experimental. Their aim is not only to place China in their own world of changing cognition, but to enter China's changing world by every means of cultural communication.

Such talk will be dismissed by some elderly Sinologists as ingenuous. But just where have the hard core Pekinologists got us? The young radicals are withdrawing from Cold War fun and games to chart the freedom at least to make their own mistakes. They are in it for culture, not for conquests. I wish them good luck on their independent journey, which offers exciting prospects between now and the year 2000. In an old Red China Hand such as myself it arouses admiration mixed with skepticism and some green-eyed envy.

Envy, because today's opportunities for systematic study of China did not exist when I first tried to penetrate beneath the surface of living Chinese society. My interest in Chinese communism began in the early nineteen thirties, when I was a journalist in Peking. I shifted to a job as a part-time lecturer at Yenching University, hoping to study there. I don't remember quite why, but I had become intensely interested in, and wished to write a book about, the "Chinese agrarian crisis." That was the euphemism we used to disguise illicit attempts to "understand" the nature of "Red-banditry." Unfortunately Yenching was as poor as I was; my wages were just enough to pay our house rent. In the hope of financing myself in a two-year program of Chinese language and field study I sought a grant from the Guggenheim Foundation. I believe only Guggenheim then gave fellowships for that kind of endeavor, but their grants were limited to one a year and provided barely enough to live on.

Jimmy Yen (Yen Yang-ch'u), who led the Ting Hsien (County) rural reform project, was my enthusiastic sponsor. Yen was successfully demonstrating—with Christian support—that cooperative social, economic, and political reforms could "save" rural China. He predicted that if the Kuomintang did not carry out his program on a nationwide scale the Communists would soon impose much more radical solutions by revolutionary means. The Generalissimo could not hear him. Nor was Guggenheim impressed by my own plea. Despite my formidable list of sponsors, that year the Guggenheim award went to a psychology professor at Columbia for "a study in Chinese racial and psychological characteristics as revealed by Chinese facial expression." That was, mind you, already several years after the Japanese conquest of Manchuria.

At the time I needed it, therefore, I was unable to get anyone to fund me for a year or two of study at the North China Language School, the missionary institution I wished to attend. I drew a line at becoming a missionary to learn the language and returned to Peking and full-time journalism. I soon began to write for the *Saturday Evening Post* and was then able to hire a Chinese tutor, but my lessons were intermittent and the results were meager. It was not until I lived for months in the Red regions of Northwest China in 1936 that I began to "think in Chinese" and for a period really had some practical grasp of the language. The moral of this story is simply that a generation ago it seemed impossible to one impecunious, nonofficial, nonmissionary young American to find anyone except the Red-bandits who would help him to a useful education in Chinese.

Diverted by the great war, work in Russia, Europe, and at home, until I "lost the United States" during the McCarthy years, I did not return to China again until 1960. Today the situation is vastly altered: Chinese Communists are providing no language courses for American students, but any patriotic American from President Nixon down (or up) would cheerfully dig into his jeans to finance any American youth to do a bit of China study in Peking if he could get a foot through the door. In days when almost any American could travel nearly anywhere in China, Washington politicians were not interested in Sinology; we were isolationists and had no plans to save China except through the missionaries and Standard Oil. Today we have thousands of non-missionary Americans qualified as Chinese language students, many by virtue of funds handed down through the C.I.A. and other official cultural organizations, to promote a rash of East Asia centers across the nation. Their chances of seeing China from within still remain, after twenty years of hostility toward Peking, rather bleak. It is better, of course, for non-Americans—but not much better.

These ironic reflections remind me of one of Chairman Mao's favorite dialectical truisms. "In given conditions a bad thing can lead to good results and a good thing to bad results." What is bad about our situation and what is good?

United States policymakers decided that the Communist victory in China was an extension of Russian power, pure and simple. The Chinese were puppets of the Russians, said John Foster Dulles, and Dean Rusk echoed him. In that belief Washington adopted Dulles' strategy of armed containment, aimed to isolate the People's Republic and bring about a counterrevolution. That eventually led to murderous assaults against the Vietnamese, rationalized for President Johnson by Dean Rusk as necessary to halt *Chinese* Communist aggression. If, at the start, Dean Rusk "had a bug up his ass about China," as the *New Republic* once asserted, the bug was soon joined by a Vietnamese variety. To contain the double itch in the twitch of the Secretary of State and those who suffered with him cost about a million casualties and destroyed hundreds of billions of dollars worth of treasure and property, representing thousands of billions of manpower hours of wasted effort. By 1970 the patent result of the illegal and immoral operations was (as even laymen such as myself were predicting in 1964) a very great political, spiritual, and military humiliation for the United States abroad and social degeneration at home.

Then what is "good" about the situation? For one thing, relevant here, the Americans were obliged to train thousands of new students to help carry on the task of containing Asian Communists in particular, and revolution in general. History has now revealed, to many of those trained, the magnitude of the American policymakers' ignorance about both Asia and revolutions. The new generation of Asian scholars is one very expensive but potentially valuable end product of bad strategic judgments.

It is a good thing for the United States to have a brush of China experts if Washington ever decides seriously to seek peace with China. Have the lessons of Vietnam and China at last been understood? If so, it may not be too much to hope that better use will be made of the younger China specialists than was true when Mr. Dulles so profligately threw our own best "China men" into the dust bin reserved for dissenters from his doctrines about Absolute Evil. (See Ross Terrill's trenchant review of the case of John Carter Vincent in these pages.)

One other good result could be a return to more civilized prewar American concepts which favored self-determination for China—and, theoretically, for all—and sought an independent and united China as the keystone to Asian peace and progress. Those were the phrases our Embassy bandied about in the thirties (and I liked them). But then our Ambassador in Peking also kept above his desk the Taoist maxim, *wu wei erh, wu pu wei*—roughly, "through not doing, things are done." So let us not end on a note of fantasy; miracles are not forecast for tomorrow.

Even if the United States were to demonstrate a maximum reasonableness and good will toward China, it would be no easy matter to reach the Chinese people with that news unless their leaders found it appropriate to their needs. Never has that country been more inaccessible to external influence, and never more on guard against liberalism and heterodoxy. During the twenty years lost in America's pursuit of chimeras in the Taiwan Straits and beyond, the rough draft of our good intentions was smeared with blood and tears but little brain sweat. Chinese leaders now often refer to "collecting their blood debts." Are they to be taken literally? Perhaps not entirely. But it is already too late to reach any understanding that would not involve a painful degree of humiliation for all those who still believe that American armed intervention is the right action in Vietnam and Taiwan. At the very least the terms must be the withdrawal of U.S. forces from

Chinese territory and complete recognition by our government of the People's Republic as sovereign over all China and sole representative of its people.

Geneva

Introduction

I

The authors of the following essays are younger than those who normally write books about China for Western readers. Most of them have recently completed, or are still at work on, doctorates. None of them saw China before 1949. None is old enough to have had any involvement, practical or emotional, with the *Kuomintang versus Communist* drama. They have known no trader's China or missionary's China. Having no vivid remembrance of the Communist "takeover," they do not have the consciousness that older observers have of China having moved out of the orbit of the West into that of a Communist "bloc." The China that first impinged on their minds was, in most cases, the China of the middle to late 1950s. In some respects this was the point of highest achievement for Mao's China; certainly China looked very good when compared, as it often was then, with India. To be sure, they are not ignorant of the past drama of China's relationship with the West: their teachers have seen to that. But over and above questions of knowledge or ignorance, each generation, or group within a generation, makes its own emotional point of entry into a problem. For these writers, it is a point of entry which takes Communist rule in China for granted.

The authors are, in a sense, inevitably children of Vietnam. They have taken up their intellectual task at a time when the American nation has appalled the world by its Vietnam crusade. Consequently, they are naturally more suspicious of United States policy in East Asia than a generation which grew up when the United States was generally anticolonialist in its attitudes. They tend to look again at the origins of the Cold War, in Asia as well as in Europe, to try and find the seeds of what became the Vietnam War (and related events). With Vietnam in the forefront of their minds, they appraise the foreign policy of China, on whose doorstep the war rages, more sympathetically than commentators who have long been convinced that it is China which threatens the United States and not the United States which threatens China. Having read daily for five years about the view of the world held by Lyndon Johnson and Dean Rusk, as well as that held by Ho Chi Minh and the NLF, they are not impressed with the dogma of the "End of Ideology" which was the political gospel of the 1950s in the West.

To be a new generation is not to be wiser or more correct than preceding generations. Each generation has its own illusions (as the next will soon remind *us*). There is a particular danger that young Western leftists may get into their heads the kind of notion of China that Voltaire had two centuries ago: China, not as it is, but China as a weapon with which to assault the unflattering *status quo* in the West. Against such a danger, research and rational, open discussion is one shield. A firsthand acquaintance with China can perhaps be another; Maoism can seem very different in Peking or Canton than in Paris or New York.

II

It cannot be said that this volume presents new and unified conclusions about China. There may, however, be a certain unity of method or perspective, which the above sketch anticipates. Members of a younger generation have to peer further into the future than their elders. They face a lifetime of living with China. Makeshift solutions to the problems posed by the tensions between China and ourselves will therefore not suffice. This concern for "tomorrow" lies behind the skepticism of many younger scholars about the policies of their governments toward China. It also explains their impatience with the fixation of public discussion on short-term problems, such as diplomatic recognition, the status of Taiwan, and the seating of Peking in the United Nations. Behind such problems lie much more fundamental ones like the cultural abyss involved in the hostility between China and America and the wielding of American power in the Far East.

It is not that policy problems are unimportant. Undeniably, the resurgence of China poses substantial problems of international relations. But when these problems are construed in the way they have been since the Korean War, the answers are almost certain to be unsatisfactory. Mostly we have shifted the focus of discussion from the policy questions to what one might characterize as the "human" questions. Of course, practical politics is hardly separate in fact from the human realities. Yet today abstractions like "Communist menace" and "balance of power" and the "domino" theory have taken on an independent reality of their own, and have made it almost impossible for us to deal justly with the human reality. As C. Wright Mills observed in *The Causes of World War Three,* a kind of Cold War metaphysic has crept into our thinking. Our attempt to get away from the metaphysic does not mean, of course, a permanent withdrawal from politics and policy issues. Rather, the conviction is that the policy questions must be subjected to a prior return to first principles. New policies can only be devised when the problems they are meant to answer have themselves been reformulated. Only thus can we transcend the absurd situation of treating diplomatic recognition or exchanges of newsmen as prime goals of international politics.

One frequent reason for the inadequacy of our policies is that they are based on assumptions that grow out of the application of norms external to China. Negative judgments are rendered because the questions asked and the norms applied are derived from other civilizations. Thus the politics of the People's Republic is decried because it fails to conform to cherished Western notions, like the rule of law, separation of powers, and institutional pluralism. And where it is seen that China simply will not fit the preconceived notions of the foreign observer, it is branded as "lunatic" or "incomprehensible."

For a new generation this will not do. Not only must we rethink the policy questions, we must rethink our assumptions about China. We must try to come to an understanding of modern Chinese history which appreciates the Chinese understanding.

Words that D. H. Lawrence addressed many years ago to a European audience bear repetition here:

It is hard to hear a new voice, as hard as it is to listen to an unknown language. We just don't listen. There is a new voice in this message. The world has declined to hear it. . . . Why?—Out of fear. The world fears a new experience more than anything. Because a new experience displaces so many old experiences. And it is like trying to use muscles that have never been used, or that have been going stiff for ages. It hurts horribly. (*Studies in Classic American Literature*, p. 11.)

The new experience of which Lawrence speaks is the American experience. Let the American experience speak on its own terms, he says; try to understand it on those terms. This is the only way to reckon with what is new in a lasting way.

So it may be today with the Chinese Revolution and ourselves. Both the "Chineseness" and the revolutionary quality of the new Chinese experience make it alien to most of us. To appreciate the terms which the Chinese themselves use to interpret their modern experience is not to accept the official Chinese Communist view. Mao is unlikely to achieve all that he is trying to do. But if he fails it will not be because he has failed to heed the doubts of Western liberalism. It would be more likely that what he is up against is the *Chinese* past, or certain persistent human weaknesses, or the pressures of a hostile military encirclement.

III

The appeal for perceiving China "on her own terms" is not simply a moral appeal. There is a more practical reason. As Professor Owen Lattimore put it in his inaugural lecture at Leeds University in England:

> Major events and significant developments in China can no longer be determined by other nations, friendly or hostile, which look in on China from the outside, assess its problems, and decide what to do. What matters now is how the world appears to the Chinese, looking outward, and what they decide to do about the world in which they are the largest nation.

Perhaps Lattimore slightly overstates the point, but it is an especially important one. An enormous change has come about in the last half-century: less than fifty years ago foreigners played on the body politic and spiritual of China as if China were primarily an object of other people's ambitions. Today she is once again master of her own affairs, and the views of the Chinese will be of major significance in determining the fate of us all.

To see China on her own terms will require a sense of history, in the double sense of memory and vision. In this area as in others, humane politics requires a broad sense of where we have been and where we are headed. The two are related; the farther we can look back, the farther we are able to look into the future. This is particularly important in approaching the Chinese, who are acutely conscious of history. Not only is there a consistent looking back and a continuous rehearsal of the liberation drama, there is also the neverending appeal to a vision of tomorrow. So we cannot understand China when our memories are confined to the Cold War.

The uniqueness of China can be overemphasized. If one error is to obscure its distinctiveness, another is to obscure the common humanity that the Chinese share with the rest of us. The writers of this volume have twin, dialectically related concerns: the commonality of the human condition, and respect for diversities. Somehow we have to "walk on two legs" with regard to these two concerns. There are certain dilemmas that China shares with all other human societies. As an international group, the authors of *China and Ourselves* have tried to keep these dilemmas in the forefront of their minds. The commonality has a very practical meaning today: the interdependence of all nations (symbolized by the power of nuclear weapons) puts China and ourselves in the same boat, as it were, facing whatever destiny the sober hopes of late twentieth century man may afford.

This implies a comparative perspective, but one somewhat different from that which has produced the Cold War conventional wisdom about China. Application of foreign concepts to China has usually been done only to show China in a bad light and to enhance the status of her antagonists. The attack on China's politics has usually carried the implicit message that the problems with which the Chinese Communists were attempting to cope had already been solved by the liberal democracies.

But China's antagonists struggle with problems just as deep as those of China. We must be ready to turn our critical eye on our own societies no less than upon China, and to see Chinese problems, where appropriate, as illustrative of the problems of modern societies in general.

At the same time it would be historically naive to talk too readily about "models"; to assume that what suits China would also suit India or France. This is what makes it somewhat absurd for non-Chinese to think of themselves as "Maoists." To be Maoist—when far from China—is hardly helpful to China, one's own society, or the relationship between the two. The editors of this book are certainly not Maoists. They admire the Chinese Revolution. But it is quite another thing to make China one's cause, or to allow the Chinese experience to dictate one's entire political stance. We would hope to be at once sympathetic toward and critical of the Chinese Revolution.

IV

Of the contributors, Stephen Fitzgerald is the most recent visitor to China, and his essay seeks to blend observations of China in 1968 with some assessment of the meaning of the Cultural Revolution then at its height. Utilizing his command of spoken Chinese, he became aware of the tensions and confusions in China today. He looks at the turbulent dynamics of the Cultural Revolution in some detail and on this basis draws some sober conclusions.

Taking a long-term perspective, Ray Wylie concerns himself with the aims of the Cultural Revolution. Though not unaware of its turbulent dynamics—he was a resident of Shanghai throughout the first stages of the Cultural Revolution—Wylie is not greatly disturbed by them. He believes it remained essentially under the control of the Maoist leadership. Since this leadership has evidently emerged triumphant from the Ninth Party Congress, it can be expected that the worthy goals of this upheaval have, at least in part, been achieved. They will thus become permanent features of Chinese Communist society, marking it off from, and making it superior to, other varieties of Communist society.

If the Cultural Revolution has been an extraordinary event, its elements were nevertheless in many instances previously present in the theory and practice of the Chinese Communist

Party. It is Jon Saari's purpose to analyze the "modernization" process in twentieth century China as a whole. In what respects has it been similar and dissimilar to the processes of modernization in other countries? As an historian, Saari is conscious of the characteristics—and limitations—which traditional Chinese society has bequeathed to China's revolutionary construction. Unlike Wylie, Saari is not sure that the Maoists will succeed in all, or even most, of what they are trying to do.

Scholarly work on China's place in the world has concentrated mainly on China and the West, very little on China's links with Asia. Feliciano Carino, who is from the Philippines, sees the Chinese Revolution from the standpoint of a region which is itself in the middle of an "unfinished revolution." The political triumph of the Chinese Communists over the twin enemies of feudalism and imperialism engages his attention. He is mindful of the problems China has in the past posed for the rest of Asia (infinitely greater than any China has posed for the West). But his admiration for the Chinese Revolution is stronger than his apprehensions about Chinese power; he sees its success as paradigmatic for all of underdeveloped Asia.

Tom Engelhardt's subject is American observers in China during the last year before the "Liberation" of 1949. Representative of the young radical students of Chinese affairs who have recently appeared in American universities, Engelhardt tries to expose the fallacies of the assumptions and perceptions of these American journalists, officials, and educators. He believes that their main concern was to promote a China that would "face West," and that their social experience of China (limited largely to the cities) made it impossible for them to understand Chinese communism.

Ross Terrill studies the case of the leading American "China Hand," who was accused of helping to "lose" China and subsequently purged under McCarthyist pressures. Utilizing the papers of John Carter Vincent, who had served in China and as director of the Far Eastern Office of the State Department, he reviews the reasons why U.S. policy met the fate it did, and asks to what extent Vincent was responsible. Pursuing comparisons with John Foster Dulles (who was instrumental in Vincent's departure from government service), Terrill concludes that Vincent was attacked essentially because he remained a professional diplomat at a time when the ideological crusades of the Cold War temporarily made ideological zeal a higher qualification for the U.S. Foreign Service than professional skill.

With Ed Friedman's essay, we pass to a "revisionist" assault on a piece of conventional wisdom about Chinese-American relations. With his eye close to the documentary record, Friedman asks if it is really true that the Taiwan problem—more particularly Peking's attitude toward it—is a brick wall blocking any improvement in U.S.–China relations. His answer is "No": that Peking is reasonably flexible about the future of Taiwan, that Washington has shown diplomatic ineptitude and a strange sense of priorities in allowing Taiwan to loom more important in U.S. foreign policy than China itself and the future of U.S.–China relations. Friedman also looks at the processes and pressures within America which have brought about this situation.

The last three essays take a comparative and theoretical approach to China. Neale Hunter, who found himself in 1966–67 in the striking situation of being a Roman Catholic living amidst the Cultural Revolution in Shanghai, raises the question of the relationship between Christian social thought and the social thought and practice of Chinese Communism. He argues that Western Christianity, leaning on Platonist Idealism, has lost its understanding of the Incarnation, and that the particular kind of materialism found in Marxism and Chinese tradition alike is both a rebuke to an abstracted Western Christianity and a fulfillment of certain aspects of the Christian gospel. Hunter's essay represents an attempt to transfer Christian approaches to the observation of China today to a quite fresh angle of vision.

Kazuhiko Sumiya applies the categories of the sociology of religion of Max Weber to the Long March. He points to Weber's preoccupation with socialism, arguing that Weber considered the idea of "emissary prophecy" to be central to true socialism. This idea, found in the *Communist Manifesto,* was abandoned by German socialism. Later, however, it was revived in Russian socialism, and, through the Revolution of 1917, it eventually found its way to its most dramatic contemporary expression in the

Thought of Mao Tse-tung. In a finely spun argument, Sumiya proceeds to compare the Long March of Mao with the Exodus of Moses from Egypt. He concludes that the historical and human significance of the Long March—not only for China but for the world—may come to match that of the Exodus.

Bruce Douglass also discusses socialism, attempting to assess the significance of the Chinese socialist construction in the light of the European socialist tradition. In an argument which moves from Fourier and Owen to Marx, then to the Bolsheviks, and finally to the Maoists, he seeks to demonstrate that the socialism of the Chinese Communists can be viewed as a return to the original wholeness of the socialist idea. Their roots in the countryside and the characteristic Chinese preoccupation with social relationships help account for this. The return is, however, seen as incomplete and ambiguous, partly because of the heavy Marxist-Bolshevik influence in Chinese Communist thought.

v

We are grateful to Edgar Snow for his Preface. This prince of China-journalists, author of the classic work on the Chinese Communist movement in formation (*Red Star Over China*) and of perhaps the best firsthand account of China today (*The Other Side of the River*), who first went to China in 1928 and has watched it with a steady eye ever since, has in several ways extended his hand across the generations to encourage us.

The impetus for *China and Ourselves* came from the China Study Project of the Political Commission of the World Student Christian Federation. The Project, which began in 1966 and ended in 1970, was designed to provide a forum for younger scholars to confront afresh the larger issues raised by the Chinese Revolution and the resurgence of China as a major power. Four international consultations were held under the Project's auspices, and many of the essays which appear in these pages are outgrowths of those meetings. Kazuhiko Sumiya's essay, for example, was first presented in 1966 at the consultation in Geneva, Switzerland, prior to its publication in *Tenbo* (Tokyo). Jon Saari's essay represents an elaboration of the themes first presented to the consultation in

Montreal, Canada, in 1968. The editors have been involved in the Project in each of its four stages. Others who have been a part of the Project at one point or another include Ray Wylie, Feliciano Carino, and Neale Hunter.

We wish to express our appreciation to the W.S.C.F., to the many people involved in various aspects of the Project, and to those churches whose financial support made the Project possible.

—B. D. and R. T.
Cambridge, Massachusetts
January 1970

CHINA AND OURSELVES

China visited: a view of the Cultural Revolution

STEPHEN FITZGERALD

Before the Great Proletarian Cultural Revolution revealed to the outside world the existence of deep divisions within the Chinese leadership, China specialists generally believed that the Chinese Communist Party had been able to preserve the fraternal solidarity of the revolutionary period and had established a unique record of monolithic unity. There had been challenges to the leadership of the Party Chairman, Mao Tse-tung, notably in the "anti-Party conspiracy" of Kao Kang and Jao Shu-shih in the early 1950s and in the circumstances surrounding the dismissal in 1959 of the Defense Minister, P'eng Teh-huai. But the top echelons of the Party had remained remarkably stable, and Mao appeared to have maintained his position without having to resort periodically to massive purges and without even feeling the need to create a secret police. This assumed special importance because of the example of the Russian Communists, who after a similar length of time in power, had experienced extraordinary intra-Party struggle.

The Cultural Revolution, therefore, took most professional observers of contemporary China by surprise, and for a time they were unable to discern what was happening or to predict how things might develop. This was not the case with some foreign news agencies and correspondents. In reporting the spectacular and disturbing events which marked the course of the Cultural Revolution, many of them hastened to advance "explanations" that were speculative and misleading. The Cultural Revolution was "China's Stalinist purge." Lin Piao's essay on the People's War published in September 1965 was "China's *Mein Kampf*"; the Red Guards were a kind of Hitler Youth Corps. The "Maoist Dynasty," following the pattern of the feudal dynasties of the past, was exhibiting the classic symptoms of imminent collapse. China had reverted to the warlordism of the Early Republic. The Chinese people were in revolt against the "oppressive dictatorship of the Chinese Communist Party." The news media in Taiwan and the Soviet Union were possibly the most inventive, and when invention failed them they pirated each other's ideas; in this way, rumors originating in Hong Kong arrived back in Hong Kong as the authoritative judgment of informed sources in Moscow!

Some of these explanations could of course be supported with reports from China and from what was being written on the wall posters and in unofficial newspapers. But they were misleading in that they almost always sought for precedents, attempting to explain the Cultural Revolution in terms of movements or events which had nothing to do with it directly. In my view, parallels with China's past or with the Soviet Union are, for the most part, not relevant.

The Cultural Revolution has been a singular event in the history of China as well as in the history of communism, not so much for what the leading participants hoped to achieve, but for their manner of achieving it. In the very simplest terms, the Cultural Revolution was a power struggle. It was not simply a struggle for personal ascendancy, although it did revolve around the personalities of Mao Tse-tung and the former head of state and designated successor to Mao, Liu Shao-ch'i. According to the official interpretation which emerged from Mao's camp, there had been serious divisions among the Party leaders on fundamental questions of doctrine and socialist construction in China. When these divisions developed into a struggle over which line should prevail, it became, by necessity, a struggle fought in ideological terms which do not necessarily reflect the actual nature of the differences. Instead of being characterized as a struggle between socialists, it was alleged to be a "struggle between two lines," the pure Marxist-Leninist line of Mao and the "counterrevolutionary revisionist" line represented by Liu Shao-ch'i (which the supporters of Mao claim had prevailed for half a decade before the Cultural Revolution). Liu and his supporters were accused of being "class enemies," of having "taken the capitalist road," and of seeking to restore capitalism in China. There is little evidence to substantiate this claim, and the accused certainly denied it. They did not, however, argue that Mao was wrong. They accepted, as the yardstick, loyalty to Mao's person and the socialist line embodied in his Thought, and asserted that, while they may have been guilty of mistakes, they were loyal to Mao and his Thought and innocent of the charge of seeking to overthrow communism.

To dismiss the Cultural Revolution as a typical Communist power struggle, however, would be to ignore its unique features. Two are of particular interest, both as extraordinary phenomena in themselves and as illustrations of personal idiosyncrasies in Mao's rule of China.

First, the struggle was not confined to the Party elite, or even to the broad mass of Party members. Mao and his supporters went outside the Party and appealed directly to students, factory workers, peasants, and laborers. In a one-party state, the people were exhorted by the Party leader to attack the ruling Communist Party. They were urged in a big character poster written by Mao himself to "bombard the headquarters." They were told to seize power from the Party elite, to expose and "drag out" the "capitalist-roaders" in positions of power, and to establish their own "revolutionary" organs of power.

This was an original and daring maneuver. According to Mao, control of the Party had been usurped by Liu Shao-ch'i, and his bourgeois philosophy had spread its corruption throughout the Party. It seems possible, however, that Mao could have chosen equally to wage an inner-Party struggle, since he himself claimed that the overwhelming majority of Party cadres were "good or comparatively good." In seeking to destroy the existing Party structure from without, Mao was risking a united opposition from the "powerholders," who had a vested interest in maintaining themselves in power. Moreover, despite six years of political tutelage of the army by Mao's "closest comrade in arms," Lin Piao, there was the possibility that regional commanders might take the side of "law and order" and support the powerholders against the revolutionary masses. An alternative possibility was that a popular assault on the Party might lead to civil war and the destruction of the Communist system in China. Mao's decision on this course of action was a measure of his confidence in his own appeal to the Chinese people, in the general acceptance of communism in China, and in his ability to reconstruct a discredited and demoralized Communist Party. In some respects, the course of the Cultural Revolution has shown that his confidence was not mistaken.

The second, and related, feature of the Cultural Revolution involved an even greater risk. The mobilization of forces against the Party elite was by no means a rigidly controlled operation. For a brief period, almost all the conventional controls which the Chinese Communist Party had imposed on the Chinese people were removed, and the people were free to criticize the Party itself: its decrees, its policies, and its organization. People were able to express themselves publicly in the wall posters which covered the cities and towns. At all levels, in every organization, meetings were held almost daily. These were not the carefully arranged meetings of the past. Some of them were convened by the existing Party committees, but mostly they were dominated by "Revolutionary Rebels," including many non-Party people, and the masses were urged to participate and speak out. Those who disagreed with the way the Cultural Revolution was being conducted in an organization formed their own faction and held their own meetings. The contending factions published their own newspapers that, together with the wall posters, provided the Chinese people with full and uncensored accounts of what was happening in all parts of China, and, incidentally, furnished the outside world with the most detailed information about events in China since 1949.

Clearly this was not a Stalinist purge. Although many people have fallen in the Cultural Revolution, it did not proceed by secret trials and sudden physical elimination of opponents, but by mass meetings, public criticisms and self-examinations, and investigations of personal histories conducted by, or at least made available to, all members of the organization or unit concerned. According to directives emanating from "Mao's proletarian headquarters," those accused of having committed mistakes were to be given the opportunity to defend themselves, or at least to admit to their mistakes, and to undergo correction. There was no officially sanctioned mass killing, and up to the time when the flow of unofficial newspapers from China dried up, it appeared that the few reported official executions concerned people guilty of "crimes against the state" rather than ideological deviations. The official denunciation in October 1968 of Liu Shao-ch'i, who until then had been referred to as "China's Khrushchev," was not followed by a massive purge within the Party. On the contrary, developments since then, and particularly since the Ninth Party Congress in April 1969, have been quite the reverse. Cadres accused of having committed mistakes, even serious mistakes, have been reinstated and are not to be subjected to further criticism.

A FIRSTHAND LOOK

In 1968, at the beginning of the third year of the Cultural Revolution, I went to China with a group of Australian and New Zealand students. This was the beginning of the period of consolidation for Mao and his supporters. Throughout the country there had been "power seizures," a process by which people who came to be known as Revolutionary Rebels replaced the established Party committees and the leading cadres in state organs. The powerholders who had been ousted were those described as bourgeois and revisionist elements and capitalist-roaders. Not all those subjected to attack were overthrown, and members of the established Party committees could themselves join forces with the Revolutionary Rebels. The situation varied tremendously in different areas and organizations, but in many cases the same people continued in power. Since early 1967, Mao had been attempting to formalize the power seizures through the Revolutionary Committees, provisional organs of power based on a "three-way alliance" of representatives of the People's Liberation Army (PLA), Revolutionary Rebel organizations, and revolutionary cadres, those who had joined in the power seizure or otherwise demonstrated their loyalty to the Thought of Mao Tse-tung. Approval from Mao or his Central Cultural Revolution Group had to be obtained by the Revolutionary Committees in the provinces and regions, which in turn approved the composition of committees at lower levels. The process of forming Revolutionary Committees that were acceptable both to the center and to the contending factions proved to be one of the most difficult problems of the Cultural Revolution.

In early 1968, although the first of the provincial Revolutionary Committees had been established (the crucial preliminary to the resolution of the conflict within each province) there was still serious fighting in many parts of China. The period of the most widespread disorder and uncontrolled physical violence had already passed, but there was still disruption in industry and dislocation in communications. In some provinces sporadic armed struggle was to continue for at least another year, and the whole country was still very much preoccupied with the business of making Cultural Revolution. The Red Guards, who had been in the vanguard of the criticisms and attacks and power seizures, were responding with reluctance to the instruction to return to their schools and universities. It was more than a year later before Mao felt sufficiently confident to convene the Ninth Party Congress to sum up the experience of the movement, to elect a new Central Committee, and to initiate discussion of new Party policies for a post–Cultural Revolution era.

Twenty-five days in company with fifty-six people was not an ideal way to visit China, but it was at that time the only way possible. Even without the Cultural Revolution, a short visit to China can be frustrating, even overpowering, frequently resulting in superficial generalizations. It is always difficult for a tourist to obtain a view of China as a whole, even if there are opportunities to travel widely and to talk with key Party figures; in this case there were no such opportunities. For those of us who had a professional interest in China, however, it was possible to distill some meaning from observations at ground level.

There were, moreover, certain advantages to traveling in China at this time. One was the power seizure in the China Travel Service. The old policy of carefully shepherding visitors from hotels to selected points of scenic or historic interest, model communes and factories, and so on, had been repudiated. This was interpreted as a deliberate attempt to isolate the visitor from the masses, to minimize politics, and to suppress the Thought of

Mao Tse-tung. The new line required that the visitor be given maximum exposure to the masses. Hence we were able to spend some time staying in students' dormitories and peasants' houses and a day with a unit of the PLA. More important, it was quite acceptable to miss scheduled visits, to wander off alone and talk to people in back streets without the aid of guides or interpreters.

A second advantage was that, due to the uneven progress of the Cultural Revolution in different parts of China, we were able to get some impression of the way in which it had developed and of the direction in which it was heading. There were striking contrasts among various places we visited, and particularly among the four provincial capitals of Chinan in Shantung Province, Wuhan in Hupei, Changsha in Hunan, and Canton in Kwangtung.

POLITICAL CORRECTNESS IN AN UNCERTAIN TIME

The most advanced of the provincial capitals was Chinan, where the provincial and municipal Revolutionary Committees had been established for almost a year. There were very few PLA to be seen, despite the presence of large crowds in the streets for the New Year holiday. Apart from the façade of wall paper, the city appeared to have returned to "normal," an appearance subsequently confirmed from the official and unofficial press. The powerholders had been overthrown and a new revolutionary order created. Mao's purpose had been achieved, apparently with a minimum of fighting between factions. It would have been difficult to form an adequate impression of the Cultural Revolution from Chinan alone.

By contrast, Changsha, the capital of Mao's home province of Hunan, was very backward, and in some ways revealed more about the Cultural Revolution than any other place we visited. This was not only because there was a serious struggle in progress, but also because there we experienced the culmination of a series of incidents involving our group, which in themselves gave an insight into Chinese society in the Cultural Revolution and the way in which factionalism and violent physical fighting developed.

For seventeen years, the Chinese had been accustomed to a

very strict ordering of society and to a dominant political doctrine to which they were required to demonstrate their fidelity
in words and actions. Even when there were radical changes in
Party policy, they were introduced through the established institutions. Through the normal state powers of control, particularly
the Party cadres and the communications media, the leadership
had been able to insure that the authority of the Party remained.
There may have been deviations from the Party line and doubts
about the Party's infallibility in some quarters, but it had been
relatively easy for cadres to survive by developing a sensitivity
to changes in the Party line, and for the ordinary people to live
with the system simply by going through the motions which the
Party required. Even the tendencies toward regionalism, which
the Cultural Revolution has revealed to have been greater than
previously suspected, did not necessarily lessen the importance
of doctrine, the authority of the Party, or the necessity for positive demonstrations of correct political thinking.

In the Cultural Revolution, there was still the pressure, greater
than ever before, for people to declare themselves in word and
deed. But how could they demonstrate their ideological purity
and political correctness when the Party itself was under attack?
Its policies in the years preceding the Cultural Revolution stood
condemned as the work of the "top capitalist-roader," Liu Shao-
ch'i. What was to be done when the "Great Helmsman" was no
longer steering a straight course or preparing the populace in
the established way for changes in direction? From the shifting
alliance of forces gathered around Mao's proletarian headquarters
in Peking there came a succession of confusing pronouncements.
Many who had "dared to rebel" early in the Cultural Revolution,
apparently with Mao's blessing, subsequently found themselves
accused of "left extremism," of "waving the red flag to oppose the
red flag," of being "left in form but right in essence." The pattern
of events may have been more clearly perceived by those involved in the struggle at the center, but most people, particularly
at lower levels, found themselves not only without a reliable
guide for action, but uncertain whether their past records might
conceal some unwitting deviation or serious mistake that would
render them vulnerable to criticism and attack.

This state of uncertainty was one reason for the plunges into extremism and violence. The Revolutionary Rebels attacked; the accused sought to defend themselves; those uncertain of their position launched preemptive attacks against the nearest available target; and all those involved strove to establish their fidelity in a situation where fidelity was no longer certain in any way other than reading, reciting, or acting out the Thoughts of Mao Tse-tung. Nor was there any guarantee that one's actions would be interpreted by others as consistent with the spirit of Mao's Thought. As a result, people were constantly involved in situations in which a statement or action would trigger off a spiral of responses in which everyone tried, with increasing intensity, to demonstrate Maoist purity to those around them, often with no concern whatever for the initial incident. It was extremely difficult to put a stop to this kind of cycle, for to do so might invite charges that one opposed Mao, or supported whatever was being criticized. This was the difficulty faced by those, such as Chou En-lai, who sought to exercise a moderating influence.

As a group, we became entangled in this kind of situation when one of our number said or did something which prompted a Chinese witness to set the cycle in motion. If it involved Revolutionary Rebels or the masses, nothing could be done to arrest it until justice seemed to be done. Justice, in this case, usually meant an apology in the form of a self-criticism, first written out and approved and then read aloud. The incidents which prompted these reactions ranged from the trivial to the provocative. There were straight breaches of Chinese laws or regulations, like photographing wall posters or construction sites. These were regarded as acts of hostility to China. There were thoughtless acts, construed as insults to China, to the Chinese people, and particularly to Mao. These included inking a false beard and moustache on a pocket calendar portrait of Mao, dropping a Mao badge on a radiator and burning a hole in Mao's face, leaving a Mao bookmark in a hotel wastepaper basket, and drawing a cartoon of the dog Snoopy (from the comic strip *Peanuts*) leaping in the air and shouting the slogan "Long Live Chairman Mao." There was also one deliberate provocation when one of the group went by himself into the Tien An Men square in Peking carrying a poster reading "Stop Interfering in Vietnam." Mindless of the possible consequences for the group or for the two Chinese involved, he persuaded two passers-by to take photos of him with his camera.

With one possible exception, the Chinese reaction to these incidents was not one of wild hostility or xenophobia, or a desire to "get" the foreigner. They simply expected conformity with a practice which was then standard in China, to which Chinese had to conform, and which to them, under the prevailing conditions, was the natural consequence of error. It was pointed out, moreover, that a Chinese in similar circumstances might be expected to submit to more than token self-criticism.

AN INCIDENT IN CHANGSHA

The possible exception occurred in Changsha. The Cultural Revolution had produced extreme reactions in Hunan Province. There were deep factional divisions, and an organization known as the *sheng-wu-lien* had established itself as the revolutionary authority in the province, with liaison centers in other parts of China, and had issued a manifesto which criticized, among other things, Mao's direction of the Cultural Revolution. The wall posters in Changsha revealed that the day before our arrival there had been a mass rally to denounce the *sheng-wu-lien* as a counterrevolutionary organization, and throughout the city there were posted handwritten copies of directives and denunciations from the leading members of the inner circle of Mao's supporters, the Central Cultural Revolution Group. The streets were full of armed soldiers, a car full of troops armed with rifles and submachine guns followed us on all arranged visits, and returning from an inspection of Mao's birthplace we encountered a military roadblock on the outskirts of the city. Part of our hotel was being used as a billet for units of the 47th Army, which is Hunan-based and would normally have its own permanent camps. The hotel itself was in the hands of a new Revolutionary Committee made up of very militant Revolutionary Rebels. From unofficial newspapers which reached Hong Kong after we left China, it appears that this was one of the most critical periods of the Cultural Revolution in Hunan Province.

In the course of the day spent at Mao's birthplace, there were a number of incidents which suggested a state of extreme tension. Returning to the hotel in Changsha, one of our group was confronted with a Mao bookmark which he had left in the wastepaper basket that morning, and accused by a hysterical Revolutionary Rebel of a gross insult to Mao and a crime against the Chinese people. The China Travel Service interpreters were holding a meeting in another part of the hotel, and the rest of our group were scattered in their hotel rooms. On the basis of our previous experience of such incidents, I suggested to the accused student that he agree to everything that was demanded until we could summon help. He agreed to do so, but the Revolutionary Rebel kept raising the demands, until finally he demanded nothing less than a complete self-examination before a full-scale mass rally of the Changsha masses. Despite the fact that even this was agreed to, the Rebel continued to shout abuse. When I suggested that continued abuse seemed unnecessary since his demands had been accepted, he became incensed, and, calling on a succession of irrelevant quotations from Mao, finally accused us both of being enemies of China: "Make trouble, fail, make trouble again, fail again . . . until their doom; that is the logic of imperialism and all reactionaries." I attempted to counter this quotation with others about making one-sided judgments and the need to conduct thorough investigation before having the right to speak. In other situations, arguing like this in their terms would have been acceptable, but to the Rebels in this hotel we were enemies and, therefore, did not have this right. In the meantime, the room had filled with Rebel reinforcements, and when the case was put to them, we came very close to being physically assaulted. Some of the more violent had to be dragged away from us; as they withdrew to consider our fate, the PLA arrived to show the flag at the end of the corridor. Since we were due to leave that night for Canton, we were hurried off to the station to wait for the train. The next morning the China Travel Service spokesmen apologized for the incident, agreeing that, while the student had made a mistake, the Rebels had been wrong in their handling of the case and in branding us enemies of China.

This incident illustrates how the conflict and much of the

violence occurred. There was a state of extreme tension, which followed the discrediting of an organization which many had supported, believing it to be Maoist and revolutionary. People were seeking to identify with a new, correct Maoist line, possibly with no clear idea of how this might be done. It was a time when accusations and counteraccusations caught up everyone involved in the Cultural Revolution in Hunan Province, a time of insecurity and uncertainty. It is quite possible that this particular Rebel was himself under some kind of pressure. Discovering a real imperialist, identifiable by his white skin, would be an almost foolproof and safe way to prove one's boundless love for Mao. Once it had started, others followed suit, outdoing each other in their quotations and verbal attacks, until some rushed forward to strike down the enemy, all in defense of Mao. The trifling incident which had sparked the affair appeared to have been forgotten.

This incident took place almost in the presence of the PLA and officials from Peking, and despite a sternly worded directive from Chou En-lai forbidding attacks of any sort on foreigners. It is not difficult to imagine, therefore, how Mao's Cultural Revolution, instead of being a united onslaught by the masses against the "handful" of bourgeois revisionists, capitalist-roaders, and other class enemies, resulted in the formation of contending factions. The development of factionalism, subsequently condemned as petit bourgeois, was further compounded by the suspension of the controls which normally operate in China, and by personal animosities and personal power ambitions which come to the surface in any fluid political situation. Nor is it surprising that factional fighting frequently resulted in physical violence and armed struggle.

Not all of the violence was political. Some of it came from the criminal element of society, released either from prison or from the strong political and social restraints which had made crimes of violence unusual in Communist China. This was apparent both from the unofficial newspapers reaching the outside world and from the official notices for wanted criminals which were to be seen everywhere in the Chinese cities and towns. From the notices I was able to study, it appeared that, while some of the accused were said to be speculators, profiteers, and "Chiang Kai-shek agents," the great majority of wanted criminals were accused of capital crimes and crimes like assault with violence, looting, and arson. The remarkable thing about this kind of violence, which is common in Western societies, is that it broke out only when the normal functioning of the government was disrupted.

Political violence appears to have occurred in most parts of China and to have been initiated both by the contending factions and by the capitalist-roaders and "class enemies." It ranged from fist fights and beating of people undergoing struggle and criticism to pitched battles between factions fought with weapons stolen from the PLA. The attitude of Mao and the Central Cultural Revolution Group toward political violence was ambiguous. At no time did they actually advocate the use of physical violence, although some of their slogans and directives could have been interpreted as condoning the use of force. From time to time they issued strict injunctions against the use of violent struggle and physical fighting. In many cases they were unable to control outbreaks of violence, and in the early stages they were reluctant to do so for fear of suppressing the revolutionary ardor of the masses. Moreover, the Cultural Revolution struggle had been cast in the form of a revolution against sections of the ruling party elite; thus it was possible to apply Mao's dictum that "revolution is not a dinner party, or writing an essay, or painting a picture, or doing embroidery."

WHY NO CIVIL WAR?

Throughout the Cultural Revolution, and particularly in 1967, many commentators believed that the movement would end in civil war, or warlordism, or otherwise destroy everything the Chinese Communist Party had built up during its seventeen years in power. This was not an unreasonable point of view, since there was abundant evidence of factional fighting and bloodshed and breakdowns in the administrative system, and the Chinese media were full of reports about regionalism and the establishment of "independent kingdoms." The question that should be asked now is why this did not happen.

One answer is that the Cultural Revolution was primarily a struggle between Communists. If there had been as many American or KMT spies and saboteurs in China as the official interpretation and the unofficial newspapers suggested, then the Party would have encountered major problems in controlling the Chinese people long before the Cultural Revolution, and the outside world would have been fully informed on what was happening in China, including the discussions of the Party Central Committee. The accusations against spies, traitors, agents, and saboteurs must be understood as a stratagem in the power struggle and not as a reflection of fact. Moreover, not only did those accused of being bourgeois revisionists or capitalist-roaders protest that they were loyal Communists, but some of the leading targets of Mao's attack are generally believed to have represented views within the Party which were the exact opposite of bourgeois revisionism at home and capitulationism abroad. They may not have been loyal Maoists; they may have been opposed to Mao personally or to his brand of socialism. But there is very little evidence to sustain the claim that there was within the Party a conspiracy working for the overthrow of communism and the restoration of capitalism.

Another reason why the country did not disintegrate was that the level of violence and chaos varied from province to province; within each province physical struggle occurred in isolated incidents or waves, with periods of relative quiet in between. This enabled Mao to concentrate his energies where the problems were greatest, and on occasion to transfer units of the armed forces to areas where violent struggle threatened to develop into civil war. Should the situation deteriorate once more, the events of the Cultural Revolution seem to indicate that collapse of the present system, disintegration into full-scale civil war, or regional warlordism is unlikely unless there are outbreaks of faction fighting simultaneously in most areas of China. Such a situation almost occurred in the middle of 1967, and it was avoided only when Mao decided to involve the PLA.

The People's Liberation Army was a crucial factor in Mao's campaign. He was at first reluctant to involve the armed forces. They were instructed not to intervene, and at one point there were reports that armed soldiers offered no resistance when their weapons were seized by Red Guards and others. When it became necessary to impose some order on the contending factions and to insure the political survival of the approved candidates, the Public Security forces were unsuitable, and they were also by this time regarded as politically suspect. The PLA was ordered to intervene, at first "to support the left, but not any particular faction." Increasingly, the army functioned as the most significant political force in China by virtue of its dual political and police functions. On the one hand, PLA representatives comprised the third, and in many cases the leading component in the Revolutionary Committees; on the other, the PLA was responsible for maintaining law and order and preventing physical fighting by all factions, not simply those opposed to the "left." By early 1968, while it was not possible to see anything of the political function, the police role was very much in evidence. In addition to guarding communications and public buildings, armed soldiers were on traffic duty and patrolling the streets, and small units were stationed in factories, schools, universities, and offices. Although there is known to have been considerable opposition in some areas to the reimposition of law and order, from the limited range of observation available to us it seemed that the PLA is held in genuine esteem and that a good relationship exists between the masses and the army personnel involved in civilian duties. This relationship is, of course, part of the tradition which has been nurtured in the PLA since its early revolutionary days, and one of the most important aspects of its role as a peacetime army.

There were two important reasons why Mao was able to mobilize the PLA in his own support. Following the dismissal of P'eng Teh-huai in 1959, the armed forces had been "remolded" under the guidance of Mao's closest ally (and now his nominated successor), Lin Piao. They were subjected to intensive political training, and in the years immediately preceding the Cultural Revolution there were a series of campaigns to "Learn from the PLA" and emulate a succession of revolutionary PLA heroes.

During the Cultural Revolution, although there were some instances of open opposition, the majority of the armed forces appear to have continued to support Mao, or at least Lin Piao. They became a symbol of loyalty to Mao and his Thought, and they were not supposed to be criticized or attacked. For foreigners at least—and, judging from the responses whenever the subject was mentioned, for Chinese also—it was not permissible even to suggest that there might be capitalist-roaders within the PLA.

The second factor that operated in Mao's favor was that the role he required of the PLA was that of a moderating and stabilizing force. By the time the PLA was fully engaged, the Cultural Revolution had already passed the stage of "pulling down" and "dragging out" and "daring to rebel," and had reached the point where Mao was ready to begin constructing a new revolutionary order. Despite its revolutionary origins, the PLA tended to be a conservative force, opposed to extremism and violence. The known instances of PLA resistance to the Cultural Revolution appear to have been based partly on opposition to the anarchist tendencies which the Revolution encouraged. The task of restoring and maintaining order, therefore, was quite acceptable to the regional commanders, and there have been indications that the right to exercise this function was the price demanded by some regional commanders in return for their commitment to Mao and the "proletarian headquarters."

One other element which may have helped to prevent a total breakdown during the Cultural Revolution was the influence of the so-called moderates in Mao's camp, particularly Chou En-lai. Chou's political survival has caused some speculation, since he had been closely associated with many of the policies condemned as the work of Liu Shao-ch'i, and in the early 1930s, before Mao gained control of the Party, he was even aligned with forces opposed to Mao. It could be argued that the Cultural Revolution was no more than a personal power struggle cloaked in ideological verbiage, that past records were important only as a weapon to be used against present enemies, and that Chou's survival was not regarded as a threat to Mao's supremacy. But Chou did more than survive; he was a major actor in the Cultural Revolution. Part of his strength lay in the fact that he had not indulged in theoretical writing; he was very powerful, but he had not attempted to establish himself as a Party theoretician, a potential rival to Mao (or anyone else) for the mantle of correct interpreter of the Marxist-Leninist canon. More important, it seems that Mao may have regarded Chou as essential to his purpose. He had the respect of the Chinese people as well as administrative and negotiating ability that would be useful in holding the country together and in rehabilitating the shattered structure when the struggle was over. But presumably Chou could have chosen not to side with Mao; he could hardly have been happy with the prospect of tearing down the structure which he had done so much to fashion. But Chou was also an old revolutionary, and his judgment may have led him to the conclusion that Mao would prevail. In that event, he may have decided that his only recourse was to join forces with Mao in order to be able to exercise influence wherever possible and to salvage what he could.

It is difficult to estimate the effect of Chou's influence in the Cultural Revolution. In some ways he was in his element. Since 1949, he has become known as an international diplomat and negotiator, but his experience in this field goes back to the 1920s when he acted as mediator between contending and deeply divided Communist and leftist factions among the Chinese in Europe. His attempts to exercise a moderating influence in the Cultural Revolution were not always successful, but many of the directives calling for restraint and forbidding excesses were issued in his name. When he was attacked by zealous revolutionaries, he was protected by the personal intervention of Mao. From the unofficial newspapers, a picture emerges of Chou's efforts at mediation. He appears to have worked constantly, at times around the clock, to reconcile the warring factions. He spent his time in long meetings and discussions with representatives from Peking and from the provinces, displaying an amazing knowledge of personalities and details of local situations. There were other central leaders involved in these discussions, but none seemed to have the understanding of the problems and the grasp of detail that Chou displayed, and some, including Mao's wife Chiang Ch'ing, were more concerned with obtaining support for their own views than with mediation. Respect for Chou's authority and admiration for his personal qualities was apparent everywhere I went in China. His role was possibly the most difficult and demanding in the Cultural Revolution, and there is considerable justification for the view that he emerged as the outstanding figure in China.

CULTURE AND CULT

The term Cultural Revolution seems highly inappropriate to the political struggle and violence which provided the central drama. The field of education, literature, and the arts, nevertheless, was one of the major areas of struggle, both because of the terms in which the struggle was being waged and because of the strategic role of propaganda, education, art, and literature. In a report to the Central Committee in 1962, Mao had said that "to overthrow a political power, it is always necessary first of all to create public opinion, to do work in the ideological sphere. This is true for the revolutionary class as well as for the counterrevolutionary class." The thrust of Mao's attack, therefore, was directed at those responsible for molding "public opinion" in the fields of propaganda and culture, which were alleged to have been taken over by Liu Shao-ch'i and his supporters. It was in these areas that the lines along which the Cultural Revolution was to develop were first given a public airing through attacks on leading historians and literary figures in 1965. They were accused of glorifying China's feudal past and, in their writings about the past, of making veiled attacks on Mao. In 1966, the attack was extended to "the den of the revisionist clique—that impenetrable and watertight 'independent kingdom,'" the Peking Municipal Party Committee, which was said to have fostered and protected the counterrevolutionary revisionists in the literary and art world.

Questions of education and culture, therefore, were major issues in the ideological struggle; and since the struggle was waged in terms of the Thought of Mao Tse-tung, it was in these fields that the effects of the development of the Mao cult were most apparent. The cult was not entirely the product of the Cultural Revolution, but previously it had been in very low key; according to Chinese sources, it was officially discouraged. The extent to which the cult had developed by early 1968 was surprising, even when one had watched it closely from the outside. We were introduced to it as soon as we crossed the Chinese border, in a session with a Mao Tse-tung Thought Propaganda Team. Most organizations have their own Propaganda Team, but there are also roving Teams, particularly for the countryside, and, more recently, special Teams composed of politically acceptable workers and peasants stationed in schools and universities. They disseminate the Thought of Mao Tse-tung in a variety of ways, but for the foreign visitor at that time, their only method of propaganda was a performance in which the actors recited, sang, danced, mimed, or acted the Thoughts, the Poems, and the Deeds. They were very active in railway stations, trains, airports, and planes. I confess to a moment of terror when the crew of our plane began a kind of soft-shoe shuffle up and down the aisle, singing and banging a tambourine, the unmarked grey uniforms making it impossible to tell whether the pilot and navigator were among the performers.

Rituals had developed to the point where it was difficult not to interpret them as part of a religious worship. In some places it was the custom to salute portraits of Mao, in others people were bowing from the waist, and I was told that many people outside Peking face in the direction of Peking when they recite or think about the Thoughts, since that is where the "Red Sun" lives and breathes. Every meeting or discussion begins and ends with quotations from Mao, introduced as the "supreme instructions," and read aloud, often at breakneck speed. Meetings are also accompanied by incantations shouted in unison; for example, Mao is wished "A Long, Long Life" three times, while Lin Piao is wished "Eternal Health" twice. In private houses, portraits or busts of Mao now stand where the portraits of ancestors once stood; and the range of acceptable items of decoration and ornamentation was narrowing to Mao artifacts. Mao portraits and quotations adorn the public buildings and temples as well as stationery, newspapers, and buses and trains. Chinese officials, questioned about delicate points of Chinese policy (for example, why did China not go to the support of the Hong Kong Communists and liberate the Hong Kong masses), often replied with the enigmatic response that this was part of Mao's "great strategic plan." No one knows what Mao's great strategic plan is, but it was a convenient response, rather like saying something is the Will of God.

Mao's birthplace at Shaoshan, about 100 kilometers from Changsha, is now a national shrine. Since part of the ritual of the pilgrimage to Shaoshan is a symbolic Long March, we were asked to walk the last three kilometers into the village; many Chinese, particularly at the height of the Red Guard movement, walked from much farther afield. The village was full of pilgrims, adding to the growth of the cult by their presence and by little refinements, like burying Mao badges or copies of three of Mao's essays known as the "Constantly Read Articles" at the back of his parents' house. The house itself is quite spacious, appropriate to his parents' middle peasant status. This has not, however, deterred the guardians of the shrine from downgrading their class status; they have not yet reached poor peasant status, but were described as "ordinary peasants," a classification which does not exist in Mao's analysis of the classes in Chinese society. Inside the house we were shown the bed on which Mao is alleged to have been born, and informed that this was the bed on which the "reddest, reddest sun first rose."

The village also boasts a Mao museum, in which photographs had been tampered with, a practice which does not appear to have existed before the Cultural Revolution. One photo of a Party Central Committee meeting in 1958 had more blank spaces than occupied seats. Another shows a procession of Party leaders riding in jeeps through Peking, including one jeep carrying a grey smudge. When questioned, the guide could only reply that the person in question was politically suspect, with a phrase which might be freely translated as "that man's got problems." Also in the museum were paintings of the young Mao in a white flowing robe and sandals, his head illuminated by a mysterious light, extending his hand in a gesture of benediction toward a group of adoring masses.

The achievements attributed to Mao in the history of post-1911 China were quite staggering. From Shaoshan and from conversations in other parts of China, I learned that Mao is held responsible for most of the important revolutionary developments, having personally led the May Fourth Movement in 1919 and the great strikes of the 1920s. He is said to have been the first Marxist-Leninist in China, and to have personally created and led the Party from the time of its inception. The process of expanding Mao's role in the history of the revolution is less evident in the post–World War II period. What has been done is to omit all reference to Mao's part in those policies which are now considered unsavory, like the overtures made to Chiang Kai-shek at the end of the war, now one of the "crimes" of Liu Shao-ch'i. In the words of one group of revolutionary activists in Shanghai, Mao is not just the greatest man in Chinese history, or simply the greatest Marxist-Leninist of all time, but the greatest man the world has ever known.

To a certain extent, the cult was a necessary component of the Cultural Revolution. To achieve his purpose, Mao had to establish that he was right and that everyone who opposed him was wrong. He had to establish the absolute supremacy of his line as embodied in his writings or Thought. His immediate supporters promoted his Thought, not only as doctrinally correct, but as the "creative development" of Marxism-Leninism, containing eternal truths. From this it was only a short step to the personality cult, the elevation of Mao to semidivine status. In discussions of the cult and its various manifestations, I was told repeatedly that Mao did not encourage it, but that it was the spontaneous expression of the boundless love of the masses. There was little evidence, however, that he discouraged it. It was politically useful during the Cultural Revolution, and presumably it will continue to be so, both for Mao and for his successors, if similar struggles develop in the future.

One interesting feature of the cult is that it does not seem to be based on fear. In the popular mind, Mao's elevation above the ranks of ordinary men tends to remove him from the arena of sordid power politics and absolve him of responsibility for "excesses" committed in his name. It is difficult to tell how deep the cult goes in the minds of the Chinese people. For some, observance of the ritual may be simply a matter of survival. But recent reports suggest that it may be taking root as a kind of popular religion, and that it may have developed a momentum which could persist even if the Party leadership should decide to discourage it. If the extreme manifestations of the cult of Mao could be tempered with practical leadership, it might prove not to be the sinister or ridiculous phenomenon which some Western commentators believe it to be. It has the potential to provide the Chinese people with a general guide for action, and as a source of inspiration it is by no means unsuitable for meeting China's problems.

THE SHRINKAGE OF CULTURE
AND THE PARALYSIS OF EDUCATION

In literature and the arts, the influence of the Cultural Revolution and the cult of Mao was most clearly manifest in what was available for mass consumption. The doors were closed, literally, on the culture of the past, but it was not destroyed. When it was realized that the Red Guards were tempted to accept at face value the injunction to "destroy the old," all libraries and museums were closed and guarded. In the only library I was able to see, at Futan University in Shanghai, the collection, ranging from classical Chinese texts to pirated copies of Western scientific journals, appeared to be untouched. It was not possible to visit the museums in Peking, and the Ming Tombs were open only to foreigners, a sore point with some of the masses, who had scrawled their opinions on the outside wall. Where the Red Guards had managed to daub slogans before the authorities stepped in, as in the Summer Palace, their handiwork was being removed. This leads one to suspect that Mao and his supporters have no intention of repudiating or destroying the culture of the past; it has simply been quarantined until such time as a politically acceptable approach to it has been worked out.

Contemporary culture for the masses is a different question. So much of the post-1949 literature has come under criticism that anyone who puts pen to paper can no longer be sure what is printable; thus he tends to write straight Mao or nothing at all. The bookshops I visited were full of Mao's writings in one form or another; some of them had nothing else, and those that did had only a limited range of technical and scientific works. The secondhand bookshops were either closed or converted to Mao shops. The writings of Lu Hsun were the only examples of pre-1949 literature of high literary merit that survived the Cultural Revolution, but despite the fact that he was extolled for his social and so-called revolutionary writing, I could not find a collection of his works for sale.

The range of theatrical performance was reduced to eight "outstanding examples" of revolutionary drama, produced either as operas, ballet, or plays. Most of them concern the period before 1949, relying on black and white issues like fighting the KMT or the Japanese. In Chinan we saw a splendid production of one of these operas that retained many of the traditional features of Peking opera, from the makeup of the actors to the responses of the audience, and that appeared to be concentrating on the artistry and neglecting the political content. Film studios were producing nothing but documentaries on the Cultural Revolution. For entertainment, the masses had the eight outstanding dramas, the performances of the Propaganda Teams, and a handful of old films about the war against Japan.

The educational system was completely paralyzed, not only because the students were called out to be the vanguard of Mao's attack, but also because the system itself and the philosophy that is alleged to have guided it were under attack. When the time came for the students to return to their schools and universities, the Mao cult presented a serious obstacle to the resumption of classes. Since all traditional subjects were suspect, what could be studied other than Mao? Yet the whole country was supposed to be a "great school for the study of Mao Tse-tung's Thought," so what was the point in having educational institutions? Temporary arrangements operating in 1968 were heavily weighted in favor of Mao study. One suggested timetable posted on a wall in Futan University solved the problem of what to do with Thursday after three days of Mao study: it left Thursday blank.

Some commentators have seen the impact of the Cultural Revolution on education as an unqualified disaster, but this may not, in fact, be the case. In recent years, China, like other underdeveloped countries, has suffered from overproduction in certain fields. This was evident in the competition for jobs and in the efforts of the Party to send graduates, not only to the countryside or remote areas, but to posts for which they were overqualified or for which their training was unsuitable. Moreover, it is not as though the disruption of education meant that a whole generation missed out completely on education, and it is possible that a new approach to education may prove to be beneficial in the long run. Despite the Cultural Revolution demand to abandon the teaching of "useless" subjects, Mao's pronouncements on education have left the door open for the training of technicians and experts. A draft program for primary education circulated officially in 1969 is interesting, not for the time it reserves for Mao study, but for the amount of time it proposes to devote to technical subjects. University education will present the toughest problem, but technical and scientific research, which in China is conducted in separate institutes rather than in institutions of higher education, appears to have enjoyed a certain immunity from the ravages of the Cultural Revolution.

THE POLITICAL EDUCATION OF YOUTH

The most visible influence of the Cultural Revolution on China's youth was the Red Guard movement. Mao himself appears to have become disillusioned with the outlook and behavior of the Red Guard activists; he ordered them back into the schools and turned to the workers and peasants as his most reliable support. The Red Guards were not a unified organized body of Communist youth. They had a hard core of "Mao's little generals," disciplined and authoritarian, who earnestly went about the task of attacking the Party elite and anyone else they judged to be opposed to Mao. They exercised their power with cruelty and often with violence, and when they had finished they turned to fighting among themselves. That was what persuaded Mao to order them back to the schools. There were also those who took advantage of their unfettered power to strike out in all directions against authority and society, who indulged in wanton acts of destruction, and who led the Red Guard movement toward anarchy. Finally there were those, possibly the majority, who took the armbands and student identity cards that entitled them to free travel and meals and went out to enjoy their freedom.

The reaction to the reimposition of restrictions on their freedom, and the subsequent movement to send vast numbers of educated youth to the countryside, varied according to the motivations and experiences of the individual Red Guard. Many of them resented the fact that they were relegated to a very minor position in the new revolutionary order, and many have resisted. From the official press, it appears that many more have taken the criticisms of the educational system to a point where they are convinced that formal education is worthless. A byproduct of the Red Guard movement, and possibly part of Mao's "great strategic plan," was the experience of the students in their period of freedom and power: they traveled all over China. Many of those I spoke to had been to every province; others had walked over the trail of the Long March. To some extent this experience may have overcome the "softness of youth" that Mao complained about to Edgar Snow in 1965. More interesting was that the students I spoke to, admittedly a minute sample of the total student population, seemed to have acquired a very real sense of identity with their country. Student life in China, because it was demanding and constricting, tended to set the students apart from the Chinese masses, despite periods of compulsory labor, a requirement that Mao claims was ignored more than it was observed, and that peasants described as a token, an excuse for a holiday. From their Cultural Revolution travels, the Red Guards gained some idea of the huge size of China and the vast problems it faces. They were able to witness firsthand the problems of poverty and underdevelopment and the way in which a bureaucracy can become bogged down, corrupt, and inefficient. Those who had been selected to participate in the administration of the schools and universities appeared to have accepted the role with a sense of dedication and responsibility. Mao may have found the Red Guards wanting in the Cultural Revolution, but he may find that their experience proves to be a valuable asset in future programs for construction and development, in the rebuilding of the Party, and in the reconstruction of the state bureaucracy.

"TWISTS AND TURNS
ON OUR WAY FORWARD. . . ."

At the Ninth Party Congress in April 1969, Mao said: "We hope that the present Congress will be a congress of unity and a congress of victory and that, after its conclusion, still greater victories will be won throughout the country." The Ninth Congress may have signaled the formal conclusion of the Cultural Revolution, but it was neither a congress of unity (it took ten days to appoint a Central Committee) nor an end to Mao's problems. The economy was barely beginning to recover. For almost three years economic planning and capital investment had been suspended and there had been a decline in foreign trade. Not surprisingly, economic problems had caused increasing concern as the Cultural Revolution progressed, a concern reflected in the slogan "Grasp Revolution and Promote Production," and economic rehabilitation was one of the first priorities after the movement had passed its peak. Among the members and alternate members of the new Central Committee, there were the Chairman and Vice Chairman of the State Planning Commission and nine of the Ministers and Vice Ministers of economic ministries. There is no guarantee that future economic policy may not produce radical experiments or a second Great Leap Forward, but the survival of some of these men suggests that, for the time being at least, there may be some compromise on the question of economic development. There have also been indications that policies and programs that were denounced during the Cultural Revolution as the work of Liu Shao-ch'i may now be providing the guidelines for economic planning.

Political problems remain on a number of levels. If the suspicion is correct that many key figures at the center and in the provinces joined the Mao camp only as a result of compromise, then Mao will have to hold the Party together in a spirit of compromise or face the prospect of open resistance to his authority, renewed regionalism, and a resurgence of factional fighting. This would seem to militate against a reappearance of the forces of the "extreme left" which dominated the Cultural Revolution for a time, but these forces are by no means extinct. There are those within the Party, including Chiang Ch'ing, who encouraged militant struggle and resisted attempts to bring the Cultural Revolution on to a more moderate tack. There is no reason to suppose that they are fully reconciled to the present trend, and both the so-called moderates as well as Mao and Lin Piao are sensitive to the dangers from this direction. At the Ninth Congress, Lin warned that "in the course of carrying out our policies at present, there still exists the struggle between two lines and there is interference from the 'Left' or the 'Right,' " and he predicted that there would be "difficulties and twists and turns on our way forward."

In the provinces there are signs of continuing discontent and resentment among the Revolutionary Rebels, who, having been eased out of their positions of power, are witnessing the wholesale rehabilitation and reinstatement of the cadres they had "dragged out" and criticized and overthrown. There have been reports of a reemergence of factionalism and some instances of open fighting. If the radicals at the center were to decide to move, they would find a ready response among the disappointed power-seekers in the provinces.

Against this must be set the new power of the PLA, which is now firmly entrenched at all levels. The army has not taken over, but it has strong representation in the new Central Committee and in the provincial Revolutionary Committees, and it has established a position as the guardian, not only of Mao's Thought, but also of law and order. There seems no immediate prospect that the PLA will attempt to become an independent political force so long as the present trend continues. But it seems certain that the PLA will resist any developments that may result in lawlessness, and that it will attempt to suppress factional fighting wherever it occurs. With its new authority and power, it might be difficult for even Mao to order the PLA to stand aside as he did during the Cultural Revolution.

One serious obstacle to the mobilization of the Party and government bureaucracies, despite the rehabilitation of cadres, is a tendency to inertia, an unwillingness to take decisions or responsibility. This is hardly surprising, given the cadres' experience in

the Cultural Revolution. The complete revitalization of the Party
and the government will not be possible until the Cultural Revolution is well and truly over, and this cannot be said in the
late 1960s.

The final resolution of the Cultural Revolution struggle will
be in sight when creative artists are free to test their abilities on
something other than Mao and the Cultural Revolution; when
historians are once more able to investigate the past; and when
the study of traditional subjects is resumed, particularly in higher
education. When that time comes, it may be assumed that the
Party leaders are sufficiently confident of themselves and of each
other to permit writing about China's feudal and more recent
past, plays and films of low political content, and teaching of
something other than Mao's Thought or basic practical skills,
without the fear that such activities represent heretical doctrines,
hidden attacks, or the preparation of "counterrevolutionary
public opinion" for the purpose of the overthrow of the existing
order.

To the outside world, the most immediate signs of an end to
the Cultural Revolution will be seen in China's foreign relations.
Despite the violent assaults on foreigners in China, the extraordinary behavior of some Chinese diplomatic missions, and the
vituperation leveled at China's "enemies" abroad, foreign relations were peripheral to the central struggle, and there is little evidence to support the view that excesses were part of a consciously
formulated policy. The violent responses of 1967 were part of
the Cultural Revolution reflex, a reaction geared to the domestic
situation rather than to the outside world; and some of the worst
excesses were the work of people in the Foreign Ministry and in
the Central Cultural Revolution Group who were subsequently
condemned and removed. The end of the Cultural Revolution
should result in confident and coordinated initiatives and the
emergence of a consistent line in foreign policy. The direction this
line will take is not yet clear. The lingering influence of the Cultural Revolution radicals may push it in a militant direction, or
at least restrict the maneuverability of those who would prefer a
more flexible policy, particularly in relations with imperialists,
revisionists, and reactionaries. Foreign observers were quick to

point out the militant aspects of Lin Piao's remarks on foreign relations at the Ninth Congress. But the tentative initiatives that began in 1968, while they are as yet too insubstantial to constitute a cohesive pattern, suggest that the ultimate trend may equally be in the other direction, and that Lin's reference to "peaceful coexistence" may not be irrelevant to future foreign policy. The Chinese leaders are confronted with grave domestic problems. To the potential threat to China's security posed by the United States there has been added a new threat from the Soviet Union, which is regarded in China with extreme concern. It is not an ideal time for revolutionary offensives or belligerence, but a time for seeking international support and creating a new balance by means of new alignments—possibly, if both sides are prepared to compromise, even with the United States.

The meaning of the Cultural Revolution

RAY WYLIE

Whither China? This question has plagued generations of Chinese intellectuals and has dominated the life of Mao Tse-tung. In Mao's youth China was an unhappy country, wracked by internal chaos, foreign domination, and intellectual confusion. With the Communist victory of 1949, however, all seemed to change for the better. The nation was united, the foreigners expelled, and the awesome task of reconstruction begun. In an address to the nation on September 21, 1949, Mao declared confidently that the Chinese people had "stood up," and that China had entered a new historical epoch.

Yet today people around the world remain confused about the nature of the Chinese Revolution. In recent years, their confusion has been deepened by the upsurge of the Cultural Revolution, a gigantic political movement now entering its fifth year. Without a doubt, the single most important issue at stake in the Cultural Revolution was control of the Chinese Communist Party (CCP). As far as we can discern, the supporters of Mao Tse-tung (Maoists) have definitely gained the upper hand in the struggle, and have effectively won over, neutralized, or destroyed all rival groups, including the followers of Liu Shao-ch'i. Certainly this is indicated by Liu's dramatic decline as an effective political figure and by the Maoists' domination of the Ninth Party Congress in April 1969. It seems clear that the Maoists are in an unusually strong position in China today, and they are likely to maintain this supremacy for some time to come.

But while it is quite possible to chronicle the rise and fall of individual leaders during the Cultural Revolution, this does not explain what has happened in China during the past few years. People are not content to leave the issue here; they want to uncover the origins of the Cultural Revolution, and to arrive at some estimate of its significance for China. In light of the dominant role of the Maoists, an understanding of their motives in the Cultural Revolution will very likely provide us with valuable insights into these aspects of the movement. Accordingly, we shall examine those aspects of Maoist thought and policy which throw light on the origins and significance of the upheaval that burst upon China in the spring of 1966.

By the 1920s most intellectuals were convinced that China must follow the path of revolution. Sun Yat-sen was an active revolutionary all his life, Chiang Kai-shek regarded himself as one, and Mao Tse-tung became a Marxist-Leninist early in his political career. So by the early decades of the twentieth century China was clearly headed along the road to revolution. What was not so clear, however, was the *kind* of revolution this was to be. Mao's victory in 1949 settled this key issue; the Chinese Revolution was to emulate the Russian Revolution of 1917. As Mao phrased it, China was prepared to "lean to one side," the side of the Soviet Union.

So in broad terms the question of China's destiny had been answered; the former "Middle Kingdom" was to follow the path of the Marxist-Leninist revolution. But still a great deal remained uncertain. First, what should be the model for the revolution? Second, whom should the revolution serve? Third, what kind of society should the revolution build? The answers to these questions did not come easily. For years before 1949, Mao and his fellow revolutionaries quarreled over the appropriate responses. But with victory the quarrels were put aside and a workable consensus reached on the basis of "leaning to one side." The immediate tasks confronting China's new leaders were to reunify the country, end foreign domination, get the economy moving, and launch an extensive program of social reform. By 1965, however, the consensus had floundered and these three questions were posed anew: China entered the period of the Cultural Revolution.

A REVOLUTION ON WHAT MODEL?

During the Cultural Revolution, the Chinese press has denounced with equal vigor "American imperialism" and "Soviet revisionism." Chinese opposition to American foreign policy is nothing new; what is new, however, is the degree to which the Soviet Union has been castigated for both its internal and external policies. Back in 1949, at the very moment "American imperialists" were hastily packing their bags in Shanghai, "Soviet comrades" were being invited to Peking. Today few Russians are to be found in China; they have joined their American counterparts in exile from the People's Republic.

Why? The question of the leadership of the revolution has been approached by the Chinese Communists from two sides, that is, as a class question and as a national question, the second of which concerns us here. The Communists generally attacked the Nationalist Party (KMT) on the grounds that it was not only a reactionary party, but it was also a "lackey" of foreign imperialist states. In an age when Chinese political values and systems were crumbling, it was difficult for Chinese leaders to be truly independent either intellectually or organizationally. If Chiang Kai-shek chose to seek inspiration and assistance from the West, Mao Tse-tung quite openly leaned to the side of the Soviet Union. Both leaders, of course, ran the risk of becoming puppets of foreign interests, and CCP charges that Chiang had "sold out" to Washington were countered by KMT accusations that Mao had become the "tool" of Moscow.

Indeed, one of the early problems of the CCP was that of maintaining its independence vis-à-vis the powerful Communist Party of the Soviet Union (CPSU). This is not to say that early Chinese Communist leaders consciously served Russia at the expense of China, but only that they often felt Moscow's judgments and policies to be superior to their own, and ultimately beneficial to China. While recognizing the "leading position" of the CPSU, however, Mao Tse-tung in particular came to insist that China must find her own path to socialism. As early as 1925, for example, Mao fell afoul of the Moscow-oriented CCP Central Committee for the heresy of believing that the peasants, not the urban proletariat, were the key to success in China. In the early 1930s he struggled against the leadership of the "Returned Student" clique, who had arrived from Moscow armed with much revolutionary theory and little else. And in an interview with Edgar

Snow on July 23, 1936, during the early stages of the Sino-Japanese War, Mao declared that "we are certainly not fighting for an emancipated China in order to turn the country over to Moscow." [1] With the signing of the Sino-Soviet Friendship Treaty in 1950, Mao's policy was clear: China should lean to one side, but should not lose its footing.

But events soon proved that this was a most difficult stance to maintain, for the relationship that developed was in the nature of things one-sided. From being the student of the West, China now became the student of the Soviet Union. Soviet ideas, Soviet techniques, and Soviet experts flooded into China, and thousands of Chinese students and intellectuals flocked to the universities of the Soviet Union. In the light of Mao's career, it could not be expected that he would look upon this development with uncritical approval; in its effort to lean to one side, China was perhaps in danger of losing its balance. "Learn from the Soviet Union!" was an appropriate slogan for the day, but hardly a permanent orientation of China's development.

By late 1959 Mao had apparently concluded that further close cooperation with the Soviet Union was not desirable. The basic differences between the Soviet and Chinese roads to socialism were becoming agonizingly clear, and the Soviet leadership appeared unwilling to tolerate Chinese political experimentation. The agricultural communes, for instance, were denounced by Nikita Khrushchev himself. More important, however, the Russian leaders were interfering in Chinese domestic politics. In 1959, for example, Defense Minister P'eng Teh-huai, who had increasingly fallen under Soviet influence, entered into communication with Russian leaders without the knowledge, let alone approval, of the CCP Central Committee. As in Germany in the 1930s, there were many Communists in China who were amenable to Soviet influence on both domestic and foreign issues.

THE BREAK WITH THE RUSSIAN MODEL

By 1960 Mao and his supporters appear to have decided to loosen ties with the Soviet Union and go it alone. Cooperation with Russia dwindled, the CCP entered into open polemics with

the CPSU, the "Thought of Mao Tse-tung" began to assume prec-
edence over orthodox Marxism-Leninism, and Soviet influence
in all spheres of life began to recede. Having rejected the uncritical acceptance of all things Western, the CCP now took steps to
cast off the Russian embrace. With Mao at the helm, China was
moving swiftly into uncharted waters.

It was not unnatural that such a radical venture should generate a good deal of opposition throughout the country. When
China departed from the Western path in 1949 there were many
Chinese who had much to regret. Likewise, many influential
people throughout the country probably thought it foolhardy to
stray far from the side of the Soviet Union and the "socialist
camp." From the available evidence, it appears that ex-President
Liu Shao-ch'i was one such individual. A former student in the
Soviet Union, a revolutionary who spent much of his career in
the urban trade union movement, an organization man who was
deeply involved in the administration of the CCP, Liu no doubt
had more in common with the Soviet leaders than had Mao. In
any case, the strong support the Soviet leadership gave Liu during
the Cultural Revolution would indicate that they had much in
common with him.

In launching the Cultural Revolution, the Maoists claimed they
were making a major contribution to the theory and practice of
Marxism-Leninism, and were in fact elevating it to a "completely
new stage." Lenin and his contemporaries, it was claimed, had
effectively solved the question of the revolutionary seizure of
state power by the proletariat, but had not been able to solve the
problem of preventing a "capitalist restoration" in later years.
Consequently, the Russian Revolution of 1917 had been progres-
sively subverted from the time of Khrushchev on, with the result
that the Soviet Union today is not a legitimate Marxist-Leninist
state. Hence, the present Soviet leadership can no longer command the support of the Russian people, let alone that of people
abroad. With the Cultural Revolution, however, Mao Tse-tung
has solved the problem of preventing a "capitalist restoration,"
and has thus preserved the Marxist-Leninist character of the
Chinese People's Republic. In effect, the Maoists were declaring

the Russian road to socialism bankrupt, making China the new center of international Marxism-Leninism.

Indeed, it seems clear that the Cultural Revolution represents the "qualitative leap" from Russian Marxist traditions to a distinctive Chinese or Maoist variety. During the initial upsurge of the movement, young people especially were called upon to "sweep aside" manifestations of "Soviet revisionism" in China, and they eagerly responded. In addition, the works of Marx, Engels, Lenin, Stalin, and other non-Chinese Marxist theorists became increasingly difficult to buy, Soviet and East European publications were removed from public sale, and people from all walks of life were encouraged to denounce "Soviet revisionism" at every available opportunity. There was also a distinct tendency to minimize the Soviet contribution to China's development in the years after 1949. In the words of the official press, China has drawn a "sharp line of distinction" between its brand of Marxism-Leninism and that of the Soviet Union.

There are probably two major forces at work in this assertion of Chinese independence from the Soviet Union. One is the Maoists' obvious sense of Chinese individuality, of national distinctiveness. The other is their ideological zeal, their desire to "carry the revolution through to the end," to use Mao's own phrase. The former would insure that allegiance to any foreign state or party would be tenuous at best. The latter would guarantee that loyalty to a foreign Marxist-Leninist party that was corrupt (i.e., "revisionist") would be impossible to maintain indefinitely. The branding of Liu Shao-ch'i as "China's Khrushchev" was an effective move by the Maoists, for it held Liu up for contempt not only because he was a revisionist, and hence a bad Marxist-Leninist, but also because he was a representative of Russian influence in China, and hence a bad Chinese.

A RENAISSANCE OF CHINESE CULTURE

The Maoists' desire to establish their intellectual and organizational independence from the Soviet Union was both a direct cause and a major theme of the Cultural Revolution. In his report to the Seventh Party Congress in 1945, Mao stated emphatically that "Russian history has created the Russian system . . . Chinese history will create the Chinese system." [2] From their statements it seems clear that the Maoists do not want to create a social system so distinctively Chinese in nature as to render it irrelevant to the rest of the world. They are equally reluctant, however, to restrict China's future development within the confines of the Soviet Union's past experiences. In the eyes of the Maoists, the Russian model becomes daily less significant: "Mao Tse-tung's Thought" has become the lodestar of China today.

In 1949, the victory of the Communists ended over a century of Chinese intellectual dependence on the Western capitalist states. Now the Cultural Revolution has brought a second "liberation," this time from the intellectual domination of the Western socialist countries, especially the Soviet Union. In a sense, the Cultural Revolution represents at least a partial "renaissance" of Chinese civilization. From this point on, we should expect to see China go her own way, to depart further and further in both her domestic and foreign policies from practices in the Western socialist states. The Maoists have declared that not only do they have the freedom to "creatively develop" Marxism-Leninism, but they also have the right to spread their ideas abroad. This development is symbolized in the person of Mao Tse-tung, who has been elevated in the official press from an "earnest student" of Marxism-Leninism to the "greatest Marxist-Leninist" of the present era.

While the Maoists have rejected foreign attempts to interpret Marxist theory on their behalf, it is worth emphasizing that they have not rejected Marxism itself. Thus in the years ahead this body of thought will serve as an important link between Chinese and Western civilizations. It is of great significance that the Maoists, while turning their backs on the prevailing social systems of the Western capitalist and socialist states, have accepted a comprehensive social philosophy that is part of the intellectual heritage of both.

WHOM SHOULD THE REVOLUTION SERVE?

For Mao Tse-tung the answer has long been clear: the Revolution must serve the "overwhelming majority of the people of China." From time to time, the composition of this group has been subject to change, but its core has always been the workers, peasants, and soldiers. In actual fact this means the peasants, for the workers and soldiers make up only a small proportion of the population, while the peasants themselves constitute approximately eighty per cent. So when we speak of the "average Chinese" we mean the peasants; they are the "overwhelming majority" of China's people.

From mid-1925 on, Mao came to realize that the peasants and the revolution were intimately linked together. Himself the son of a moderately well-off peasant, Mao as a young man came to know firsthand the suffering of most of the peasant population. He felt that the peasants were the "real" people of China, that they suffered most under the old system, and that therefore the revolution should serve their interests first and foremost. At the same time, he realized it was the peasants who had the least to lose and the most to gain by a radical change in the social order. Given the correct leadership, these multitudes could be forged into a mighty revolutionary force that would sweep all before it. Writing in 1927, Mao summed up his feelings by firmly declaring that "without the poor peasants there can be no revolution. To reject them is to reject the revolution. To attack them is to attack the revolution." [3]

This was a radical departure from the orthodox Marxist-Leninist suspicion of the peasantry as a latent bourgeoisie, but Mao was vindicated when his peasant armies achieved victory in 1949. This peasant orientation, which differed sharply from the Soviet experience, was reaffirmed in the years following the establishment of the People's Republic. To the Russian revolutionaries, the peasant masses were a major obstacle to the realization of communism. But to Mao it was entirely different; when the rural communes were launched in 1958 the CCP claimed this step was a giant leap toward communism. That is, far from being obstacles to the realization of communism in China, the peasant masses were perhaps the chief agents of such a realization. Moscow scoffed at the suggestion, and Mao apparently ran into stiff opposition from ranking members in his own party.

Ex-President Liu Shao-ch'i appeared to figure prominently in this opposition. As we have already seen, Liu, although like Mao of peasant origin, had a personality and career pattern very unlike those of Mao. Whereas Mao set much store by the revolutionary nature of the peasants, Liu displayed much more interest in the urban proletariat. In early May 1926, speaking at an important meeting of workers and peasants, Liu declared quite bluntly that in the revolutionary struggles that lay ahead the workers must "take the peasants by the hand" and lead them forward.[4] In any case, the communes were less successful than had been expected. In the ensuing months Mao's star waned, and Liu appeared to take a more commanding position in the party and government. In 1959, for example, he assumed the chairmanship of the Republic, a post formerly held by Mao.

With the coming of the Cultural Revolution, however, Liu has been swept from power. With his departure, a decided swing to the countryside has been noticed. It appears that Mao, once again in full control, is trying to direct the revolution back to its rural origins. During 1969, for example, the Maoists reemphasized the need for cadres and intellectuals to live and work in the countryside for certain periods of time. In addition, they announced that the rural communes should be given greater financial independence, and that the medicare system prevalent in the cities should be extended to the countryside. To get some sense of what this reorientation of the revolution means, we can look at the widespread changes which are now being introduced into the educational system. We shall confine our comments to medical education, but this should be sufficient to indicate the general trend.

WESTERN MEDICAL EDUCATION IN SOCIALIST CHINA

In 1949, when the Communists came to power, the prevailing system of training doctors and other medical personnel was virtually maintained intact. That is, Western-trained teachers carried on with Western techniques and Western curricula with little change. As the years went by, Soviet influences began to play a bigger role, but these differed little from those of the West. After some years of observation, however, it became clear to the Maoists that this system of medical education was far from satisfactory. Indeed, it tended to operate so that the part of the population that needed medical services the most—the peasantry —was least likely to receive them.

First, the time required to train an individual doctor was simply too long, amounting to seven years for a general practitioner and even longer for a specialist. This, of course, was identical to the Western practice: two years of premedicine, four years of medicine, and one year of internship. For a country crying out for medical personnel and faced with a rapidly increasing population, some faster method of producing doctors had to be found. Second, the doctors who graduated under this system were mistrained, for they were trained according to the standards and needs of highly industrialized urban populations in the West. In addition, they were taught to use—and demand—sophisticated equipment and supplies that the country simply could not produce in sufficient quantity to meet their needs.

These are in part technical problems, but it was probably the psychological and sociological dilemmas posed by this system of training doctors that caused the most serious problems. True to Western and Soviet practice, most medical students in China came from urban areas and attended large medical colleges in the major cities. They were trained to high standards, and were often encouraged to look forward to additional years of specialization or research. It was not unnatural, therefore, that when they completed their formal studies they often wanted to remain in these cities. After all, such urban centers as Peking, Shanghai, and Canton were much more appealing to the average graduate than life in the countryside. The cities could offer higher salaries, better living conditions, a more satisfactory cultural life, as well as opportunities for advanced studies.

This attitude may be understandable, given the conditions, but it was regarded by the Maoists as a betrayal of the revolution.

As we have pointed out, Mao made it clear throughout most of his career that the revolution must serve first and foremost the "overwhelming majority of the people of China," that is, the peasants. Accordingly, any truly "revolutionary" system of medical education would produce doctors who would give first priority to meeting the needs of the peasantry. Yet the existing system was doing the very opposite; it was turning out doctors who were professionally trained and psychologically motivated to serve the interests of the cities. The system had to be changed.

"SERVING THE PEOPLE" IN MEDICAL EDUCATION

And the system *is* being changed. As a result of the Maoists' victory in the Cultural Revolution, the entire educational system is being transformed in accord with the realities and needs of rural China. The victorious Maoists have intimated that the time required to train a doctor is going to be halved from seven to perhaps three or four years. The premedical years, for instance, are going to be dropped, and the final year of internship is going to be integrated into the normal course of study. In addition, the students are going to spend more time studying the types of diseases, illnesses, and injuries common to the Chinese peasantry, not to foreign urban populations. And, given the scarcity of sophisticated medical equipment and supplies in rural China, students will be trained to function effectively with simple resources.

Several decisions have been made to facilitate moving the doctors out of the cities and into the countryside. First, most, if not all, of the large medical colleges in the major cities will be reduced in size, and a part of their faculties, libraries, and facilities moved to provincial cities and towns. These off-shoots will then become the nuclei of smaller provincial institutes of medicine which will offer the new short practical course. Second, most of the students chosen to attend these new colleges will be the sons and daughters of peasants in the adjacent district. Third, as part of their formal course of study, these students will be required to keep in close touch with their native villages or similar villages nearby. For instance, each year the students will probably spend some time there, either working side by side with the peasants or attending to the simpler of their medical needs. Finally, when they graduate they will return to the countryside to work among the *lao pai hsing,* the common people of China.[5]

Mao has often been criticized both at home and abroad for his obsession with the countryside, and his "rural style of work." His ideas have been considered anachronistic in an age when China has crossed the threshold of industrialization. However, China is still a land of peasants, and any national planning that does not take this into consideration is dubious at best. But Mao has never advocated that the cities be dragged down to the level of the countryside; on the contrary, he has always argued that China's key developmental problem is to elevate the level of the peasantry. During the Cultural Revolution, for example, one of the chief aims of the Maoists was to establish the political conditions under which the differences between the cities and the countryside could be narrowed and ultimately eliminated.

It is in fact the Maoists' desire to modernize the countryside that has motivated them to reform the educational system to conform with the "concrete situation" in the vast rural areas, and to "send down" hundreds of thousands of intellectuals (high school students and higher) to play a key role in developing the countryside. Because of China's huge population, any plans for development that are not carried out on a mass scale have little chance of success. The proposed reform of the educational system during the Cultural Revolution has a twofold purpose. One, it is expected to make the intellectuals more aware of the needs of the rural population, which accounts for eight out of every ten Chinese. Two, it hopes to give the intellectuals an education appropriate to the actual conditions in the countryside today. Thus the reform of the educational system to serve the needs of the peasantry is a natural byproduct of the general reorientation of the Chinese Revolution that has taken place during the Cultural Revolution.

WHAT KIND OF SOCIETY
SHOULD THE REVOLUTION BUILD?

Revolutionaries have seldom argued over the need to reject the society into which they were born. It is usually on the question of building a new society that agreement breaks down. Among socialist revolutionaries, however, egalitarianism has perhaps been the dominant theme in their conception of the new society. Their overriding concern has been to restructure society in such a way as to prevent the fragmentation of society into separate, and unequal, classes. This concern led Karl Marx to condemn the inequities of his own times and to set about constructing the theoretical basis of a society where men would be equal, hence free. Unfortunately, penning one's thoughts about revolution and *carrying out* a revolution are two different things, as Lenin in Russia and Mao in China were to discover.

In spite of the obvious accomplishments of the Soviet Union over the last fifty years, few independent thinkers would maintain that a truly egalitarian society has been constructed in Russia. On the contrary, it is only too apparent that new privileged classes have gradually emerged over the years to replace those destroyed in the first impetus of the Revolution of 1917. It may be less surprising to us that the Russian revolutionaries failed to build an egalitarian society when we consider that they were pioneering a new kind of social project and that they worked under conditions of extreme hardship.

Nevertheless Mao has determined that the same fate shall not happen to China: hence the Cultural Revolution and the gigantic struggle against "revisionism" at every level of society. The Maoists are attempting to reassert the egalitarian ethos of the revolution in the face of increasing social stratification. In the CCP there are doubtless many individuals who are prepared to accept growing social stratification as an "inevitable" phenomenon of development, much in the same way as the Russians have accepted it. This is true to some extent of the old revolutionaries who struggled through years of hardship prior to victory in 1949, but it is probably even more true of the millions of individuals who were hastily admitted into the Party in the years just prior to and just after victory. No doubt many of these new members were "rice communists," more appreciative of the benefits of Party membership than of the ideals for which the CCP stood. Today, in the Cultural Revolution, these Party members are being reexamined and, if found wanting, removed from positions of power.

Speaking of the tempestuous peasant uprisings in rural China in the 1920s, Mao put the case rather bluntly:

> All revolutionary parties and all revolutionary comrades will stand before them [the peasants] to be tested, to be accepted or rejected by them. To march at their head and lead them? To follow in the rear, gesticulating at them and criticizing them? To face them as opponents? Every Chinese is free to choose among the three, but circumstances demand that a quick choice be made. . . .[6]

Likewise during the Cultural Revolution a "quick choice" had to be made; the nation had entered a period of intense struggle, and every Chinese had to make a decision: to support the Maoists or to support their opponents. There was no middle path. Given this choice, the overwhelming majority supported the Maoists, and they emerged victorious.

What do the Maoists have in mind for China? Do they intend to undertake the construction of an egalitarian society? Let us look closely at the People's Liberation Army (PLA), for the Maoists claim that the army has become a "great school of Mao Tse-Tung's Thought," and a model for the rest of society. In the years prior to and during the Cultural Revolution, people all over China were exhorted to learn from the PLA, and a whole series of young army heroes was held up as examples to be emulated.

THE ORIGINAL EGALITARIANISM OF THE PLA

When the Nationalist and Communist armies came face to face immediately after World War II, many foreign observers commented on the PLA's élan, its morale, its will to fight. More so than most Chinese armies in the past, the PLA knew both *how* to fight and *why* to fight. Contrary to the opinions of many old China hands in Shanghai, it was not "just another Chinese army." The PLA's morale was high largely because its leaders consciously adhered to the principle of egalitarianism in the life of the army. This was not the pure egalitarianism of a Utopia; there were leaders, there were followers, there was discipline. Nevertheless the attempt was made to reduce as much as possible the distinctions between officers and enlisted men.

In the first place, efforts were directed toward keeping officers' salaries, living standards, and privileges within reasonable limits. In the second place, the soldiers were encouraged to put forward their opinions, voice their grievances, and to discuss tactics and strategy with their officers. Finally, everyone in uniform was exhorted to take part in small group study of national and international affairs. More so than in other countries, the PLA was a "politicized" army; its individual members were to be both "red and expert": that is, politically knowledgeable and militarily competent.

After victory in 1949, however, things began to change. With China leaning to one side following the signing of the Sino-Soviet Friendship Pact, Soviet ideas and practices began to filter into every aspect of Chinese life. The army was no exception. In 1955, in a sharp departure from tradition, Defense Minister P'eng Teh-huai announced that the Soviet style of uniforms and the Soviet system of ranks were to be introduced into the PLA. As in the Soviet Red Army, egalitarianism was to be sacrificed in the interest of a privileged officer class. In addition, the army was to be gradually "de-politicized," with greater attention paid to professional military competence. The army of the revolution was to become the army of the state, along Russian lines.

The details of the struggle within the Party's Central Committee are not known, but it is reasonable to assume that the Maoists did not look favorably upon this transformation of the PLA. We do know that four years later, at the Lushan Central Committee meeting, the Maoists were able to strip P'eng of all his offices and have him expelled from the Political Bureau of the Party. In his place was put Lin Piao, who at the age of fifty became the Minister of Defense and the top man in the PLA. Lin was not unfamiliar with the job, for he had long been one of the PLA's outstanding commanders, and was the man who captured Peking. Most Western observers have regarded the outcome of the Lushan meeting as a defeat for Mao, but Lin's key role in the Cultural Revolution may necessitate some reassessment. If Mao did not in fact engineer Lin's appointment at this meeting, he quickly won Lin's loyalty to his cause.

Soon after his appointment to the defense post, Lin inaugurated an intense program of education for all the armed forces. The egalitarian traditions of the early Red Army were evoked, more time was set aside for political, as opposed to purely military, studies, and special attention was paid to the study of Mao Tse-tung's writings. In succeeding years the army was heralded as an active political force, the most loyal supporter of Mao Tse-tung's Thought, and worthy of emulation by the whole population. "Learn from the PLA!" became a national slogan for young and old alike.

A REVIVAL OF EGALITARIANISM

By early 1965, Lin estimated that the army had been won over to Mao, both in the sense of loyalty to Mao as a political leader and to his Thought as a political ideal. With the bulk of the army on his side, both ideologically and organizationally, Mao felt strong enough to strike back at those in positions of power whom he felt were betraying the principles of the revolution.

Accordingly, in May 1965 Lin announced that the Soviet style of uniforms and the Soviet system of ranks were to be abolished in the PLA. And the implication was that all "revisionist" (i.e., Soviet) influences in the army were to be combated. This sweeping announcement met with some opposition within the officer class in the army; nevertheless the reforms went through. The officers lost their ranks and many of the privileges that went with them. Mao and Lin were determined to revolutionize the army, and by 1965 they had largely succeeded. Now the task was to revolutionize the Party and all of society; hence the Cultural Revolution.

What we have seen in the army is a striking example of Maoism at work: the attempt to extend egalitarian principles to that part of society which is generally regarded as inherently anti-egalitarian. What has happened in the army is important to an understanding of the Cultural Revolution for two reasons. First, the army was in effect the pilot project for an experiment that Mao hopes to effect in the entire social system, both during and after the initial upsurge of the Cultural Revolution. Second, the substantial control of the army resulting from Lin's years of work gave Mao the freedom to launch a gigantic political struggle without the danger of precipitating a civil war. It is true that some officers did come out in opposition to Mao, but in general the army remained loyal and responded well to Maoist direction.

Thus Lin Piao's work in the PLA should be seen as an integral part of the Cultural Revolution; without this advance preparation in the army, the Maoists might never have been in a strong enough position to launch the Cultural Revolution at all. Given its ideological and political importance to the Maoists, it is not surprising that the PLA has occupied such a prominent position in Chinese politics over the past few years. Yet in spite of this exalted position, the available evidence does not suggest that the tail is wagging the dog; the Maoists appear to be in control of the army, and not vice versa.

Of course, it is not only in the army that we can see evidence of egalitarianism in Chinese society. At the universities, for example, professors were called upon to renounce their academic titles and to accept reductions in salary. In the factories, directors were required to take their turn at the bench, and demands were made for the abolition of piecework. In the communes, officials who seldom worked in the fields were denounced, and the peasants called for more voice in local government. If this egalitarian spirit at times led to foolish extremes, its main thrust was essentially healthy and was a major source of dynamism in the Cultural Revolution.

The Maoists certainly favored this egalitarian spirit, but at no point did they confer approval on anarchy. Like most Chinese intellectuals (and most successful revolutionaries), they have a strong sense of authority and discipline. Nevertheless, the Red Guards claimed that they had "lifted the lid" off the political system, and one hopes it will not again be screwed down so tightly. In their encouragement of the widely used wall posters, in their experiments with the new "revolutionary committees," and even in their abolition of the carefully ranked leadership lists, the Maoists have indicated a desire to break at least partially from the elitist politics of the past.

THE YEARS AHEAD

In this discussion we have attempted to look at Maoist thought and policy over the years insofar as they illuminate the origins and significance of the Cultural Revolution. We have assumed that the Maoists conceived and launched the Cultural Revolution in order to accomplish certain well-defined goals. First, they hoped to reassert what they considered the fundamental principles of the Chinese Revolution: independence from foreign—especially Soviet—control, orientation toward the peasantry, and maintenance of an egalitarian ethos. Second, they determined to remove from power those individuals within and without the CCP who were thought to be betraying these essential principles, and thus subverting the Revolution. Third, they planned to launch a program of reform designed to embody in actual practice these basic principles of the Revolution.

At the present time, it is impossible to say whether or not the Maoists can succeed in all of these aims. We shall have to wait and see. Nevertheless, we cannot escape the conclusion that Mao and his supporters have triumphed over their immediate opponents both within and without the Party. This victory is of course crucial, for without it the Maoists would be unable to carry out the policies they feel are essential to China's future development. It is important to an understanding of the Cultural Revolution to realize that the struggle for power is not merely a struggle for position. Above all, it is a struggle for policy, a struggle between two different lines of action. As the official press puts it, the "revolutionary line" of Mao Tse-tung has triumphed over the "revisionist line" of Liu Shao-ch'i.

If this is true, it seems reasonable to assume that China's immediate development will be characterized by continuing efforts to find a Chinese road to socialism, to elevate the peasant masses in the countryside, and to construct an essentially egalitarian society.

NOTES

1. Stuart R. Schram, *The Political Thought of Mao Tse-tung,* rev. ed. (London: Penguin Books, 1969), p. 419.

2. *Ibid.,* p. 299.

3. *Ibid.,* p. 255.

4. Stuart R. Schram, *Mao Tse-tung* (London: Penguin Books, 1966), p. 91.

5. This account of the reform of the medical system is based in part on an interview I had with staff and students at the Nanking Medical University in July 1967.

6. Schram, *Political Thought of Mao,* p. 250.

China's special modernity

JON SAARI

Old-style imperialism, for better or for worse, bound the various regions of the world inextricably together and inaugurated world history. The first written commentaries on this phenomenon of "world history" reflected the basic nature of the relationship: the strong vs. the weak, the conquerors vs. the conquered. Given the seemingly one-directional impact of the West on the rest of the world in this modern era, the condescending habit of mind has proved hard to eradicate; it is painful to unlearn the assumptions of mastery and dominance.

Historical understanding by nature follows rather than antici- pates the direction of events, and American interest in studying world history is no exception. Before World War II our interest in the rest of the world was marginal. But since the United States assumed the role of guardian of the "free world," such studies have flourished. Now, of course, old-style imperialism is un- tenable, and the relationship between the haves and the have-nots has grown more subtle. Missionary tracts have been replaced by AID bulletins; gunboat coercion has given way to counterinsur- gency operations. Our language has been "modernized" as well. Gone are such terms as heathen, pagan, backward, primitive, uncivilized, enlightenment, and even westernization. They have been replaced by social science jargon: modernization, traditional societies, the dynamics of growth, and the development syndrome (developed, developing, less developed, underdeveloped, unde- veloped).

Beneath the surface changes, however, many of the old biases live on. One is ethnocentrism, or attachment to the familiar. As virtually the whole of American national history coincided with the Industrial Revolution, it is hardly surprising that our particu- lar capitalist route to modernity has been felt to be "natural" or "inevitable" or even "right." The inclusion within our perspective of the more diversified historical experiences of the European nations, which weren't "born modern," corrects this bias somewhat, but we are still tempted to think of the rest of the world as following in our footsteps, as being "Westernized." Gradually, however, the net is being thrown even wider, incorporating the experiences of societies recently wrenched out of their centuries-old ways. In these societies, the persistence of old institutions and habits has taught us the complexities of the process. Environmental factors such as institutional reform, capital accumulation, and expertise now seem secondary to such internal factors as value systems, motivation, and early socialization. Men, unlike the steel plants that can be imported, are the product of generations of inherited ways transmitted in the most uncontrollable of settings, the primary family. There is no five-year plan for modernizing men.

The peril we face is smoothing over the crooked, devious nature of this passage to modernity. "Growth" or "development" are wretchedly inadequate words to describe what has been happening in this modern period. The last two hundred years in the West have seen untold brutality and violence—witness the two world wars alone—whose deeper causes lie rooted in the strains of the process of modernization. It is doubtful whether the modern experience of the non-Western world will prove any less uneven or violent. Indeed, considering the contrast between much of what modernity brings and their own traditions, our expectation should be that their experience will be even more painful and chaotic. It might, as Cyril Black has urged, be well to begin to think in terms of ten revolutions a year.[1] Whether these societies will have the wisdom and resources to divert their struggles into less violent forms remains to be seen. We in the West did not have such wisdom, and it is quite hypocritical now for Western commentators to talk about violence as though it were a foreign virus.

The late modernizers have not enjoyed the luxury of evolutionary change, and this fact has shaped their understanding of what "change" is, making it quite different from our own. Our attitude toward "change" has not been one of fear but of drift. We have been content to let change flow from thousands of private visions, and then having to deal with problems of waste and exploitation through reform after they have become intolerable or threatening to the social order. In much of the non-Western world, "change" has broken in upon traditional ways in a painfully abrupt manner. It has been perceived as an alien force from the beginning, feared yet respected because of the wealth and national power it seemed to promise. "Change" meant "change to modern ways," and became an issue against the background of traditional cultures, generating a wide range of reactions from staunch traditionalism to a complete acceptance of things Western. These visions of the future have varied a great deal. The present vision in the People's Republic of China represents in an extreme form the aspiration to *master* "change," to bring this alien, unknown, feared phenomenon under control.

One essential step in mastering change is to fit it into an interpretative scheme that explains it, that makes the past comprehensible and tames the future. In this connection, the promise of certain "scientific" knowledge has been one element in the wide appeal of Marxism in the twentieth century. The irony is that after almost fifty years of struggling to react to changes, to anticipate changes, and to introduce changes into Chinese life according to Marxist categories, the aging revolutionaries on the mainland have come to know just how untamable "change" is. Their effort to keep ahead of "change," not only in terms of economic and political planning, but also philosophically, has pushed them to the ultimate doctrine of permanent revolution. This doctrine, with its cry for endless struggle against the evils in society and within oneself, reflects the hopes and fears generated over a lifetime of constant battling to master modern problems.

Needless to say, the majority of Westerners are far from appreciating the pains of aging revolutionaries, who see that their historical triumphs can never be secured once and for all for future generations. We have so little to share with them. Our society is highly mechanized and urban, with high levels of production, *per capita* income, and consumption. Theirs is working to complete the basic modern infrastructure (roads, harbors, communication networks) for economic development, and to bridge the gap between the modernizing coastal strip and the peasant hinterland.

In ours the individual is left alone or isolated in the nuclear family amidst large impersonal public and private organizations. In theirs the individual scarcely exists, save as a building unit in various social groupings or as an example from the masses and for the masses. In our societies, government is becoming administration, which might be interpreted as the withering away of the state as it has been known in recent history. Ideological appeals are greatly reduced, if heard at all. In theirs, politics attempts to be "in command" of all areas of life and bureaucratism is castigated as a great evil. The mastery of an ideology, such as Maoism, and its creative application to any task (from ping pong to nuclear engineering), is the beginning and end of education and work.

Looking only at these present contrasts, the distance between us seems enormous. Perceived historically, and with due appreciation for the different modes of modernization, the distance is still enormous, but it is more manageable. Through such an approach we can gain greater empathy and a sense of proportion.

This essay will attempt such an approach to the modern history of China. Utilizing insights derived from recent modernization studies,[2] I want to discuss several factors that have contributed to the distinctiveness of China's modernity.[3] I want also to discuss how China's strong cultural tradition might influence her modern future, and in that connection to point to a basic point of divergence between China's experience with modernity and that of the West.

CHINA AS A CONTINUOUS TERRITORY AND PEOPLE

One factor affecting the Chinese transition to modernity is that, unlike so many other nations undergoing rapid modernization, China has enjoyed a significant continuity of territory, population, and history. The Chinese trace their unity as a state back to Chin Shih Huang Tih, 221 years before Christ. Though there were many dynastic changes and periods of disunity, often involving outside groups such as the Manchus and Mongols, the Heavenly Order itself remained constant; only the Heavenly Mandate passed from one ruler to another. Below the Emperor were a small elite of scholars and scholar-officials who maintained their position as mediators between imperial authority and the peasant masses from one dynasty to the next. They mastered and preserved the classical literature, interpreted the signs of Heavenly grace and displeasure, and by their monopoly of literacy and official roles they were able to contain history, literature, and philosophy within an orthodox thought framework. Chinese histories—family, clan, local, regional, and dynastic—were voluminous, and the sense of connection was kept alive from one generation to the next through the intense consciousness of being a small part of a much longer continuum. In the *Three Character Classic,* memorized by millions of children under the old system, the study of history begins with genealogical tables and a list of emperors from 2953 B.C. to the present. During the modern period, this consciousness of a long and glorious history was one source of China's energetic response to the colonial challenge.

Although the territorial extent of China has varied over the course of her long history, contracting and expanding within East and Southeast Asia by cultural diffusion, military conquest, and trade, still the Chinese or the dominant "Han people" have a comparatively well-defined geographical homeland. Mao Tse-tung and Chiang Kai-shek agree on China's general shape. The challenge of modernity brought about an involuntary contraction of this territorial unit. Whole chunks were detached from Chinese influence, including Indochina, Korea, Taiwan, and Manchuria, and sections of the mainland itself were appropriated by forced concessions and leases. In fact Sun Yat-sen feared the ultimate subjugation and extermination of the Chinese territory and people, whom he saw falling behind population trends in the West. These fears confirmed him in his ardent nationalism, which he felt was one of the only defenses available to the Chinese in fending off this ultimate disaster.

The continuity of territory and people has had a number of implications for China's recent history, some advantageous and others disadvantageous. First, it provided a base upon which a nation could be built. The process of nation-building was relatively easier in China than in those societies without such continuity of territory and people. In this latter situation the nation, such as it was, had to be built from the ground up with foreign powers usually acting as the major constructors. Israel is a dramatic example. The major obstacles to nation-building in China were those posed by the sheer size of the polity and by the great inertia of a tradition that had defined a cultural world rather than a state. The transition from culturalism to nationalism, from *T'ien Hsia* (All under Heaven) to *Kuo Chia* (state-family) is thus a major chapter in the intellectual history of modern China. Once this concept was firmly established, by the late years of the nineteenth century, the progressive integration of China's many regions into the new concept could begin. The task, to use Sun Yat-sen's metaphor, was to take a heap of loose sand and cement the grains through new principles into a solid rock. This struggle for political unity raged for decades from the end of the Ch'ing dynasty until 1949. Even now, of course, there are two governments claiming to be the legitimate inheritors of the territory and people of China. During this long period of political disunity, however, the Chinese people, in mind and emotion, have been united as heirs to a long past lived out on the mainland, seas, and islands of East Asia.

The existence of a continuous history, despite its eventual contributions to cohesion and a sense of identity, also provided obstacles to the efforts of modernizing leaders to bring something new into the Chinese experience. The past had long determined norms of behavior, and even after some Chinese began to free themselves from this yoke, many continued to be governed by old habits. Indeed the major struggle in the first quarter of the century was not among modernizing groups (left, right, or center), but between the traditionalists and the modernizers. The traditionalist intellectuals not only rejected republicanism—witness the first President of the Republic, Yuan Shih-k'ai and his attempt to crown himself Emperor in 1915—but also modern science and technology.

But the greatest bastion of traditionalism was the peasant masses who were so little touched by the modernization proceeding in China's thin coastal strip. One key to the success of the Chinese Communist Party (CCP) was its ability to recognize the traditionalist tendencies in peasant attitudes. In this regard, it is worth looking at an article by Li Ta-chao (one of the founders of the CCP and a teacher of Mao when Mao was a librarian at Peking National University). Impressed by the spontaneous peasant uprising of the Red Spear societies of Shantung, Honan, and Shensi in the summer of 1926, Li defines a way of relating the Party and Communist objectives to the peasant movement. The peasants must first understand that they *do* have the capacity to liberate themselves, that they must not wait for outside saviors, whether gods or emperors. Their "narrow racial view" must be broadened so that they realize that the "revolutionary peasant masses of the whole world are their friends." Superstitions against modern weapons and reliance on bamboo poles, swords, Confucian signboards, and images of gods had to be stopped. Parochial loyalties had to be transformed into true class consciousness. All this could be accomplished, he felt, by cadres working in the villages to bring more order, understanding, and effective organization into the peasants' own movement.[4]

CHINA AS A LATE-MODERNIZER

Lateness in beginning the modernizing process meant that modernization proceeded under the indirect influence of the ideas and institutions of the early-modernizers: Europe, the United States, Russia, and Japan. Whereas the early-modernizers could proceed gradually and empirically, adapting their traditional institutions to changing needs and conditions, the late-modernizers imported a distracting array of foreign models, which misled as often as they enlightened. The early history of the CCP (1921–31) offers a clear example of this tyranny of form, in this case orthodox Marxist–Leninist categories over empirical observation and experience. According to orthodox Marxism, the major base of support for the socialist revolution would be the industrial proletariat in the cities. Even after the virtual destruction of its urban base in 1927, the CCP continued to plan strategy on this assumption. Mao developed his strategy for peasant rebellion on his own against the official line.

The reliance on foreign models also posed an identity problem for Chinese leaders. How could they relate their own traditions to the alien modern imports? Few intellectuals were so iconoclastic as to reject totally the Chinese past. The psychological cost of such a total negation was insupportable for the majority of Chinese nationalists; they felt the need to establish the relevance of the Chinese past to the "modern" Chinese future. These Chinese nationalists, whether tradition-oriented, such as Chiang Kai-shek, or revolutionary, such as Sun Yat-sen or Mao Tse-tung, asserted links that made it possible to move into the modern world while bringing at least one part of the Great Tradition along with them. Sun and Mao dramatized the heroic struggles of the poor and oppressed classes throughout Chinese history, especially those of the T'ai-p'ing rebels of the 1850s and 1860s. Chiang tended to emulate the imperial officials of the T'ung Chih Restoration (1862–74) who put down that rebellion. One appeal of communism was as a solution to this identity problem: it placed China in the vanguard of world history ahead of the early-modernizers who had been China's oppressors (as well as teachers).[5]

Another consequence of the lateness of China's modernization was that the struggle for political consolidation outstripped the slower and more gradual accompanying developments in economic and social life. For example, by the early 1920s, industrialization in China had barely reached the point where it could generate large labor organizations. Trade unionism and a strong independent social-democratic movement as they existed in the West never had time to develop in China. For this reason the CCP was freed from the challenge of a powerful social-democratic movement. The liberal movement in China, in turn, was denied the mass base of support an independent labor movement could have provided; it found no mass allies and remained an ineffective elitist pressure group.

CHINA'S INDIRECT COLONIAL EXPERIENCE

The role of imperialism in modern Chinese history is keenly felt by all Chinese nationalists, but their interpretations frequently distort the role of foreign exploitation in modern Chinese history.[6] China's experience with imperialism and semicolonialism probably did more to hasten than inhibit the process of internal political consolidation.

China did *not* experience the direct and pervasive foreign tutelage which we call colonialism. In the nineteenth century she did experience foreign penetration against her will, and she did witness the steady creation of a foreigner's world in her coastal cities under the protection of gunboats and extraterritoriality. After 1860 the Christian missionaries gained access to the Chinese interior and the foreign presence became a reality in the inland village; missionary schools and hospitals followed not far behind. New confrontations brought new treaties and protocols that strengthened the foreigner's stake in the modernizing coastal strip through outright land concessions and leases, developmental and indemnity loans, and control of the Chinese customs and post office. In developmental terms, however, there is considerable difference between a state of subjugation and a state of dependence. Subjugation means development dictated by an external force, through invasion, occupation, or colonization. It means a more complete substitution of alien for traditional institutions, a sharper and more complete break with the past. In contrast, dependence allows for considerable interplay between internal and external forces. It is within this latter pattern that China's modern history took shape.

More important than investment statistics and missionary schools was the quality of the human relationships that developed in the unequal contact between the foreigners and the Chinese. Implicit in these relationships were many of the feelings and ties that bind the colonizer to the colonized: deference and suppressed hatred by the latter, guilt, mixed with paternalism and contempt, by the former.[7] It was this psychological dimension of foreign exploitation that perhaps explains the liquidation of the entire foreign enterprise in China—economic, cultural, religious, and philanthropic—after 1949. There was a layer of feeling in many Chinese—in some suppressed, in some highly visible—that demanded as complete a separation from foreigners as possible in order to restore a sense of dignity and equality. Subjectively, there is not much difference between the state of dependence and the state of subjugation. It is true that the state of total dependence, if analogies from American slavery and German concentration camps are at all applicable, can in fact destroy the very capacity and desire for individual response. The semicolonialism and semidependence that China experienced was enough to convey a sense of violation, but not enough to produce permanent incapacitating effects. To the reader of the foreign press in China or abroad, the revolution seemed to drag on hopelessly, with no direction or purpose. Yet in retrospect it is clear that China was one of the first *independent* modernizing nations, and since the breakup of the colonial empires after World War II we can see the enormous problems that independent modernization poses. It is true that it took almost sixty years, until after the defeat by Japan in 1894–95, for the traditional elite to become alarmed about the nature of the challenge confronting China; it was another decade before the fundamental break with the past was made by the dynasty itself, that is, by the abolition of the old examination system in 1905. But from then until 1949 there were continuous political struggles of the first magnitude among the competing modernizing groups.

THE VIGOROUS INTERNAL POLITICAL STRUGGLE

Because foreign imperialism was limited and divided in China, political consolidation was achieved mainly through the competitive struggles among various Chinese groups. Only twice did "united fronts" form: once during the concerted KMT drive to oust the Peking regime (1924–27) and again during the War of National Resistance against the Japanese (1937–45). Yet both were tenuous, barely masking internal struggles for advantage. Each came to a quick end once the immediate objective was realized, with the factions moving quickly to renewed struggle against one another. In China's twentieth century political history, the capture of the nationalist banner in the battles against imperialist aggressors was not the decisive feature in the struggle for power—as, for example, it was in India. Differences of ideology, leadership, organization, and social class consistently were more important as the factions struggled against one another. The story of their interplay during the fifty years prior to the Communist rise to power is one of the most fascinating chapters in modern history.

The decline of the Manchu Dynasty in the late nineteenth and early twentieth centuries was characterized by large-scale rebellions and desperate revenue problems that weakened the relationship between the central government and its traditional gentry base.[8] The revenue problems led increasingly to the sale of examination degrees, and in turn the quality and prestige of the scholar-officials declined. The reforms that might have been made to encourage indigenous initiatives in industry and commerce were never made, for they contradicted the system of gentry privileges. Following the Sino-Japanese War (1894–95) —a humiliating defeat for China—the internal and external pressures for change increased. The regime could still suppress the small reform party within China, but it was largely helpless in combating anti-Manchu revolutionary groups abroad, its own fanatics at home (the Boxers, who wanted to drive the foreigners into the sea in a burst of messianic zeal), and the insatiable foreign imperialists. The Empress Dowager could not rescue the situation, even though she forced through a series of sweeping reform edicts between 1905 and 1908.

At this point a new governing coalition between the politically powerful agrarian upper class and the rising commercial and industrial elite was not possible because the latter was still too dependent and weak a partner. The gentry gradually began to take control of local affairs, collecting their own taxes and allying themselves with individual militarists, who in turn became the tax collectors and the guarantors of order in the countryside. All of this could only have a negative effect on the life situation of peasants. They lost whatever protection the old imperial officials had provided and exploitation increased greatly.

The end of the Dynasty in 1911 confirmed this decisive shift in power away from the central apparatus. And the Republic declared in 1912 was unable to function because it could not overcome or incorporate the new social forces and alliances that had emerged at the provincial and regional levels. Anarchy at the center remained until the KMT reunited China in 1927–28. The decade of tenuous political unity under the Nanking government (1928–37) saw little effort to curb the increasingly arbitrary use of power on the land by the warlords and ex-gentry (now turned landlords). This abuse continued until the land reform program of the CCP. The rural reconstruction programs of the 1930s failed to change the basic relationships in the countryside.

Amidst these changes, what did the KMT in fact represent? During the early years of the First United Front (1924–27) under Sun Yat-sen, the party was able to profit from the discontent of the workers and peasants as it advanced northward. The nationalistic impulse that guided the movement, however, only thinly concealed the internal conflicts of interest and viewpoint; as success beckoned in early 1927, the coalition became increasingly fragile. Sun Yat-sen, even at the time of his death in 1925, was well aware of elements within the organization that balked at the prospect of giving any concrete meaning to the Third Principle of the People's Livelihood.

Support for the First Principle (Nationalism) was intense; the impact of the Second Principle (People's Democracy) was muted, since an indefinite period of political tutelage lay in the plans. The character of the Third Principle was ambiguous and troubling to rightist elements; the fear of an effective left wing within the KMT being able to implement radical reforms was enough to precipitate the massacre of April 1927. Following the split, an uneasy combination of ex-gentry absentee landlords from the coastal provinces and the new commercial, financial, and industrial urban elite of the 1920s provided the social base of the KMT government at Nanking. Chiang Kai-shek, however, retained control of the military arm, and through it he directed the party and intimidated the various supporting groups.

Chiang's understanding of his own role was ambiguous. He was completely preoccupied with national reunification, for which all other ends had to be sacrificed. His inclination was to use military force to solve problems and to urge moral renewal and a return to the Confucian standards of the T'ung Chih Restoration as remedies. He had no concrete program to meet the mounting social and economic problems, save acceptance of the *status quo* in the countryside and suppression of "disloyal" resistance in the cities. Thus the KMT after 1927 represented a modernizing party with conservative, tradition-oriented solutions to the problems of political consolidation and modernization. Such strategies by no means always fail, but any prospect of success was cut short by the outbreak of full-scale war with Japan in 1937 and by the continued pressure of a highly organized Communist movement in the countryside.

The crucial force in the Communist rise to power was the expanding marginal landless peasant class at the bottom of the village social structure. As the village deteriorated, these landless peasants no longer had a stake in the system and became wandering recruits for bandit groups, warlord armies, and the Communists.

But a revolutionary situation does not ignite itself. Most of the landless peasants left their home villages to join bandits of a nearby army or they remained in the village and died in the next famine. Few organized resistance in the village itself. Spontaneous resistance did not bury the old order, even though the internal decay of the upper class and the loss of deference and respect for them made the old-style exploitation less tolerable. The CCP, even in these favorable circumstances and after it had evolved a cogent strategy of peasant revolution, was able to succeed only with an assist from the Japanese conquest and occupation. This occupation in North China eliminated the old elites in the countryside and forged solidarity among the oppressed. In these circumstances, the CCP social program could be combined with its resistance to foreign oppression. The party was able to consolidate its territorial base by offering a third alternative to submission to the Japanese or starvation.

In other parts of China, the revolution came from above, by government direction after 1949. Land was redistributed from rich to poor, and to each member of the family on an equal-share basis, regardless of age and sex. This not only finished the old system of land tenure but the old family and social structure as well. The latter aspect of land reform broke the traditional connection between kinship and landed property. The new energies released by these radical changes were linked to the goals of the new national political power, whose reach now extended to the individual citizen. The new political power proceeded to draw more out of the village than the landlords or the KMT had taken. But the rationale had changed significantly: it was now the distinctively modern one of increasing national economic output, not underwriting the leisure and culture of a few.

The internal political struggle in China thus culminated in the transfer of power to a modernizing group intent upon radical change. But radical change to what ends? Partly to implement a new vision of the good society. Partly to leap over the "wasteful" capitalist phase of industrial development into the more integrated socialist phase. Partly to increase China's power and influence in the world and to blaze a path of proud self-reliance for other late-modernizing nations to follow. Economic modernization was clearly only one of several goals, and an instrumental one at that. It was not in any sense a "direction" in itself.

TRADITION, MODERNITY, AND CONVERGENCE

Given the nature of old China, the scope of the task that faces the Chinese people in their passage into modernity is enormous. The need for certain changes is clear. China must bridge the gaps between the elite and the masses, between educated and uneducated, between the cities and the hinterland. They must break out of the reliance on human muscle and simple tools in order to reap the benefits of modern technology. They must overcome the deep-rooted fatalism that has entrenched itself in the minds of Chinese peasants. The pantheon of supernatural powers on which they have relied to make the world comprehensible and tolerable must be eliminated.

What is less clear is the fate of China's traditional social morality. Whether or not this, too, needs to be jettisoned in favor of some more modern pattern is one of the more important and difficult questions of China's future. It is at this point that our distinctive Western preferences emerge most forcefully. We tend to assume that our style of political and economic organization is not only right but "required" by modern civilization itself.

The Chinese have long had a passion and a genius for social morality, and in the long run this may well prove to be the source of divergence between Chinese and Western paths of development. It has had a profound effect on her transitional experience thus far, and it could well provide a core of the future modern equilibrium that Chinese society settles upon.

The traditional social morality that is proving so durable in the present is defined best in terms of the social learning of children brought up in the traditional setting. It is less a moral code or system in the Western sense than a self-understanding. A child came to learn during his formative years that his "self" was defined principally in terms of a web of relationships with other people. The primary relationship was that with his parents, whom he was to obey and serve during their lifetime. His life and decisions were never cut off from them until their death, and that event only inaugurated another phase of respectful service in "ancestor worship." The virtue of *Hsiao,* or filial piety, had counterparts in other contexts: in service to superiors it was *Chong,* or loyalty; in relation to older brothers it was *Ti,* or brotherly deference. Countless examples of model sons and daughters and brothers and officials were recorded and circulated. Adults urged children by persuasion and punishment to contain their emotions and thoughts, or at least their behavior, in these fixed role conceptions. The ideal relationship, however, involved mutuality and reciprocity, if not equality. While inferiors were to be respectful and loyal to superiors, superiors were to respond with kindliness. Yet filial obligation in practice often did not depend upon reciprocity; in fact many of the prime examples of filial children were those who submitted willingly despite the deviant conduct of their parents.

This was not just an external social code ordering behavior, but was also a part of the inner life of the people. This ethic of absolute obedience to authority carried with it reliance on this authority in facing problems and making decisions. The carefully articulated social codes insured the security of clear and predictable relationships. Implicit in both are fear of repressed aggression in oneself and others, dread of the ambiguous situation, and extreme anxiety over "social chaos" or "confusion."

The social conflicts of the transitional period probed the weak underside of this system of social morality. After the abdication of the Emperor in the Revolution of 1911, the focus of attack shifted from state authority to family authority. The "filial sons" who went off to modern-style primary and middle schools no longer could accept the system. The powerless ones who had been forced to "eat bitterness" (as the Chinese phrase puts it) under the old system—that is, the young, the women, the misfits— became conscious of the manmade nature of their suffering, and were no longer willing to submit.

From sanctuary bases in the coastal cities and modern schools, rebels launched a sharp attack against the old morality. The older generation was puzzled and infuriated, and resisted being dragged to the chopping block on the heels of the now decapitated imperial state. These divided families produced profoundly disturbed sons and daughters. They did not accept the old filial patterns, but at the same time they were not able to live with themselves in "modern" patterns. Guilt and hostility plagued them. These personal and social tensions generated what Robert J. Lifton has characterized the "psychology of totalism." [9]

There was still the unresolved question of what would replace the authority of the old state. Traditional Chinese political culture had fostered a deferential style of politics in which the masses acquiesced and the elite prided itself on the "art of governance." In times of political stability the masses had no political voice, and probably were content to be left alone. But in times of instability politics became "the devouring tiger." It was an all-or-nothing style of politics—all order or all chaos—with none of the features of the "pragmatic," "pluralist" politics of the West. There was no conception of the legitimacy and healthiness of political opposition, diffusion of sovereignty, inviolable rights of the individual, separation of powers, constitutional procedures for resolution of conflict, and so on.

If acquiring such views is a part of what it means to become "modern," then China's politics during the transitional period was dominated by men who were not modern. Their political instincts were to expect deference from the masses. They zealously carved out a territorial power base by the traditional means appropriate to times of disorder and social chaos. The "independent kingdoms" of the warlords and the general lack of any agreement on fundamental political principles insured the failure of the first Republican experiment (1912–28). After the unification of the country following the Northern Expedition (1926–27), the Nationalist government in Nanking drew up plans to end "political tutelage." Even if circumstances had permitted the experiment, it is hard to see how a fledgling government would have stood up to the powerful independent organizations of party and army. Since the war, the end of political tutelage in Taiwan has not meant the opening up of politics to multiparty competition.

Thus in the transitional period an important change in *manners* was introduced into the old social morality, greatly affecting relationships between young and old, educated and uneducated. Yet the basic authority pattern—deference by the many and instruction by the virtuous few—has persisted in politics. And it continues to persist in the People's Republic of China. Peking denounces Western-style democracy while trumpeting its own "democratic centralism." This does provide through the mass campaigns a kind of training for political participation, but it does not, as yet, concede legitimacy to other viewpoints than that of the CCP. In the final analysis, any change in this pattern will depend less upon the self-abdication of the elite or its willingness to risk the outward forms of Western-style democratic processes (which would not be much of a risk, initially) than it will depend upon the people themselves *un*learning the habit of deference and demanding a different style of politics.

THE EXPERIMENTAL FUTURE

Mao's hope for the future is that he will be able to take the "blank" Chinese masses and impress onto them a new version of the good society in which egoism is destroyed and exploitation of man by man is ended. Such utopian visions of the good society are necessary if we are to be able to appropriate the best from the past, to view the present critically, and to move with some hope into the future. However, there are obvious dangers when such utopian visions are implemented by *state* power and the distinction between sin and crime is lost. When this happens, non-conformity becomes not only heretical but criminal. Within the closed circle of such a system, logic becomes a tyrant whose henchmen search the corners and byways to bring everyone and everything into orderly compliance. Nothing is intentionally passed by; only oversight and neglect and weakness offer respite and relief.

Apart from the rights or wrongs of utopian visions, there are serious questions that can be posed about the future of the Maoist vision of the New Man in the New Society. Can the Chinese way endure under conditions of life in a highly urban industrial society? Will efficiency, specialization, and bureaucratic rationality eventually dissipate the appeal of revolutionary values? Is Mao one of the last great political romantics whose vision is ultimately doomed? It is tempting to treat such questions as rhetorical, and predict China's future on the basis of the experience of the early-modernizers. But precedents are of dubious worth in this case. Not just in China (or in the developing countries), but throughout the world, the present is a time of great institutional flux. It seems likely that we shall see a proliferation of social experiments that will enlarge our vision of what modernity means. All we can do here is note some limiting factors which the Maoist experiment is likely to face.

One such factor is that in discrepancies between behavior and values it is the values rather than the behavior patterns that are most likely to give way. Some modern institutions unthinkingly require people to act and reason in certain ways, whatever an individual's values. Living in a modern city, for example, obliges one to acquire habits of planning regularity. Factories and complex organizations require functional specialization and output-determined definitions of "efficiency" and "waste." Modern schools immerse one in mathematics and the natural and physical sciences, which can provide a contagious style of logic and objectivity. The factory assembly line epitomizes the basic modern pattern: an endless stream of fragmented bits flowing relentlessly along, with man standing on the side, adding or subtracting little to the whole, yet finding his life dominated by the "rationality" of machine processes.

Second, the limits of human willpower and endurance are being tested by the Chinese approach to social transformation. One of the elements that Maoism stresses most is "voluntarism," or the role of human consciousness in refashioning the social environment. Only by emphasizing this human factor over objective material factors could the CCP undertake to leapfrog the historically "inevitable" phase of capitalism and construct a socialist state—even a Communist state—upon a precapitalist material and social base. Determination and willpower, whether spontaneous or stimulated, are indeed the greatest assets of the regime, and care is taken that the tempo of struggle keeps them high. There are continuous struggles and campaigns: struggles for production, for socialism, for the liberation of the world's oppressed, struggles against class enemies, against doctrinal heresies, against the "bourgeois" within oneself. These repeated exhortations and self-accusations may succeed up to a point, but they can also become self-defeating. They may end in bitter disappointment, suppressed hostility, and cynical compliance.

A third limiting factor is the inveterate tendency of large organizations—such as the Party, the government, and the army—to become professional over time and lose their dynamic political orientation. Like the layers of sediment that collect in paint jars left standing too long, the various functional units in institutions seem to settle into separate specialized domains. In the young United States Thomas Jefferson favored a new revolution every twenty years to forestall this tendency. There are signs that this problem has already presented itself in China, and that the Cultural Revolution is in part Mao's response to it. Whether the problem will be solved, it is too soon to say. Still, Mao's own remark that Marx, Engels, and Lenin might look ridiculous a thousand years from now represents a recognition that the changes in the future may be too unexpected and bizarre to be called "defeats" or "victories."

NOTES

1. Cyril E. Black, *The Dynamics of Modernization* (New York: Harper & Row, 1966), p. 166.

2. Much of the literature on modernization is in the form of "orienting statements," i.e., definitions and discussions of some aspect of the larger process. In some areas actual theories that assert relationships between

two measurable variables are being proposed. In time it is possible that enough relationships can be specified to make sense out of individual threads in the overall tapestry (intellectual, economic, social, political, and psychological). Establishing the interrelationships between these various "threads" would be the final task in giving modernization theory a "scientific" (theoretically predictive) basis. It is highly doubtful that this will ever be done, considering the complexity of the subject, the elusiveness of much data, and the limitations of the human mind and lifetime. At this point in time, it seems much more appropriate to acknowledge limitations than to tally up accomplishments.

3. The four variables I shall examine are discussed by Black, *op. cit.,* even though he does not apply them to China.

4. Maurice J. Meisner, *Li Ta-chao and the Origins of Chinese Marxism* (Cambridge: Harvard University Press, 1967), pp. 246–56.

5. For an exploration of this process of psychological adjustment, see Joseph R. Levenson, *Confucian China and Its Modern Fate* (Berkeley: University of California Press, 1958).

6. See, for example, Hu Sheng, *Imperialism and Chinese Politics* (Peking, 1955).

7. One suggestive treatment of the "relentless reciprocity" that binds together intruders and natives in such situations is Albert Memmi, *The Colonizer and the Colonized* (New York: Grossman, 1957), which focuses on North Africa.

8. The analysis that follows is based closely on the recent synthesis by Barrington Moore, Jr., *Social Origins of Dictatorship and Democracy* (Boston: Beacon Press, 1966).

9. Robert J. Lifton, *Thought Reform and the Psychology of Totalism* (New York: W. W. Norton, 1963).

China and the unfinished revolutions of Asia

FELICIANO CARINO

The encounter between East and West constitutes much of the modern history of Asia. No diagnosis of Asia's present political and social disorders can be adequate without an analysis of the political impact of the West. At the same time, the inner crisis and disintegration of Western society is best seen in its present interaction with Asia.

In the last half of the twentieth century, the dynamics of Asia's response to the West and the inner agony and hope it has created are perhaps best represented by the Chinese Revolution. If Hiroshima in 1945 marked the brutal defeat of an Asian power that posed the first major challenge to Western control of Asia's future, the birth of the People's Republic of China in 1949 is another symbolic expression of the harsh political realities of this encounter that includes the story of Western exploitation and the rise of Asian nationalism in revolt.

MODERNIZATION OR REVOLUTION?

It is this Asian nationalist revolt, still incipient in some countries but already underway in others, that the rise of China brings to the surface of Asia's contemporary political and social life. The drive to modernize and industrialize, so widespread in Asia today, cannot be fully understood apart from this unfinished political revolution. It is important to point this out initially because it has become common in recent times among Western observers to interpret contemporary Asia in terms of modernization.

By modernization is usually meant the dynamic form that the process of technological innovation has taken in recent times and the manner by which the results of such innovation have been

69

related to the resolution of social and political problems to achieve optimum use of human and material resources. While, in principle, modernization is more than economic development, and includes the adjustments in social and political organization that technological innovation brings about, it is often true that modernization theory tends to emphasize the technological and economic features.

As a way of viewing both the dynamics and the goals of Asian social and political life, modernization is rationalist and materialist in orientation. It is often characterized as a process of rationalization in all those spheres of social action—economic, political, military, educational, and so on—that lend themselves to norms of reason. It is conceived as involving sustained attention to the most appropriate and efficient methods of increasing man's ability to control nature and society. Economists have tended to equate it with industrialization because in industrial development the meaning of rationalization has been clearest. It tends also to involve a highly developed division of labor, a "functional specificity," according to which men must have a comparatively high degree of autonomy and authority within their respective areas of competence. It involves, moreover, norms of universality rather than ascription, and thus implies social mobility and the opening up of careers to talents.

This is certainly an attractive goal for most Asian societies, and no responsible Asian political leader denies the need to modernize. The rising demands of Asian peoples cannot be met without it. Nor can effective equality with the old states of the West be achieved without it. It has been the common experience of colonial peoples that all their efforts to liberate themselves from Western control failed as long as they faced the modern West equipped only with traditional techniques of warfare and social organization. Only after they have absorbed some elements of the spiritual, scientific, and material revolution that has transformed Western man and society since the sixteenth century have non-Western nations been able to free themselves.

Modernization, then, is central to any realistic picture of the contemporary Asian scene as well as to any projection of the future. However, the conditions under which it is realized and the methods and the values that shape the process vary enormously, and these differences have their effect upon the outcome. When modernization is made the overarching framework within which all else is fitted, this often not only distorts the picture but runs counter to the impulses of contemporary Asian politics. This is why modernization theory has at times functioned as a rationalization of the present pattern of Western relationships with Asia, and has been used as an ideology of Western dominance.[1] For it to be useful in the achievement of Asian aspirations, one needs to place it within the wider context of Asia's unfinished political revolution.

THE MODERN CONCEPT OF REVOLUTION

"Revolutions," writes Hannah Arendt, "are the only political events which confront us directly and inevitably with new beginnings."[2] In her analysis of modern revolutionary movements, Arendt discovers that beyond the political upheavals these have created, their significance lies even more in the manner in which they share in the faith that the course of history can begin anew, that an entirely new story can unfold in man's social and political life. Modern revolutions are such profound events in their social impact not only because of the movements they have generated and the specific issues they have inspired—such as the ideas of equality and justice under law in the French revolution—but also because they have partaken of that more basic discovery, made not too long ago, of man's capacity for historical novelty, of reality in motion, of the future as an open possibility that is more than a mere unfolding of the past.

Historically, this view of revolution is a recent one. The Greeks, for example, used the word "revolution" to mean restoration. As an event in political, social, and intellectual life, its orientation was toward the past. The idea was related to the cyclic movements of the celestial bodies, and it came to mean return to a previous state of purity. Behind this lies a metaphysics of an unchanging and eternal order to which present and future must conform. Revolution was intended to preserve the previous state of greatness, which historical development had lost through distortion or corruption.

The modern concept of revolution is thus a transfer to politics of that view of reality that first emerged through the rise of modern science. More than any other movement in history, the modern scientific revolution broke the hold of the past and opened up new areas of unexplored possibilities for man. It shifted the attention of man from his preoccupation with the eternal and unchanging orders of Being to the relative, more risky, but more hopeful, dimensions of historical existence. Truth, in all areas of life, ceased to be defined in terms of tradition, as something given; it came to be seen as something in the process of formation, something which one discovers by means of an openended search. The amazing results this yielded, and the changes it brought about in the intellectual climate, intensified the yearning for novelty and change in other areas of life as well, and raised the possibility of the relative perfectibility of human society within the bounds of history. It is no accident that modern revolutionary ideologies are, in large part, responses to the challenge of the scientific revolution and its concomitant in social and economic life, industrialization. This can certainly be said of such Asian ideologies as Indonesia's *Pantjasila* and the Thought of Mao Tse-tung, as well as the intellectual and social analysis that gave birth to "The Great Proletarian Cultural Revolution." [3]

PROMETHEUS AS IMPERIALIST

This powerful transformation first took place in the West, and the West as a result has been the shaper of world history in the modern period. This revolutionary spirit spread from the dominant nations of Western Europe, first to Eastern Europe, to America, and then to Asia and the rest of the world. The world was unified and reshaped as the West expanded and took possession of the rest of the earth. In Asia, as in other areas, this dominance brought oppression and exploitation, but it also brought a revolutionary process comparable, though not identical, to that of the West. The process is still in motion. The movements for independence were only a part of it, albeit a vital part.

Among the determinants of the modern political history of Asia, its relationship with the West has been vital. It was through

Western expansion that Asian societies were pulled into the stream of the modern industrial revolution. And it was through the West that the dynamics of modern commercial society and the politics of nationalism were extended to Asia's formerly agrarian cultures. The interaction created tensions for both Asia and the West. For while the West was the initial bearer of this revolutionary impulse, it transmitted it to the rest of the world in a mode that led to Western dominance. The Westerner, therefore, has to share a double responsibility. He is, on the one hand, the archetypal revolutionary, "the Prometheus who stole fire from heaven and set the world ablaze." Yet at the same time, he is an imperialist, a capitalist, and an exploiter—the obvious target for the indignation of those in Asia and elsewhere whom he has exploited. If it is the West that made revolution a possibility for Asia, it increasingly appears that it is also the West that prevents its realization.

During the last thirty years, all the historic empires that ruled Asia have fallen and a multitude of new nations have emerged. Many of these new states are animated by hostility to Western hegemony and an intense desire to assert national independence. But at the same time they are not opposed to the new cosmopolitan civilization that is the fruit of Western expansion. Asian peoples today wish to be active partners in this civilization and to appropriate their full share of the material benefits it has produced. They have been pressured into a new cosmopolitan civilization which is by origin Western in principles and values, and they are reacting violently in defense of their respective national identities. This reaction, however, is not necessarily directed against the new world order itself, but rather against the external powers, whose preeminence is realized at their cost.

BUILDING A NEW IDENTITY

The bitterness of the reaction against Western and other alien domination is produced in part by the upheaval that traditional politics and cultures undergo under the impact of modernization. During the last two or three generations, so many traditional institutions that seemed to be essential to Asian civilizations have begun to lose prestige and to be threatened with change or destruction. Because of the upheaval in traditional institutions, for most Asian nations the primary and most immediate task on the way to the future is the formation of a new national identity. "Among the subjects never taught adequately to a colonized people," writes Han Suyin, "is its own history." [4] The study of historical development can—under the right conditions—inspire the feeling that it is in some measure within an Asian people's power to create history. Historical study thus can be a powerful instrument of liberation. The ongoing conversation of a people with their past and their awareness of historical process become important forces in the shaping of their future.

Han Suyin continues,

by making the people aware that they are intimately involved in this vast historical process, that they can even create and guide it, the Chinese Communist Party seeks to abolish the lag in understanding which, because of the pace of material change, leaves the mind, attitude, and behaviour still fettered to a previous epoch. To create understanding of the historical forces at work in the world, is in itself to accelerate historical processes, since the mental reluctance to change is diminished. . . . It is this role of history-study as history-maker . . . which is in action today in China, where "700 million critics, 700 million statesmen, 700 million students of the thought of Mao Tse-tung" are being trained to see themselves in the historical forces and to participate in them, to hasten the process taking place.[5]

The same process is occurring in many other Asian nations. Reappraisal of national histories in order to form new national identities has become a major preoccupation. This is a necessary first step in the liberation from the humiliating effects of the Western "assault" upon the individual and corporate existence of Asian peoples. Liberation can come only as a people, long accustomed to the deadening weight of colonial rule, discover that they have a past that is their own and a future that they can create, and that therefore they may order their national life in their own way and work out forms of economic, political, and social life that are genuinely their own. This is the heart of nationalism, which continues to be the strongest driving force in the political life of Asian nations today. It has its own "circle of rationality," and evokes forms of political behavior that are often difficult for Westerners to understand. And it includes not just a transformation of political and economic structures, but a cultural transformation as well. It involves the spiritual renewal of a people.

An example will illustrate the point. Analyzing the Philippine situation under Spanish rule at the turn of the century, José Rizal, one of the leading figures in the Philippine revolution of 1896, wrote bitterly of how the Spaniards treated Filipinos with contempt, as inferiors, "mere muscle, brutes, and beasts of burden," incapable of anything else. The Spaniards

> affirmed and took for granted what they wanted to believe. They made the race itself an object of insult. They professed themselves unable to see in it any admirable quality, any human trait. Certain writers and clergymen surpassed themselves by undertaking to prove that the natives lacked not only the capacity for virtue but even the talent for vice.[6]

In Rizal's view, the wounding of the Filipino in the most sensitive part of his spiritual being, his *amor propio,* his self-esteem, was a more powerful generator of the Philippine revolution than the actual acts of tyranny and oppression inflicted by the Spaniards. What prompted the revolt against Spain was in large measure the accumulation of resentment over this attitude toward the Philippine masses. This resentment, more spiritual than economic in origin, transformed the regional revolts and local uprisings that punctuated centuries of Spanish rule into a movement that sought an overthrow of the entire social system from top to bottom.

This is not to minimize the need for economic and political development so much as to put these within a wider framework. It is to emphasize that development takes place at particular moments in time and in concrete places within the lives of nations and peoples with their own peculiar histories and cultural heritages. Given the ethnic and cultural pluralism of many Asian nations, it is clear that only as these nations are able to discover how to integrate the diverse elements around newly established goals that the new national self-identity can emerge. Thus the Indonesian *Pantjasila*—the five principles of one God, nationalism (the creation of a national personality, as Sukarno used to put it), internationalist humanitarianism, social justice, and democracy or sovereignty of the people—was projected as a means of providing a framework of national unity in the midst of diversity and the continuing power of colonialism. The purpose is nation- and character-building.

INTELLECTUALS AND PEASANTS

In this search for national identity that is accompanied by a commitment to far-reaching transformations of individual and corporate life, two groups play particularly significant roles, the intellectuals and the peasantry. Intellectuals are important because they are in the paradoxical position of bearing the values, skills, and intellectual ethos of a modern society before their societies have achieved any significant degree of modernization.

Intellectuals are also important since they are the focal point of the inherent crisis and contradiction of colonialism. While their education and training have usually been provided under Western auspices, and for this reason they have assimilated much that is Western in their values and patterns of thought, the continuation of Western dominance frustrates them to no end, and does not harmonize easily with their new-found values of equality and justice. They tend therefore to be the leaders of anticolonialist movements and the shapers of nationalism. Nowhere are the internal contradictions of colonialism—its dual nature as a modernizing and a conservative force in the underdeveloped societies—clearer than in its effects on native intellectuals. It produces these intellectuals and yet it frustrates them, thus arousing their opposition. It produces in them its own gravediggers.

If intellectuals provide the leadership for revolutionary politics in Asia, peasants provide the mass base. Asia, after all, is still primarily agrarian, and peasants constitute the downtrodden of most Asian societies. Peasants have always, therefore, played a significant role in political movements in Asian countries. The history of mass movements in the Philippines, which extends back to the early twenties, and of political revolts during the period of Spanish rule, has been dominated by peasant participation. In Indonesia, it was found necessary very early in the struggle for national independence to rely on this constituency. As Roesland Abdulgani puts it,

It should be well remembered, that since 1920, the Indonesian nationalist movement had already made a thorough study of the question: what should be the aim and how should the strategy and tactics be of the nationalist movement? In their comparative study of British colonialism towards Indian nationalist movements, the Indonesian leaders at that time came to the conclusion that the Indonesian struggle for freedom cannot be based upon middle-class people, as in India, because the Indonesian middle-class traders had been virtually destroyed during the period of Dutch finance-capitalism in the 19th century. The Indonesian nationalist had to work with the broad layer of "the little men," of the "common men," composed of the millions of peasants, fishermen, workers, vendors and lower officials in the colonial bureaucracy. Contrary to Marx's conception of the proletarian, Sukarno came to the Marhaen—the name of a poor peasant in West Java, whom he elevates as the symbol of the source of strength and power of the nationalist movement.[7]

This fact, however, is often concealed and its significance minimized by the drive toward modernization. The preoccupation with rapid industrialization has often led to a dichotomy between progress and technological advance in a few urban centers and continuing poverty and stagnancy in the rural areas. Thus, while the city has been elevated as a symbol of modernization and progress, the peasants view such developments as having been achieved at their expense and are resentful of it.

In their fascination and enthusiasm for modernization of their societies, intellectuals are often equally insensitive to this dichotomy. There is therefore increasing evidence that the relationship between intellectuals and peasants—so vital in revolutionary politics in Asia—is not always a smooth one. This inner contradiction of modernization in the still agrarian societies of Asia is perhaps the most critical issue that the triumph of the Chinese Revolution raises in any consideration of revolutionary change in Asia today. Working primarily with China's rural peasants, the Chinese Revolution has refocused attention upon the question of the mobilization and organization of the peasantry as a crucial factor in Asia's political future.

THE LEGACIES OF COLONIALISM

Finally, the political future of Asia depends in large measure upon the course of the struggle with the legacies of colonialism. Consider, for example, the American presence in Asia: close to a million military personnel, numerous bases, interlocking defense pacts, and economic trade agreements. Consider also Sukarno's oft-quoted lament that years after Indonesians supposedly won their independence, they still think like the Dutch, speak like the Dutch, and dress like the Dutch. One after another, many Asian peoples are coming to the recognition that colonialism is not just a political fact, but *a total social and cultural reality*. In the days of colonial rule, the domination and dependence were such that many of the decisions regarding the whole fabric of political, economic, educational, and cultural life were made outside the country. This culture of dependence runs very deeply into the spirit and promotes a kind of "reflexive" existence. It is this that lives on after the colonial ruler is gone, and it is in this sense that the legacy of colonialism is often more destructive to the native than colonial rule itself.

There is an economic side to the aftermath of colonialism. The West entered the twentieth century assuming the truth of Adam Smith's view that the "wealth of nations" is achieved through economic effort freed of political restrictions. His argument for international free trade, a corollary of the more general proposition that individual self-interest is the primary instrument of social progress, projected that the most rational use of human and material resources will occur automatically if people are allowed to follow their natural inclinations under conditions of free competition. This is generally true everywhere, Smith asserted, and it is particularly true in the trade relations between nations. From this it follows that the burgeoning wealth of an increasingly technologically and industrially advanced world can be shared by the less developed through free trade.

But consider this laissez-faire doctrine in the light of the findings of the United Nations Conference on Trade and Development. It has become clear that as a result of the organization of international trade according to Smith's basic principles, the "wealth of nations" has not in fact been widely distributed but has instead become more and more concentrated in the hands of the developed nations of the West. The rich nations have become richer and the poor poorer, and the gap between them has broadened consistently. This is primarily because the terms of trade are determined by prices of primary commodities set by the more powerful and developed nations.

As the Final Act of the Geneva Trade and Development Conference states, "the joint income of the developing countries, with two-thirds of the world's population, is not much more than one-tenth of that of the industrialized countries." As the world economy swiftly expands, the results of scientific and technological progress widen the gap still further. The value of world exports has more than doubled since 1950, but the developing countries' share in the profits has been declining steadily "from nearly one-third in 1950 to slightly more than one-fifth in 1962"—and at a time, we should note, when development in the poorer countries required imports of capital goods and technical skills from developed nations. The growing gap between import and export monies has put the severest strains on development plans.

Many factors in underdeveloped countries no doubt contribute to this problem. Yet even when "their plans, policies and institutions are designed to provide for maximum savings, investment and output to a predetermined order of priorities for a targeted rate of growth," their realization has been hindered "by the instability of international markets for primary products and by conditions restricting access of primary commodities and semi-manufactures and manufactures to the markets of the developed countries." [8]

The evasive and even hostile reactions of the more developed countries to some of the remedial proposals made by the Geneva Conference show that this issue will continue to plague international relations for a long time to come. The end of the colonial era has not yet come, regardless of what flags fly in Djakarta, Delhi, and Bangkok.

ASIA AND THE RISE OF CHINA

So the Asian revolution remains unfinished—stagnated, as it were, in midprocess. This is the fundamental reality to recognize when speaking of the future of Asia.

There is also the presence of the Asian giant—China—a reality with which Asian peoples have had to cope long before the Western presence or revolution. Long before the "green jade, chop suey, and laundry men" became objects of fascination for Westerners, and served as their experience and image of China, Limahong, a Chinese emigrant, landed in Lingayen Gulf in the northern part of the Philippines and attempted to take the islands from Spain. Limahong was not an expression of official Chinese foreign policy, but his coming to the Philippines was a representative event in the long history of relations between China and her Southeast Asian neighbors, relations that were as much or more commercial and cultural as political.

The long history of relations with China brought to most of the countries of Asia the Chinese resident. Reactions to this Chinese presence have ranged from assimilation (as for example in the case of Thailand, where many members of the elite have Chinese blood); to mutual commercial exploitation, accompanied by tightening of legislative controls on Chinese holdings (as in the case of the Philippines); to open hostility (as in the case of Indonesia) because of the suspicion that the Chinese resident is an agent of Chinese interference in domestic affairs.

This history of Chinese presence in other parts of Asia must not be overlooked in assessing the impact of the rise of China upon her Asian neighbors. In the Philippines, for example, the Chinese account for 17.4 per cent of the investments in single ownerships, partnerships, and corporations, despite the fact that they represent less than one-thirtieth of the population. They also account for 75 per cent of the total foreign investments in complete proprietorships, 94 per cent in partnerships, and 86 per cent in corporations. Their middleman or *comprador* activities produce much power: they are the primary distributors of rice, lumber, sugar, and other important domestic commodities. They are also the local distributors for such large foreign concerns as Ford, General Motors, Mercedes Benz, and so on. As former President Diosdado Macapagal has observed, "Some of these fears [of the Chinese] are emotional, imaginary, and irrational, while others have a foundation in fact." [9]

Because of their economic power, the Chinese in the Philippines represent a power to be reckoned with in the domestic politics of the country, and the allegiance of this power is often suspect. From both the right and the left come attacks on the Chinese merchants. From the right come attacks on the Chinese because they are seen as "foreign" competitors in commerce. From the left come attacks because the Chinese are seen as part of the establishment that must be changed.

China thus is a powerful reality that must be dealt with on two fronts: in the relations between nations and in domestic affairs. This has been going on for centuries, long before the advent of the Cold War. For this reason few Asians can be romantic about the rise of China. Yet, at the same time, this long history of intercourse with China has meant that much Chinese culture has been assimilated into the cultures of other Asian societies, and this in turn has helped nurture appropriate patterns of discourse with China. Unlike the Americans, Southeast Asian peoples have developed ways of living with China's power and influence.

THE CHINESE REVOLUTION AS MIRROR

So neither revolution nor China is new to the experience of the rest of Asia. But the *Chinese Revolution* is. Unfortunately, because of the present polarizations in Asian politics, little is being done in non-Communist Asia to undertake the much-needed look at the challenge of this revolution. And yet its impact cannot be resisted for long. The Chinese Revolution is too monumental an event and too close to the rest of Asia for anyone to contain it. And no effort at containing China can prevent its influence from being felt, especially by those who seek to build a new Asia. The reasons for this are not difficult to locate.

First, *the historical experience out of which the Chinese Revolution grew is common to the modern history of other Asian nations.* To look at Asia through the telescope of China's recent political history, and vice versa, is to see why the revolution initiated by the Western "assault" can no longer be consummated or controlled by the West, but must work itself out in bitter reaction against the West.

Rarely do men in the West understand what it means for a country like China, steeped in traditions that extend far into the past, to enter the Western genius. For those who have been raised in an industrial society, the industrial system is taken for granted. They tend to lack any conception of how industrialism affects those who are confronted directly out of preindustrial experience. Assuming their own feelings to be natural, they forget how mixed their first reactions to industrialism were in their own societies. This failure to remember accounts for the widespread conviction that the reactions to industrialism in non-Western societies reflect cultural backwardness.

Thus it has been difficult to understand the rise of China and the methods by which this has been accomplished. But when this revolution is seen in the context of Asia's modern political history, a different perspective appears. The significance of the Chinese Revolution for the rest of Asia derives not from the fact that it presents us with a model applicable everywhere, but rather from the fact that it reflects to a large degree the mood of Asia's modern history.

This is the great significance of the Thought of Mao Tse-tung. Philosopher, economic planner, politician, and revolutionary, his Thought prompts a ready response from an increasingly large number of Asians because it is attuned to some of the main aspirations of modern Asian societies: the bitter reaction against Western dominance, the radical rearrangement of social and political structures, the fascination with science and technology, and also the protest against the soullessness and inhumanity that often result from the process of transformation. The Thought of Mao Tse-tung comes not so much as a new argument that convinces with facts and figures, but rather as a focus to ideas and sentiments already engendered by the swirl of change.

Hope is a dominant theme in Mao's writings. In the context of China's recent political history, his is a faith to which people can turn who no longer can find sustenance in ancient values and institutions yet who fear the internal chaos which may result from letting these things go. This is a political faith which dares to accept the ruined past of a traditional civilization and build anew, almost from the ground up. It is a faith which people can adopt as the expression of their rejection of dependence on the West.

THE CHINESE REVOLUTION AS SYMBOL

This leads to a second point: *in the light of the unfinished character of Asia's political revolution, the rise of China and the Chinese Revolution are symbols of a revolutionary fervor which Asia still needs*. While revolution is hardly new to Asia, it is still to be consummated. The sudden bursts of enthusiasm that came through the various independence movements and the hopes these sparked for the future of Asian nations have quieted down. In many cases, they have been discredited through betrayal. Preoccupation with the demands of day-to-day existence in the post-independence period has diverted attention from more long-range and far-reaching transformations of society and state. The lesson, moreover, of the postindependence period has been that while revolution is possible, so is counterrevolution, and that while the established powers may be corrupt, they remain very strong.

It is in the midst of this postindependence reaction and lethargy that an Asian revolutionary may look at China. The revolution that Mao espouses is a total one, devoted to the total remaking of Chinese society. Nothing is to be left untouched: even the most sacred and time-honored traditions are deliberately subjected to criticism and attack. Related to this is a "conversionist" element in Mao's thought.* Revolutionary change is not simply a matter of changing the structures of social institutions but also of transforming the cultural ethos that shapes the spirit of man. "The fundamental point in Mao's thought," writes Kazuhiko Sumiya, "is the inner transformation of man which is brought about through the total transformation of the organization of society." [10] Purging China of egoism and producing a people free of self-love is the staggering goal of this process. The conviction that this can in fact happen is one of the central forces behind the Chinese Revolution.

The political aspirations of this Revolution are equally large and dramatic. "The great challenge of the modern world," writes Franz Schurmann, "is the transformation of masses who are outside of the world into individuals who become a part of it." [11] Mao teaches that social revolution is inevitable in the poor countries of the world, and that through its political organization revolution accomplishes this task. It reaches out to the most distant and poverty-stricken of the peasant masses. It is from them that revolution draws its strength, and in the course of the struggle they are transformed.

This kind of optimism has rarely been found in the recent political doctrines of the West. The emphasis on personal change as an integral part of the revolutionary process and therefore also of revolutionary strategy has been almost forgotten in the reaction against excessive individualism and pietism. Likewise, in non-Communist Asia, there is little to compare with this kind of revolutionary faith. Whether or not the Chinese will succeed is a judgment that only future Chinese history can render. But the very fact that the Chinese are trying constitutes an inspiration to those who likewise want to bring about social change.

Among the formerly colonized peoples of the world China is perhaps the only really independent nation, fully in command of

---

* Mao is one of the few political figures in the world today whose political philosophy emphasizes conversion in a sense analogous to that of traditional Christian thought. Perhaps part of the reason why theologians have such difficulty dealing with Mao's Thought (on the few occasions when they bother to discuss it) is that conversion has almost disappeared from the theologian's vocabulary.

the main processes that determine her fate. She has done successful battle with the legacies of colonialism. Compared with most
other developing nations, the pace of her economic development
has been good, especially when the size of the population and the
needs faced at the time of the revolution are taken into account.
Within a comparatively brief period of time she has achieved
military capabilities that make her a power with which both the
Soviet Union and the United States have to reckon. In having
made China strong again, the Communist Revolution has restored
a sense of national pride and dignity among its people that is a
staggering contrast to the demoralization that swept the country
in the wake of Western penetration. Despite these achievements,
however, Mao Tse-tung does not cease to press the revolution
forward still further.

REVOLUTION AND IDEOLOGY IN ASIA

Finally, *the Chinese Revolution raises in a fresh way for Asia the
question of the ideology from which the drive to change emerges
and through which it derives direction and meaning.* Ideology is a
term that is used primarily pejoratively in most American academic circles. Ideological thinking is said to fall prey to oversimplification, prejudice, psychological imbalances, distortion of
facts, and so on. It is hardly an accident, therefore, that the
deliberately ideological character of the Chinese revolution seldom
receives a hearing.

Such antipathy to ideology is itself an ideological bias. Its
advocates often overlook the objective need for ideology in
societies that are undergoing large social and political changes.
A new ideology has arisen in China because the traditional social
and political system was not capable any longer of giving unity to
individual and social life. The fact that a Maoist-Marxist framework has been projected to replace the old worldview, to receive
the same kind of commitment as that originally attached in
Chinese civilization to Confucianism, is a phenomenon that is
hardly comprehensible to those who hold the "plague on ideology" assumptions.

The Maoist-Marxist ideology has provided a new framework

in China by which reality is interpreted and made coherent and social existence is given new direction, after traditional patterns of thought and behavior have been rendered ineffective and unacceptable. The need for a total worldview remains in the developing world today. This is especially true in areas where ancient religious traditions previously have defined the terms of political life.

STANDING MARX ON HIS HEAD

The character of the new ideological framework is graphically illustrated in the Chinese Cultural Revolution, in which we can observe a dialectic between the thought of Mao and that of Marx. Mao seems at times to be standing Marx on his head in a manner parallel to Marx's reversal of Hegel. In turning Hegel upside down, Marx explained the dialectics of history in the material circumstances of human existence. The dialectic remained but was separated from Hegel's immanent Idea. The metaphors of the Cultural Revolution, on the other hand, reflect a return to idealism. Thus, *The Decision of the Central Committee of the Communist Party of China,* released on August 8, 1966, declares that the Cultural Revolution is so designed that "it touches people to their very souls." Here we have theological language, mystical and evangelical. The aim of the Cultural Revolution is "to revolutionize people's ideology" and "as a consequence to achieve greater, faster, better and more economical results in all fields of work." Ideology is clearly given priority over material circumstances. Mao is quoted as saying, "While we recognize that in the general development of history, the material determines the mental, and social being determines social consciousness, we also —and indeed must—recognize the reaction of mental on material things." [12]

In this new "Marxist" system, it is natural that a main enemy is "economism." Reactionaries are accused of offering the peasant more incentives and the workers higher wages. Likewise, it is natural that Mao relies primarily in the Cultural Revolution on students: they are the ones most likely to be moved by ideas and ideals and least likely to be preoccupied with wage increases and job benefits. Marx wanted to utilize economic motivation in order to transform society; Mao scorns it in order to transform man himself. Nothing less than this is his enormous aspiration in the twilight years of his life, and it is in keeping that some of his writings about these themes read like Christian homilies. Faith can remove mountains, insists the widely read *Foolish Old Man Who Removed Mountains.*

Mao breaks with Marx in order to stimulate fervor. Hegel saw the Prussian state as the culmination and resolution of the dialectic of history. Marx in his turn saw Communist society as this culmination and resolution. Both were convinced that the contradictions of history would come to an eventual end. Whatever lip service he may pay to Marxist orthodoxy, Mao is not much concerned with the culmination and resolution of history and the end of struggle. Even in the socialist society, he insists, "there will be contradictions after 1,000 or 10,000 or even 100 million years." Revolutionary fervor must go on without ceasing; the revolutionary cause must be perpetuated generation after generation.

The power of this idealism is certainly one of the factors to which one must point in explaining the appeal of Mao's thought to the youth of China. As I. F. Stone has written, we see in China

> that same call to struggle and sacrifice that has recruited the first followers of all great religions and revolutions. To his exasperated opponents, . . . Mao's call for supermen must seem like Nietzsche's genius streaked with lunacy. It will probably prove as impracticable as the Sermon on the Mount. If Mao fails, as all his predecessors have failed, it is because man, still half-monkey, cannot live at so high a pitch, and when the bugles die down prefers a quiet scratch in the warm sun.[13]

The power of this idealism also explains the appeal of Mao's Thought to many other Asians. For an increasing number of intellectuals in the Philippines and Thailand and Vietnam, there seems neither time nor room for the quiet scratch. The urgency of the need for large-scale social change and the power of its opponents stands in the forefront of thought, obscuring dreams of quiet pleasures. To those who struggle against "powers and principalities" in these countries, Mao's thought can only serve as an inspiration.

TOMORROW IN ASIA . . .

To sum up, this essay has tried to show that while the Chinese Revolution is peculiar to China, the history out of which it has emerged and the thought which has guided it bear marked similarities to the history and political thought of much of the rest of Asia. The immediate policy issues that China's rise to power raises are certainly of concern to her Asian neighbors, yet these issues cannot be treated adequately without a deep and sensitive look at China, both her past and her future. The future of other Asian peoples, it is becoming increasingly clear, is inseparably related to that of China. Her traditions and her new hopes must be understood if that future is to be faced positively. This is both an intellectual and a political problem which must be confronted directly and not skirted. China poses an enormous challenge to the rest of Asia. What will happen if, twenty or so years from now, China becomes the fully developed, technologically advanced nation that she promises to be, while her neighbors remain feudal, agrarian, and dependent on the West for their security?

NOTES

1. See, for example, W. W. Rostow, "Guerilla Warfare in Underdeveloped Areas," in Marcus G. Raskin and Bernard B. Fall, eds., *The Viet-Nam Reader* (New York: Vintage Books, 1965), pp. 108–16.

2. Hannah Arendt, *On Revolution* (New York: Viking Books, 1965), p. 13.

3. On this point, see Mary Matossian, "Ideologies of Delayed Industrialization: Some Tensions and Ambiguities," in John H. Kautsky, ed., *Political Change in Underdeveloped Countries: Nationalism and Communism* (New York: John Wiley & Sons, 1964), pp. 252–64.

4. Han Suyin, *China in the Year 2001* (New York: Basic Books, 1967), p. 6.

5. *Ibid.,* p. 7.

6. José Rizal, quoted in Horacio de la Costa, *The Background of Nationalism and Other Essays* (Manila, 1965), p. 34.

7. Roesland Abdulgani, "Recent Political Changes in Indonesia," speech delivered at Yale University, 1967 (New York: Permanent Mission of the Republic of Indonesia to the United Nations), p. 3.

8. *United Nations Conference on Trade and Development: Final Act* (Geneva), duplicated report. See also *Issues before UNCTAD II* (New York, 1967).

9. Diosdado Macapagal, quoted in Arnold C. Brackman, "The Malay World and China: Partner or Barrier?" in Abraham M. Halpern, ed., *Policies Toward China: Views from Six Continents* (New York: McGraw-Hill, 1965), p. 289. The statistics on the Chinese role in the Philippine economy are also drawn from Brackman's essay.

10. Kazuhiko Sumiya, "The Historical Significance of Mao Tse-tung's Thought," (WSCF China Project Document no. 28), p. 3; see also Sumiya's essay in the present volume.

11. Franz Schurmann, *Ideology and Organization in Communist China* (Berkeley: University of California Press, 1967), p. xliv.

12. Mao Tse-tung, quoted in *I. F. Stone's Weekly,* January 30, 1967, p. 1.

13. I. F. Stone, *op. cit.,* p. 2.

Long day's journey:

American observers in China, 1948–50

TOM ENGELHARDT

THE VIEW FROM THE TOP

When the Kuomintang returned to Shanghai in 1945, foreign newsmen took over the top five floors of the eighteen-floor "Broadway Mansions." There, in the "city's closest approach to a modern American skyscraper," [1] they set up their correspondents' club, arranged their lodgings, and danced "under gaily colored lights" while "White Russian mistresses mingled with American wives and both cursed the Chinese." [2] From the windows of their clubrooms, they had a "bird's-eye view" of Shanghai: the Bund, the foreign banks, the American consulate. In the cold winter of 1948 they could watch crowds of refugees in their tattered clothes, milling below; in the spring of 1949, they saw demoralized Nationalist troops commandeering transportion to flee south. They could see "agitators" executed on the street corners and clerks bicycling past, hampers overloaded with worthless money. On the morning of May 25, 1949, they awoke to see, sleeping in rows on the sidewalks in the same faded-yellow padded uniforms, the troops of an army from another China, the People's Liberation Army.

Like generations of British, French, and other European diplomats, teachers, advisers, newsmen, and businessmen before them, Americans in China came to have a proprietary feeling toward the country in which they were living. They were there for various reasons. There were some, like the reporters Doak Barnett and Jean Lyon, born of missionary parents and brought up in China, who had not even returned to the United States until sent there for college. Later they had "found the old bond with the Orient as strong as ever" [3] and had returned. Some, like Ambassador

Leighton Stuart, the ex-president of Yenching University, had not only been born and bred in China, but had worked there for so many years that they remembered little about their own country. Others, like the editor of the English-language *Shanghai Evening Post and Mercury* or the reporter Archibald Steele, though not born in China, had been there so long that they too were "Old China Hands." For these people the ties were deep.

Americans like Christopher Rand of the *New Yorker* magazine had worked for the United States in China (Office of War Information) during the war and stayed on. Businessmen came out from their home offices. Diplomats and other U.S. officials had been sent there on assignment. By the late 1940s, they tended to come from "recent service in Washington or Europe [with their] increasingly hardline attitudes of the cold war." [4] Embassy official John Melby, while not a "Cold Warrior," had been sent to China in 1945 by Averell Harriman, who believed that "officers with Moscow background should be stationed at strategic spots around the world." [5] Like Melby, few of these men knew much about China or even were particularly interested in it before their arrival. While their interest grew, their proprietary concern for China was clearly more political than personal.

Others went for the adventure itself, for the chance to overcome the frustrations of home life, to move freely, or to become someone. These people just took off—perhaps after having read a few books, studied the language a little, and made a few contacts. They were like Julian Schuman, who "saw the Dodgers go down into the dust, bought a handbook on journalism, said goodbye to my family in Brooklyn . . . [and] boarded the S.S. *Iran Victory,* a beatup service vessel turned freighter, now bound for Shanghai." [6] There was also a small group of American intellectuals who were (or planned to become) professional students of China. They went to study or to teach at China's Westernized universities. Derk Bodde, for instance, went on a Fulbright grant to translate a history of Chinese philosophy against the background of the Chinese civil war.

These Americans in China tended to live in relative comfort in the only places where such comfort could be found, China's larger cities, particularly Shanghai. Most often they lived in those areas of the cities Westerners themselves had built to their own tastes. There they conducted the business they felt important, imported (often duty free) the luxuries necessary to their daily lives, ran "Chinese" industries, parceled out their "aid," made contact with Chinese officialdom, and found the necessary interpreters for those moments when they could not get along in English.

During the late 1940s, the privileged position of any American in China was enhanced by the widening separation of the cities from the countryside, the swift collapse of the Nationalist economy, and the increasing dependence of the government on the whim of the United States for its very existence. In the cities, the social order was disintegrating. Yet the soundness of the American dollar, the protection of American power, and the noose of American aid all gave a placid quality to the lives of Americans in China's cities. They were detached from the chaos and increasing misery they saw around them. In Shanghai, which housed the greatest concentration of Americans,

> the American colony must have numbered two thousand, perhaps three, and it was a self-engrossed town within the detached [city]. The few remaining "Old China Hands" were submerged by crowds of younger Americans who regarded China as a strange but incidental background to their office work and their pleasures at parties, country clubs, or nightclubs.[7]

Among all classes of urban Chinese, there was growing resentment toward this privileged position. Even at the highest levels of government there was an undercurrent of resentment. From 1946 on, this resentment was reflected in the government-controlled KMT press. In the summers of 1947 and 1948, Chinese students (and often their teachers as well) took to the streets to protest both the way in which American aid was prolonging the civil war and the "atrocities" committed by individual Americans in China. They were, Jean Lyon commented, "only saying publicly what millions feel." [8]

However all this was felt by American observers in a limited way. "Officials tried to cushion the contacts between Americans and natives; often their efforts produced an illusion that the populace was friendly." [9] In some quarters there was worry that America's "reservoir of goodwill" was seeping away and suspicion that the growing feeling of resentment to the presence of foreigners in China bore an eery resemblance to the situation that produced the Boxer Rebellion of 1900. But most Americans passed this off. Either, they thought, the war-ravaged Chinese populace was simply using the foreigner as a "convenient" target or they were being exploited by the Communists, those ruthless elements in Chinese society who wished to use "every available group . . . to foster economic and political discontent." [10] The general feeling among Americans was that a finger had been mistakenly pointed at them as they went quietly about their daily business. On the other hand, Chinese officials, intellectuals, businessmen, students, and newsmen—all those Chinese with whom Americans had some contact—were left with a feeling of humiliation, outrage, and helplessness over America's role in China. It seemed a situation in which (in Mao's phrase) they could not "stand up."

The hinterland

There was another China, a rural China where eighty per cent of the Chinese population lived. In that China, millions of peasants under the leadership of the Chinese Communist Party had risen with great passion and bitterness, breaking the back of traditional land tenure relationships, often killing the landlords who for so long had controlled their lives. In that China a volunteer army had been created among the peasants. There, not so far from the isolated KMT-controlled cities, the whole structure of Chinese society was being torn apart and put together anew.

Yet as the Chinese civil war reached its climax and the revolutionary army moved on the cities, promising their inhabitants a new life (a "liberation"), that China, peasant China, remained a dark land for all but a few American observers. To go there, even when the distance was only a couple of hundred miles, required arduous, roundabout, and time-consuming travel. Living in the desolate and backward liberated areas was for an American journalist an uncomfortable, dirty, and tiring business. Cables could not be sent or stories forwarded. "The chief problem about covering China from [Nanking]," Gordon Walker of the *Monitor* complained, "is that practically nothing is known about the other side." [11] There had been rumors, of course—brief reports, speculations, and a vague sense that the Communists were "penetrating the villages and finding a response where for a long time no one had cared what happened or who thought what." [12] A few intrepid adventurers had actually ventured into those unknown regions and observed that a revolution was, in fact, in progress. But those like Jack Belden, who came back to tell his tale, had trouble finding magazines willing to print what they saw, while others declined to come back at all, choosing instead to cast their lot with the revolutionaries.

For the rest, peasant China was an enigma to be noticed only out of the corner of the eye. To leave the usual trails for even a brief foray into the nearest countryside was to step over a line into another world. It was not that these men did not see the injustices in the way the peasant was forced to live in rural China. They wrote of his lack of land, marginal existence, high rents, impossible taxes, and bad treatment at the hands of Nationalist troops. They reiterated the need for "reform," for the implementation of the laws already on the books of the Kuomintang regime. But there they stopped, caught up by the "complexity of the problem of achieving change and progress in China by peaceful, non-revolutionary means." [13]

When they went to verify their thoughts on rural China by seeing peasants at first hand, their forays with other Americans or KMT officials had the quality of processionals.

> Several of us made an overnight trip into the hinterland. By getting just fifty miles away from Chungking we dropped back a thousand years. . . . Breakfast in the little open air restaurant was witnessed by at least a hundred interested and respectful people who made me feel like Bourbon royalty.[14]

It is hardly strange that Americans, approaching Chinese peasants through KMT officials or the landlords who stood over them (appearing, one imagines, as another face of the ruling class), would find a countryside dotted with more or less fatalistic nonagitators. Doak Barnett, for instance, traveling to the Szechuan countryside to talk to KMT officials, landlords, and peasants, found a prototypical farmer whose

> life is far from easy . . . [but] he accepts it. There is a certain equilibrium between him and his environment, both physical and social, which apparently is quite stable. He is not agitating against tenancy, although he would like to own a plot of land. He is not indignant against the high rent he has to pay, although he would like to pay less, because that is just the way things are. He is conservative and accepts things as they are.[15]

How then to explain the murder of landlords by peasants in the Communist areas, or the "fanatic" determination of their peasant army? Under these circumstances, the natural explanation was to lay the blame on an opportunistic Communist Party exploiting the injustices of the rural areas, tricking the peasants, manipulating them in their ignorance, and riding to power on their backs.

From another planet
Even in the cities the Americans' contacts with "the Chinese people" were limited. When dealing with the masses of uneducated workers, refugees, and peddlers in the cities, they were restricted to the barest and most artificial contact. Over and over again in the American newspaper reports of the time the representative of the working class is described as somebody doing a menial job for the foreigner—the "boy" who cooks his breakfast, the maid who cleans his room, the child who shines his shoes, or the pedicab or rickshaw coolie who transports him. An endless number of rickshaw drivers comment on the problems of the Chinese proletariat. The masses of oppressed people living in China's cities and countryside—their problems, their hopes, and their endless humiliation—were of peripheral interest. As one headline said some months after the Communists entered Peking, "Peiping, Transformed by Reds, Becomes City of Drab Uniforms,

Foreigners Have Dull Time, Art Dealers Languish; Food Prices Are Low, People Are Friendly." [16]

In sum, Americans in the cities were restricted in their contacts to certain clearly identifiable groups: first, the various officials, civil servants, and military personnel of the national government; second, merchants and businessmen of all varieties, especially those most closely tied to Western businesses; third, students and teachers (especially the Westernized "liberal" intellectuals) whom some of the Americans in China had either taught or studied with. Even these relationships lacked substance. Paul Frillman of the U.S. Information Service described his job in Manchuria in 1946:

> Grandiosely, my mission was to get in touch with the Chinese of Manchuria, give them favorable ideas about America, and convince them American policy was to their best interests. . . . The only Chinese I could realistically hope to reach were the students and intelligentsia—a tiny literate minority—in Mukden and a few other cities. Even with them, contact could seem strained and hypocritical because our conditions of life were so different. . . . I had a warm flat and consular office to escape to, but I knew many of my students could keep semi-warm only by getting in bed and staying there. It would have sounded hollow to claim we were allies fighting shoulder to shoulder for democracy.[17]

As the civil war progressed, as inflation increased, and as the cry for peace in China became stronger, many in these groups, having rejected the Kuomintang, turned away as well from the United States to which it seemed to be hopelessly tied. Particularly the Westernized intellectuals, that group with whom Americans felt the greatest kinship, came to see that it was American aid and the hope for further American aid that was keeping the Nationalist government afloat and prolonging the civil war. Those sections of Chinese society with which American officialdom could associate became increasingly small. As John Melby observed,

> Little by little people we know are slipping away, dropping out of sight. The few still around are wary and uncommunicative. It

is personally sad, and officially dangerous in that it leaves us with a narrowing base of information—for the most part what the government wants us to know.[18]

In the end, American observers in China found that their strongest ties were to Americans and other foreigners. The most sensitive of them, in fact, were aware of the unreality of their experience of China. "We might, in fact, almost be observers from another planet," wrote Derk Bodde.[19] Given this separation from Chinese society, most of them could hardly understand when Chinese, even Chinese who had been close to them, began to express bitterness toward them as Americans, when they began to accuse them of being imperialists. This became even more difficult after the Communists entered the cities.

> Quite often the foreigner did not know what the Communists were talking about. He thought of imperialism in terms of his high school history course. He recalled vaguely learning something about British soldiers slaughtering Indians years ago. He remembered that foreign traders once numbed Asian people by selling them opium. He recollected that foreigners bought gold, spices, and silks in the Far East for a fraction of their worth, and sold Western goods in the Far East for many times their worth. The foreigner knew that he did none of these things. He concluded that the Communists have made him the whipping-boy for their own inadequacies.[20]

As far as they could see, they had done nothing out of the ordinary, which in many cases was true. What few of them saw was that, for an American, the "ordinary" was detrimental, if not destructive, to Chinese society as a whole (though sometimes helpful to certain small segments of that society).

The main emphases of their reporting during the civil war were the continued privileged position of foreigners in Chinese society and the necessity for China to face West. These two things were closely related. Article after article written from 1948 to 1950 concerned itself not with the Chinese people, but with the problems of foreign businessmen, foreign missionaries, foreign diplomats, and foreign correspondents in China. What the United States

wanted (though not always what it "blundered" into doing) was
ipso facto what was good for the people.

Their very "detachment" from Chinese society, their confine-
ment to the cities, their naturally accepted position of privilege,
and their limited contact with the Chinese people led them to place
priority on interests in China that had little to do with the welfare
of the Chinese people as a whole. The questions they were led to
ask about the events taking place around them, the lenses through
which they viewed the Chinese Revolution and the liberation of
the people in the cities (or to them, the "occupation" of the
cities), forced almost every one of them to reject the Communist
revolution in China. In the end, the new China as it unfolded before them was rejected as a darkest China principally because it
was to be a China without Americans. As Jack Belden wrote, in
1949,

> Neither the American government, the American press, nor
> the American people, nor many of their representatives in the Far
> East in the embassies, the military establishments and the business
> offices sought to look beyond their own narrow national or personal
> interests toward the heart of the admittedly ignorant, but terribly
> emotional, bitter men and women of China.[21]

Let us trace this process of rejection.

THE DEVIL AND THE DEEP BLUE SEA

"It is true," wrote Randall Gould, editor of the *Shanghai Evening
Post and Mercury,*

> that we had not been robbed of our life's savings, as had the
> Chinese middle class when forced to hand over its gold, silver, and
> foreign currency in exchange for the new "gold yuan" currency. . . .
> Neither had we been subjected to all the rigors of the Nationalist
> police state, including mass executions. . . . But all in all, [by May
> 1949] we had had enough of the Nationalists.[22]

By that time, Gould stood with almost every other American in
China in rejecting the Nationalist regime. In fact, most of the

Americans arriving in China in the late 1940s had had enough of the Nationalists almost from the moment they disembarked onto the docks of Shanghai. On the city's streets, the faces seemed tired and the contrasts stark.

Silent children with swollen bellies waited at the kitchen doors of restaurants to snatch a few morsels from the garbage, while patrons within dined upon delicacies like "gold coin chicken" and "Phoenix claws and water fish." Scavengers vastly outnumbered the diners.[23]

What they saw they could hardly fit into everyday language. To the reporter Darrell Berrigan, it seemed "a city through whose streets all Four Horsemen of the Apocalypse ride untamed." [24] The Chinese people appeared "driven to the wall and well-nigh without the will or the strength to fight and rebuild." [25] All they wanted was peace at any price, even the risk of Communist domination. Change was clearly in order. And as the Americans saw it, in that change Chiang Kai-shek's government—unlike the United States—would have no part to play.

Of course Americans in China had talked for years of the need for change, of reforms in the government as a prerequisite for further aid, and of the need for Chiang to include more progressive elements in his government, or even to stand aside altogether. Though this dissatisfaction with the Nationalists had begun during the war years in Chungking, by the late 1940s it had reached almost a cacophony of despair and denunciation. Among American officials, opinions on Chiang's prospects ran "the gamut of pessimism; from deep to ordinary pessimism." [26] In their newspaper reports, embassy assessments, and private conversations, Americans described the decay of a social order, the corruption, the mismanagement, the poor military tactics, the "medieval" methods of repression of intellectuals, the exploitation of the peasantry, and most of all the general war weariness of the Chinese people. In short, they saw that Nationalist China was near the end of the line. Drawing a phrase from Chinese history, they concluded that Chiang and his associates had lost the Mandate of Heaven. The questions that concerned them throughout 1948 and 1949 were "To whom would the Mandate pass?" and "What role would the United States be able to play in that passing?"

Conquerors from North of the Great Wall
At the same time, these Americans began to develop a political analysis which answered their concerns. This analysis provided them with a facile explanation of the success of the Communist Party in the Chinese civil war and the apparent American failure to promote an alternative China more to its liking. As a start it dealt with two practical problems: How could Nationalist China, with its massive infusions of American aid, with its American military training programs and advanced American military equipment, not stand up against the Communists, who had "virtually nothing but raw manpower"? [27] How could revolutionary communism get mass support from the peasants and even the intelligentsia of China? It explained why the "will to resist waned and, by [a] curious conspiracy of circumstances, Revolutionary Communism came to be associated with—of all things—order and the promise of peace." [28]

It was not, they felt, that the Communists were winning but that the KMT had abdicated. Chiang's greatest failure had been his refusal to "recognize the modernization trend." [29] "Instead of moving out to meet Communist political reforms with his own brand of what might have been superior reforms, he leaned heavily upon the weapons of repression and reaction." [30] As they saw it, any government that refused to carry out social reforms in China, to bow to the Chinese people's desire for change, could not stand long. The KMT had created a "vacuum," particularly in the Chinese countryside, by doing nothing about the basic problems of the people, by working for its own self-enrichment, and by ignoring or exacerbating the basic injustices in Chinese society. The Communists were simply entering the void left by the retreating Nationalists.

This concept of a political "vacuum" seems a natural image for men whose main contact with China was the shrinking KMT urban areas and the upper classes within those areas. At the heart of this "vacuum" lay the Chinese peasantry, whom the KMT had "seemed to regard . . . as nothing but an endlessly exploitable source of money, food, and conscripts." [31] Yet this same peasant, the Americans recognized, was the key to the control of the country. He had basic social grievances that were being cleverly exploited by the Communists, who were using actual injustices in the lives of the majority of the Chinese people to ride to power.

The passive masses, unable to express their desires, sick of the civil war, and tired of both political extremes, were caught inarticulate and helpless in the middle. As Doak Barnett put it in a visit to Yen Hsi-shan's headquarters, "The people in Shansi . . . are caught between the devil and the deep blue sea." [32]

The alien nature of the Communists was emphasized by highlighting their links to Russia. Communism was interpreted as an ideology without Chinese roots. By linking the Mandate of Heaven concept to the oncoming Chinese Communist success in the civil war, some managed as well to create the image of the Communists as a conquering dynasty.

> The evils of the Chiang Kai-shek dynasty finally are rending it apart, repeating a historic Chinese pattern. . . . Often in China's history the oppressed people have overthrown tyrant emperors with the aid of conquerors from North of the Great Wall.[33]

A third path?

This explanation of Communist success in China gave little credit to the Communists. Yet it did provide, on a theoretical level at least, a way for the United States to compete on a new basis in the struggle for power in China. If the Nationalists had lost the Mandate of Heaven, if the Communists were an alien force, if the Chinese people with their just grievances were somehow caught in the middle, leaning toward the Communists only by default, then perhaps a "third path" might be possible.* Another

---

* This "third path" might equally be called a second American path in China (support for Chiang having been the first). It was simply assumed that a China embarked on a "third path" would be a China facing West, a China in which the United States could maintain its position of influence.

Chinese group, even linked to a United States divested of the taint of Chiang Kai-shek and offering "determined moral reforms," might be able to sway the people in a different direction, to stake out the middle ground. There might yet be a reason not to write "non-Communist China" off as hopeless.

It is easy to see how this sort of analytical framework led to the "loss of China" mentality that has possessed the United States since 1949. For if the Communists could be seen as an outside force, then they were basically the coequal of that other outside force, the United States. With two outside forces, each looking on China as a first line of defense, and each struggling with the other for the allegiance of the Chinese people, one had to lose out. Thus the conclusion that when the Communists won, the United States lost China.

In their analysis of China, these observers accepted a common American self-conception, namely, that the United States represented a way in which basic social change could be brought about without excesses of violence and disorder. In retrospect a dismayed Ambassador Stuart expressed the problem this way:

> It was an ironical situation. The United States had come into existence through a revolutionary struggle for freedom, and had led the world in establishing a truly republican form of government which had in successive tests demonstrated and improved upon its feasibility. . . . Communism as standardized in the Soviet Union had degenerated into the only remaining form of totalitarianism with all its evils. Yet in China we were being accused of imperialistic assistance to the forces of reaction and corrupt bureaucracy by those who were leading in a victorious revolution based on slogans of liberation and democracy.[34]

This self-conception, at variance with America's actual position in the world and in China itself, led them to equate the United States' interests with the basic interests of the "unthinking masses" [35] of China. Americans in China pictured themselves much as they pictured the Chinese people—caught in the middle. They recognized that their government had been (and still was) the main prop of the Chiang Kai-shek regime. Yet they saw this as a colossal blunder. The United States had simply made a mistake in China. It had backed the wrong regime for all the right reasons. It had been taken in since "our Nationalist protégés wanted only munitions and money from Americans, not ideas." [36]

In reality, their position was grim, yet their political analysis held out hope. By withdrawing support from Chiang and his government (which most Americans in China felt "would be the most effective anti-Communist course"),[37] the United States would be able to capitalize on the basic congruence of her position with that of the Chinese people. But this idea had to be translated into policy. "The need—and the problem—now is to find both individuals and groups upon whom reliance can be placed," [38] argued Gordon Walker of the *Monitor* in early 1949 in a statement reflecting the fantasy world into which their special position in China had led them. At a time when all was clearly lost, they still searched doggedly for a "third path" in China, a means by which their country could retain some of its position of influence.

What were the various conceptions of the "third path" the Americans considered in 1948 and early 1949? Perhaps the most interesting, in the light of America's professed desire for a united, peaceful, and progressive China, was their encouragement of regionalism (a policy which culminated in the pathetic support of the Taiwan regime from 1950 to the present moment). There were two different approaches to the regional division of China. Each was linked to a different stage in the continuing success of the revolution. The first was to utilize certain "progressives" from the small "liberal" parties and from within the KMT itself to establish a "stable non-Communist government in Central and South China." [39]

When it became clear that the Communists would sweep across the Yangtze, some Americans emphasized a second approach. The United States should support the warlord-militarists who controlled the outlying provinces of China. American economic aid to these regional governments would "permit basic anticommunist Chinese characteristics to reassert themselves and correspondingly weaken sympathy for the Communists." [40] Of particular interest was Ma Pu-fang, a warlord in Northwest China, who claimed he was setting up a Moslem Federation in the area.

> American authorities here meanwhile are watching with close interest developments in this region. . . . American interest in this northwest region is patently strong. If nothing else, the region might provide sites for much needed weather stations. . . . Establishment of an anti-Communist buffer in the northwest might provide precedent upon which such provinces as Szechuan, Yunnan and Sikang might resist Communist penetration—at least to the point where it would seriously hamper Chinese Communists' efforts to consolidate all China.[41]

Given the Chinese political situation, this was a pathetic joke. Some months later, Ma Pu-fang packed his bags and left for Taiwan and a "pilgrimage" to Mecca. The front collapsed almost immediately. The tactics, though, were strangely reminiscent of allied support for Kolchak, Denikin, and other regional forces against the struggling new Soviet government in the Russian civil war. In China, the consequences were a good deal less serious, but the intent was similar.[42]

Besides KMT "progressives" and the regional warlords, there was another group of interest to the Americans, a vague assortment of Chinese intellectuals who had been given a Western "liberal" education at the missionary colleges and westernized universities of China. Many had studied in Western countries as well. They held a place close to the American heart. Their possibilities had been fondly discussed in China, particularly during the Marshall Mission, though even then they were a rootless and politically powerless group. Yet before 1949, the Americans had had to write them off as totally ineffectual. These men were even less likely than the provincial militarists and KMT bureaucrats to provide a mediating force between the United States and the people of China.

American intervention

These hopes for an American-sponsored "middle course" bore no relation to the actual position of the United States in China.

As the sole prop of the most repressive and antidemocratic sector of the Chinese political spectrum and the sole supplier of military hardware meant for the destruction of a popular revolution, the United States could hardly play a mediating role in China. Nor did these hopes relate to the position of any "mediating" group in Chinese society, for, in 1949, no significant middle group existed in China. Those who were amenable to U.S. "arms and ideas" had been completely isolated from the people of China. The others had gone or were waiting to go over to the revolution. The great shock, for the Americans who saw the PLA come into Peking, Tientsin, and Shanghai, was that their beloved Chinese liberals, the Americanized university professors and their students, went over to the revolution with alacrity, enthusiasm, and energy, as did the cities' workers.

There was a further possibility which was briefly considered and, of necessity, rejected. If there were no mediating groups through which the Americans could enter the Chinese "vacuum," then the Americans could enter the vacuum themselves. Certainly there were many Americans in China itching to release U.S. power to tidy up the situation. But, as Secretary of State Marshall wrote from Washington in October 1948:

> To achieve the objective of reducing the Chinese Communists to a completely negligible factor in China in the immediate future, it would be necessary for the United States virtually to take over the Chinese Government and administer its economic, military and governmental affairs. Strong Chinese sensibilities regarding infringement of China's sovereignty, the intense feeling of nationalism among all Chinese, and the unavailability of qualified American personnel in large numbers required argue strongly against attempting such a solution.[43]

Or as Dean Acheson wrote in his "Letter of Transmittal" (to the State Department's 1949 China "White Paper"), "It is obvious that the American people would not have sanctioned such a colossal commitment of our armies in 1945 or later." [44] Given the mood of the American people, the growing Russian strength, and the priority of European commitments, it was well beyond the political (and probably military) capacity of the United States to intervene directly in China on the required scale. Yet most of the Americans in China had no qualms about the justice of intervening, were it possible. They did doubt the quality of the reception they would receive. They felt that the mind of the Chinese Nationalist, "twisted and made sensitive by a hundred years of foreign exploitation," [45] and the limitations of American power stood in the way of America's best chance to stake out the "middle ground" in China.

There remained, though, a possibility that the more perceptive of the Americans had been considering for years. These men felt that factors in the Chinese political and economic situation, or in the makeup of the Chinese people themselves, would force the Communist revolutionaries to face West in spite of themselves. This attempt to use the Communists against themselves was the most sophisticated of the "third path" tactics.

THANK YOU, AMERICA!

As the first troops of the People's Liberation Army marched through the streets in May 1949, there was pathos in the position of Americans living in Shanghai. The events of the late winter and early spring had left most of them in a strange psychological state. For endless months they had been captive and helpless witnesses to the bankruptcy of American policy in China. They saw the demoralized Nationalist troops fleeing through the cities, looting, executing, burning, and robbing their fellow Chinese. They were approached by KMT officials pleading for help in fleeing the country. They saw KMT generals (the lucky ones) sitting in airport waiting rooms, their tennis rackets, their riding saddles, and their wives' American cosmetics piled in heaps at their sides. They saw foreign businessmen, not to speak of their Chinese equivalents, sitting on their hands as their businesses rotted. In their rooms, the running water did not work and the electricity stayed off. Inflation was beyond stopping. The streets were filled with starving and uncared-for refugees; and, as many of the Americans looked back on their stay in China, it seemed as though to lesser degrees it had always been like this. It was a complete debacle, a poor man's *gotterdammerung.* They began to develop a "nothing could be worse than this" mentality, which helped them to move toward a positive reaction to the new revolutionary Communist regime.

For the Americans who had waited in China's cities, the initial impact of the People's Liberation Army was traumatic. Only a minuscule group of Americans who had ventured into the countryside, into the liberated areas of North China, already knew how revolutionary the PLA was. As Jack Belden commented after his visit to the liberated areas early in 1947,

> I have seen the American, British, Burmese, Indian, French, German, Russian and Chinese Kuomintang armies in action; but I have never seen an army quite like the 8th Route Army led by the Chinese Communists. In many ways, it was absolutely unique among the armies of the world. I think this was principally due to the fact that much of it was not created from an old standing army, but out of the people themselves.[46]

But most Americans had not listened carefully to this message, and those who had could hardly be expected to believe what they heard. They credited Chiang's defeats more to his own military ineptitude than to the Communists themselves. Though they came at last to realize that the Communists had "won" the civil war, they were hardly prepared for what that meant.

In Shanghai, as the demoralized Nationalist rabble fled out one end of the city, the revolutionary troops entered the other. Rather than impose on the people, the PLA soldiers slept on their packs on the sidewalks of the city. They paid for everything they took, even glasses of hot water. These simple peasant boys lectured people who tried to offer them free food, saying they were the "people's army" and were supposed to serve the people, not burden them. They were well disciplined. They were, in contrast to the departing KMT troops, spirited and proud. "They talked, laughed, sang, whistled, whereas the Nationalists were speechless." [47] And they were tough. Equally shocking to Americans was the fact that they were almost totally furnished with American equipment. "One observer remarked [of a parade weeks later] that in the military section of the parade everything was of American manufacture except the soldiers." [48] The soldiers were proud of that as well. They held up huge banners saying: "These fine weapons have been received from Imperialist America, through the courtesy of Chiang Kai-shek. Thank you, America!" [49]

Most Americans could not believe their eyes. Who had ever seen a Chinese army like this? For the first time, they were forced to face up to the power of the forces they had been opposing, to see how the supposedly apathetic Chinese peasant could transform himself, to recognize what men like Belden had known for years. What followed fast on the heels of the soldiers was even more astonishing to them. There was neither disorder, nor riots, nor violent antiforeign agitation—none of the things they had feared. Instead the revolutionary government brought inflation under control, attacked widespread corruption with "a most un-Chinese energy," [50] stabilized wages, and began to clean up the city. As the PLA soldiers had left Americans incredulous, so did the cadres of the new regime. All agreed they had an "unprecedented integrity," that they were "scrupulously honest" and "thoroughly incorruptible."

Ironically enough, the Americans were being presented with what they had thought they had been searching for all along: a dynamic movement that, in the words of the U.S. Ambassador, was

> fostering among millions those qualities of which China had stood so palpably in need, qualities which [in his view] Christian missions and other cultural [i.e., Western] forces had been slowly inculcating among so pitifully few.[51]

But how, American observers wondered, could these values (self-sacrifice, democratic participation, discipline, desire to serve the people, and so on) become associated with communism? If all these values were present, was this actually revolutionary communism they were facing, or was it something more "reasonable," something with which the West could get along? A familiar pattern of thought appeared again: the primary consideration was the new regime's treatment of foreigners, foreign interests, and foreign value systems. What mattered most were "relations with the local foreign diplomatic representation, large-scale foreign and Chinese business operations, and the operation of the foreign press." [52] The question of what was best for the Chinese people was subordinated to what was best for the West in China.

You can't eat an ideology

Yet whatever ambivalence Americans may have felt during this early period of the revolutionary takeover in Shanghai, a strange euphoria came over many of them. They walked around with unbelieving eyes, saying to each other, "When our families and home offices read our reports they will say we all have gone Communist." [53] Much to their surprise, they felt more at home than the most optimistic of them would have expected. But what was it that pleased them so much? What did they see in this situation that left them still feeling hopeful in the new China?

The simple explanation is that they did not see what was happening in China as a revolution. The cities had been "occupied," not "liberated." There had been no violence, except from the Nationalists, or any of the expected antiforeign excesses. The policies of the new regime cautiously entering the cities (consulting with Chinese businessmen and guaranteeing foreign properties) were clearly "go-slow" policies. As they saw it, the new regime was "promoting evolution rather than revolution and mutual respect between labor and management rather than class warfare." [54] Or as the conservative Randall Gould explained a week after the takeover, "the world's largest Communist city, is making a high-gear effort to revise and renovate its economy—along lines thus far orthodox and capitalistic." [55] Over a long period of time, the Americans thought, well, who knew . . . ? Of course, had they been in the countryside, they might have reached quite different conclusions:

> Certainly any movement which overthrows property relationships, turns out the governing class, changes the tax system, assaults

the cultural and religious patterns, arouses bloody passions among millions of people and produces a social convulsion of continental proportions can hardly be called anything but a revolution.[56]

From all this the Americans in the cities had been shielded.

While they saw few "Communist" aspects to the takeover, they thought they saw certain tendencies that could be exploited to their own benefit. They had made several political projections, moreover, which prophesied that over time, the Communist movement itself would turn out to be a "third force." The first projection, considered in both Washington and Shanghai, is reflected in this State Department leak to James Reston of the *New York Times*:

> [China] is a vast, unconnected, poorly organized, continent of a country populated by undernourished, highly individualistic people.
>
> If our officials' information is correct, the Communists do not have the administrative personnel to deal effectively with the economic problems of the country. Winning the war, the State Department feels, will be easy for the Communists; running the country will be extremely difficult, and probably cannot be done without enlisting legions of non-Communist officials who may very well, in the long run, prevent the effective communization of the area.[57]

This "fifth column" strategy seems to have been favored by our embassy in Nanking. As one reporter commented in January 1949, "There had been a regular procession of KMT politicians to the offices of Ambassador Leighton Stuart, asking for his help in transplanting a core of the present regime into a future coalition."[58]

This touched upon a real problem for the Communists. Their entry into the cities left them face to face with technical problems completely new to them. There was an overwhelming drain on the limited number of technically trained personnel they had. They were forced to turn immediately to the enthusiastic student population for help and, for the running of the cities, to already existing administrative and technical personnel. For the Americans, the question was "whether this will have the effect of diluting and corrupting the communist policies or whether the Reds will find it necessary to resort again to terrorism and intimidation [sic] to gain their ends." [59] Given their perception of the revolution and their experience with that other "revolutionary" force, the Nationalists, it was natural that they should expect the cities to "corrupt" the Communists—a prospect to which some looked forward with hardly disguised relish.

This sort of a corrupting process would be an American meal ticket back into China. But there was another, more important factor that the Americans generally saw as limiting any Communist policy of "dewesternization." This was the economic power of the United States. The leaders of the revolution had bound themselves to a vigorous and far-reaching reconstruction and industrialization program. Yet their position was desperate. "You can't eat an ideology," commented the *New York Herald Tribune's* Archibald Steele.[60] As the Americans saw it, even to stay on their feet, no less to begin such a program, it was axiomatic that they would need "aid." Though they had "constantly denounced post-war American aid as 'imperialistic,' the fact remains . . . that China [i.e., KMT urban China] has been living since the end of the Japanese war on a margin of American economic assistance." [61] In Shanghai, particularly,

a Communist government or a coalition regime . . . will also have to act with a realization that American cotton, provided by the E.C.A., is all that keeps alive this city's great textile industry.[62]

The situation, as many of the Americans analyzed it even before the PLA entered Shanghai, was that the Communists simply could not begin an ambitious industrialization program "while at the same time indulging in the luxury of kicking Uncle Sam around." [63] Russia, committed to her own industrialization program and that of its East European allies, could not provide the necessary money and machines even if she wanted to. "As to other industrial equipment, it is impossible to see how it can be kept up at all, much less added to, by anyone save the United States." [64]

Almost all the Americans in China saw this need for American aid as a wedge that, if nothing else did, would force the new revolutionary regime to adopt a businesslike attitude toward America. Its potential, though, went far beyond that. It would help to drive a wedge between the Chinese and the Russians. It would help force Mao to become "Asia's Tito." It might even force a continued moderation in any "revolutionary" domestic programs. In sum, it would help to retain, in somewhat altered form, the Western presence in China, Western capital in China's industries, and a certain Western hand in China's political development.

These factors—the orderly, nonviolent, and go-slow nature of the takeover; the incorporation of a "fifth column" of old administrative and technical personnel; the supposed need for U.S. aid—all these singly or in various combinations were discussed by most of the American observers with hope during the first three weeks of the new regime in Shanghai.

A nightmare of morality

Yet, two months later, in August, these same Americans, almost to a man, were whistling a totally different and more virulent tune. "Mass 1950 Famine Foreseen in China" read the headline in the August 12 New York Times.

> Conditions of misery and disruption unsurpassed in this century are foreseen . . . for China in the coming year by experts of the United States and other countries in Chinese affairs.[65]

"Recent developments indicate . . ." wrote Lieberman of the Times on October 6, "that present-day Communist China has not just one Achilles heel, but many." [66] As seen by American observers, the problems were almost endless. There were rumors of "isolated peasant uprisings . . . [that] may be a portent of things to come." [67] There were claims of widespread dissatisfaction in the cities. There was the problem of feeding an exhausted Chinese people and of industrializing without Western aid. And on and on. "Grave doubts" were pompously raised about whether the revolutionary regime would be able to solve "China's basic problems." [68] (They are still being raised twenty years later.) If not, "Many Western observers predict their regime will go down. . . . Don't expect a big upset in Peking soon. If one is to come it probably won't occur for from five to twenty years. Things move slowly in China." [69] Within two months they had come to reject the regime; and someday, they hoped, it might fall. This rejection suffused everything they looked at. Education became indoctrination, self-sacrifice became fanaticism. And as for honesty, integrity, and incorruptibility,

> Having lived through Shanghai's disastrous post-war inflation and then through four months of Communism, most of us were glad to be going away. On deck a British passenger, one of those who had known and loved Shanghai as 'the wickedest city on earth,' mumbled his feelings about the trying months just past: 'a nightmare of morality,' he said.[70]

What had happened between June and August which convinced so many of them that they had to reject the new China? The attitude of the Chinese Communists toward the United States (and Americans in China) had hardened. It could not be said that the new revolutionary regime had ever been warm and friendly to Americans living in China. But upon its arrival in Shanghai, as in other cities, it established "correct" if distant relations. It promised to protect foreign property and foreign lives, though admonishing foreigners to remember that the Chinese people had "stood up."

All Westerners, not just Americans, were equally brought under Chinese law, a transformation of major significance. Secondly, the central place of Americans and other Westerners in Chinese urban society disappeared overnight. "We were not regimented," wrote an English teacher, "nor were we bullied. Something much more galling happened to us: we were ignored. . . . Perhaps the most important thing to realize about the foreign colonies in present-day China is their absolute insignificance—from the Chinese point of view." [71] Not that the foreigner had not felt detached and isolated in Nationalist China. He had. But his relationship to Chinese society was now different. If he was a newsman, for instance, he could not find Communist officials to interview. If a diplomat, he was no longer privy to the councils of the Chinese government. English was no longer a "universal" language. He could no longer push a pedicab driver who annoyed him.

The Chinese Communists themselves had changed. Between the "salad days" at Yenan and Chungking and the liberation of Peking, they had seen a face of the United States generally played down by the American observers in China. They had seen humanitarian America's bombs and bullets. Whatever illusions they had held about the United States in the earlier 1940s were gone. It was clear to them that America's anti-Communist face was implacable. They knew from experience which country had been the main arsenal of arms, aid, and advice to their adversaries, which was their main enemy.

When they entered the cities, as one observer remarked, they saw their situation as "comparable to the early blockaded days of the U.S.S.R." [72] They did not look on Americans in their public roles as simply harmless and detached individuals but as representatives of a power which was out to destroy their revolution. "They regard American consulates as virtual enemy bases within their territory and American newsmen as possible spies." [73] They justifiably had a siege mentality. They were aware that the beginnings of a *cordon sanitaire* was being thrown up around them by the United States, that they were on the front lines of what might soon be World War III. They saw their Chinese opponents (and Americans near them) openly speculating on a Russo-American war as a new opening for an American-sponsored KMT return to power. They knew that the very personnel with whom they had to work in the cities were a possible fifth column in time of war.

In the face of such hostility, it is surprising that they retained as much openness and flexibility toward the West upon entering Shanghai as they did. It is surprising that they were so "correct" and "aloof" rather than hostile to Americans living there. The speed with which they cleaned up Shanghai harbor, the anger with which they treated the rumor in an English paper that the KMT had mined the harbor, showed their interest in trading on an equitable basis with Western nations, including the United

States. They even allowed the ship, the *China Victory*, whose hold was filled with American bombers for Taiwan, to do business in Tientsin.[74] Naturally, in postrevolutionary China, they were not likely to accept the dominance of Western capital in the coastal (i.e., industrial) sector of their economy. Yet they seemed willing to go quite far (even to the point of having Huang Hua, head of the Foreign Personnel Bureau, discuss the possibility of an American loan with his former teacher, Ambassador Stuart).

On the other hand, their posture in Shanghai changed significantly about three weeks after the entry of the PLA when the Nationalists declared a blockade of the port.[75] This blockade, while not officially upheld by the U.S. government, was supported by U.S. insurance companies, whose soaring shipping fees made it financially disastrous for American firms to trade with China (though the KMT itself had few planes or ships with which to enforce the blockade). In effect, China's window on the West was closed. The new regime was forced to take drastic steps to turn Shanghai inland (by cutting the population, dispersing industries, and so on). For the Americans, Mao Tse-tung's July 1 "lean-to-one-side" speech was a crushing blow to their hopes in China. "One could see the effect of the speech on Dr. Leighton Stuart," commented the Indian Ambassador.

> That good man had hoped against hope that the Communists, many of whom had been his students in Yen Ching university, would take a moderate line. But Mao Tse-tung's speech finally shattered that hope. Dr. Stuart was a broken man.[76]

Yet, given the context of an economically powerful, inflexibly hostile United States, the speech was hardly surprising. Later in July, the U.S.I.A. offices were closed on the grounds that the United States had no right to pass out its propaganda when it had not recognized the new regime, stringent restrictions were placed on American correspondents, and, in October, Angus Ward, the American consul at Mukden, was sequestered in his consulate. The freeze was on: the American presence in China was treated with increasingly cold hostility.

Darkest China

Most of the American observers denied the existence of "American imperialism." They felt they were being used as convenient targets for Chinese frustrations. When they looked at their lives —writing for newspapers, studying at universities, preaching the gospel, running a business, or whatever—they could not see how they had done great harm to China. They had certainly meant their best. While some of them were willing to castigate their government for its tragic blunders in China and its shortsightedness, they no more doubted the basic motivations behind its policies than they did their own motivations. They understood Chinese attacks on "American imperialism," their application of the law to foreigners, their insistence on humiliating apologies for "minor" offenses by foreigners, as evidence of Chinese "xenophobia," of the irrationality characteristic of an insulated and humiliated "peasant mentality." For some, it was also evidence of the way Communists could exploit the grievances and frustrations of a people that had been unable for a hundred years to face up to the pressures of the modern world. Once more the Americans saw themselves as innocent scapegoats.

But as the months passed and the Communist regime reacted to America's policies in Asia, American observers felt increasingly insignificant in the new China and increasingly rejected by it. They could not accept the idea that China could "shun" the West and at the same time benefit the Chinese people. Yet, as Jean Lyon commented, "The questions which are so uppermost in American minds seemed hardly to be questions at all to the Chinese I knew." [77] On a personal level most of them were tired and fed up.

So the new People's China had won the first round. American observers had predicted doom and despair for the new China. In Shanghai, a summer typhoon, the worst drought in years, and the blockade had fed their fancies. But the new regime had been neither corrupted nor undermined. "Today [October] it is clear that their 'Shanghai experience' has not affected the Communists, unless to make them even more revolutionary . . . a leaner, harder Shanghai awaits Western recognition." [78] They had, in fact, retained the support, "in many cases the enthusiastic support [in Shanghai], of the two groups they consider most important, the workers and students." [79] Already they had begun to move decisively toward creating a better life for the people of China. And "the unhappiest people in North China [were] the foreign business men and industrialists." [80] For the road China had chosen, though her own, was one which excluded the West.

Many of the American observers were sympathetic and sensitive men who wished the best for China and its people. Yet that sympathy had taken most of them only a small distance along the road to understanding of the revolutionary upheaval that had occurred right under their noses. The role their country had played (and continued to play) in the economic and political life of China had limited them. The standards they used to judge social and political events in China had limited them. What they had desperately wanted was a set of circumstances in which their interests, those of their country, and those of the Chinese people would be fused. This was why the notion of the "third path" had appealed to them.

When the Chinese Revolution turned its back on a hostile America, these men began to leave China. Some left for Hong Kong where their transformation into China-watchers began on arrival ("A high source from the mainland reports . . ."); some went to Rhee's Korea ("After six months in North China, three of them under Communist occupation, it is gratifying to be back in a relatively free world") [81] and on to Japan; some went back to the United States, and some to Taiwan, America's China, where the pitiful remnants of the KMT held sway:

> "Hey look!" [the sailor] shouted. "We're back in [Nationalist] China! There's a slopehead Chinaman begging for cigarettes! Here!" The crewman drew one cigarette from a pack and threw it on the pier. Everyone at the railing laughed as the sentry and another who had suddenly appeared scrambled for it. I thought of the Communist guard . . . [in Tientsin] who had proudly turned down the seaman's cigarette. [82]

The ones who left were not happy. What had happened in China had split their lives apart. In the end they had naturally chosen what they knew and understood best. They left drumming the drums of danger. They warned of the "millions of Asiatics [who] will be lost irretrievably to the Soviet orbit by default," [83] that already "almost a third of [Asia's] vast human mass has been swallowed up in Communism's glacial advance." [84] They called on the United States "to provide an alternative to Communism" [85] in Asia, and they bemoaned what had happened in China as "a blackout for the flickering American picture of a China working painfully, but surely, toward the kind of society that would be politically and economically complementary to that of the United States." [86] Unwillingly, for the first time in a century they left China to her own people. From the border at British-held Kowloon they looked back for some hint of movement in the peasant fields beyond, but for them night had descended on darkest China.

NOTES

1. Ronald Stead, "From a Shanghai Window," *Christian Science Monitor* (magazine), May 7, 1949, p. 5.

2. Jack Belden, *China Shakes the World* (New York: Harper & Bros., 1949), p. 366.

3. Jean Lyon, *Just Half a World Away* (London: Hutchinson & Co., 1955), p. 16.

4. John F. Melby, *The Mandate of Heaven, Record of a Civil War* (London: University of Toronto Press, 1968), p. 273.

5. *Ibid.*, p. 17.

6. Julian Schuman, *Assignment China* (New York: Whittier Books, 1956), pp. 15–16.

7. Paul Frillman and Graham Peck, *China, The Remembered Life* (Boston: Houghton Mifflin Co., 1968), p. 271.

8. Jean Lyon, "Chinese Students," *The Nation*, June 28, 1947, p. 768.

9. Thurston Griggs, *Americans in China: Some Chinese Views* (Washington, D.C.: Foundation for Foreign Affairs, 1948), p. 42.

10. Peggy Durdin, "China's Dark Destiny," *The Nation*, February 8, 1947, p. 152.

11. Gordon Walker, "China's War Rumbles on in Maze of Peace Reports," *Christian Science Monitor*, April 12, 1949, p. 15.

12. Melby, *op. cit.*, p. 47.

13. A. Doak Barnett, *China on the Eve of Communist Takeover* (New York: Praeger, 1963), p. 154.

14. Melby, *op. cit.*, p. 105.

15. Barnett, *op. cit.*, p. 115.

16. Archibald Steele, "Peiping Transformed," *New York Herald Tribune,* April 28, 1949, p. 1.

17. Frillman, *op. cit.,* p. 268.

18. Melby, *op. cit.,* p. 198.

19. Derk Bodde, *Peking Diary: Nineteen Forty-Eight to Nineteen Forty-Nine, a Year of Revolution* (New York: Fawcett Publications, 1967), p. 38.

20. Lynn and Amos Landman, *Profile of Red China* (New York: Simon & Schuster, 1951), p. 175.

21. Belden, *op. cit.,* p. 5.

22. Randall Gould, "Shanghai During the Takeover, 1949," *The Annals of the Academy of Political and Social Science,* vol. 277, September 1951, p. 182.

23. Landman and Landman, *op. cit.,* p. 6.

24. Darrell Berrigan, "Shanghai Woos the Chinese Reds," *Saturday Evening Post,* May 7, 1949, p. 158.

25. Berrigan, "Is Our Navy Trapped in China?," *Saturday Evening Post,* September 25, 1948, p. 145.

26. Schuman, *op. cit.,* p. 37.

27. Walker, "How and Where to Buttress Aid to China: Can West Find Effective Ways?," *Christian Science Monitor,* January 8, 1949, p. 13.

28. Robert Doyle, "The Conqueror from the Caves, China's new boss, Mao, holds his land in the tight vise of Communism," *Life,* January 23, 1950, p. 84.

29. Walker, *op. cit.*

30. Walker, "Chiang Drops Reins in Nanking," *Christian Science Monitor,* January 21, 1949, p. 1.

31. Frillman, *op. cit.,* p. 261.

32. Barnett, *op. cit.,* p. 176.

33. Walter L. Briggs, "From Canton to Canton," *New Republic,* December 6, 1948, p. 8.

34. John Leighton Stuart, *Fifty Years in China* (New York: Random House, 1954), p. 221.

35. *The China White Paper, August 1949* (Stanford: Stanford University Press, 1967), p. 246.

36. Frillman, *op. cit.,* p. 262.

37. Briggs, "Merely Irritating," *New Republic,* December 27, 1948, p. 10.

38. Walker, "How and Where to Buttress Aid to China," *Christian Science Monitor,* January 8, 1949, p. 13.

39. *The China White Paper, op. cit.,* p. 268.

40. *Ibid.,* p. 279.

41. Walker, "Northwest China: Moslem State Pushed," *Christian Science Monitor,* April 15, 1949, p. 1.

42. For the source of this idea see Belden, *op. cit.,* pp. 451–52.

43. *The China White Paper, op. cit.,* p. 281.

44. *Ibid.*, p. x.

45. Christopher Rand, "Between the Bear and the Dragon," *Collier's*, March 6, 1948, p. 63.

46. Belden, *op. cit.*, p. 346.

47. Gould, "Shanghai: New Day Brings New Regime," *Christian Science Monitor*, May 25, 1949, p. 1.

48. Walter Sullivan, "Reds in Shanghai Show Off Might," *New York Times*, July 8, 1949, p. 8.

49. Harrison Forman, *Blunder in Asia* (New York: Didier, 1950), p. 4.

50. Andrew Roth, "How the Communists Rule," *The Nation*, November 19, 1949, p. 488.

51. Stuart, *op. cit.*, p. 243.

52. Walker, "Vital Rail Line Won," *Christian Science Monitor*, January 17, 1949, p. 1.

53. Gould, "Shanghai: Communists Release Imports," *Christian Science Monitor*, January 2, 1949, p. 9.

54. Sullivan, "Red Moves Please Shanghai Bankers," *New York Times*, June 4, 1949, p. 4.

55. Gould, "Shanghai: Communists and Capitalism," *Christian Science Monitor*, May 31, 1949, p. 6.

56. Belden, *op. cit.*, p. 463.

57. James Reston, "U.S. Will Now Follow Hands-Off Policy in China," *New York Times* (review section), April 24, 1949, p. 3.

58. Roth, "Sauve Qui Peut," *The Nation*, January 29, 1949, p. 127; or see his "The Crumbling Kuomintang," *The Nation*, May 21, 1949, p. 579.

59. Steele, "Chinese Reds Plan Peace on Own Terms," *New York Herald Tribune*, January 10, 1949, p. 1.

60. Steele, "Chinese in New Red Territories Keeping Their Fingers Crossed," *New York Herald Tribune*, February 2, 1949, p. 11.

61. Henry Lieberman, "Communists Confronted with Great Task in China," *New York Times* (review section), January 16, 1949, p. 5.

62. Allen Raymond, "Shanghai Hope Rises as Chiang Is Reported Out," *New York Herald Tribune*, January 22, 1949, p. 3.

63. Gould, "Cross Purposes in China," *Christian Science Monitor*, May 9, 1949, p. 18.

64. *Ibid.*

65. Tillman Durdin, "Mass 1950 Famine Foreseen in China," *New York Times*, August 12, 1949, p. 1.

66. Lieberman, "Communists Face Pitfalls in China," *New York Times*, October 6, 1949, p. 14.

67. Barnett, *Communist China: The Early Years 1949–55* (New York: Praeger, 1964), p. 24.

68. *Ibid.*

69. Seymour Topping, "Making Chinese Communist State Is Viewed as a Staggering Task," *New York Herald Tribune,* October 6, 1949, p. 16.

70. Robert Doyle, "Report on Communist Shanghai," *Life,* October 17, 1949, p. 129.

71. Otto B. Van Der Sprenkel et al., *New China: Three Views* (London: Turnstile Press, 1950), pp. 21, 27.

72. Roth, "How the Communists Rule," *The Nation,* November 19, 1949, p. 490.

73. Roth, "Peiping's New Look," *The Nation,* March 5, 1949, pp. 274–75.

74. On the *China Victory* see James Burke, "The Commies Don't Even Say Thanks," *Saturday Evening Post,* October 22, 1949, pp. 113–16.

75. For an idea of the emphasis the Communists placed on the blockade see Mao's August 1949 replies to the White Paper, "Farewell Leighton Stuart!" (particularly p. 438) and " 'Friendship' or Aggression" (particularly p. 449), *Selected Works of Mao Tse-tung,* vol. IV (Peking: Foreign Language Press, 1967).

76. K. M. Panikkar, *In Two Chinas, Memoirs of a Dilpomat* (London: George Allen & Unwin, 1955), p. 59.

77. Jean Lyon, "When the Communists Entered Peking," *Harper's Magazine,* February 1950, p. 85.

78. Roth, "How the Communists Rule," *The Nation,* November 19, 1949, p. 488.

79. Walter Sullivan, "Shanghai's Red Rulers Hold Loyalty of Labor, Students," *New York Times,* November 25, 1949, p. 1.

80. Steele, "In Red China: Rich Are Poorer, But Poor Are Not Getting Richer," *New York Herald Tribune,* October 18, 1949, p. 1.

81. *Ibid.*

82. Burke, *op. cit.,* p. 115.

83. Forman, *op. cit.,* p. 189.

84. Steele, "Asia's Red Riddle," *New York Herald Tribune,* October 18, 1949, p. 1.

85. Forman, *op. cit.,* p. 190.

86. Lieberman, "Gigantic Questions for Mao—And For Us, Too," *New York Times Magazine,* January 1, 1950, pp. 23–24.

John Carter Vincent and the American "loss" of China

ROSS TERRILL

It is twenty years since the U.S. "lost" China. In October 1949, Mao Tse-tung proclaimed the People's Republic of China in Peking, as "America's" Chinese licked their wounds on Taiwan. At that time, U.S. foreign policy was in anguished transition from a sense of grandeur stemming from the great victory of 1945 to a deepening awareness of intractable problems and hostile powers in Europe and Asia alike. "After a long voyage in which the favoring currents of history bore us in the direction in which we sought to navigate," Robert Heilbroner wrote in *The Future as History,* "we have emerged into an open sea where powerful contrary winds come directly into conflict with our passage." [1] By the time Stalin had crystallized his hegemony throughout Eastern Europe and Mao had reached Peking and celebrated the departure of America's last Ambassador with his bitter article, "Farewell, Leighton Stuart," the world did indeed seem an "open sea" of swirling currents.

Fear of Communist power remolded the content, style, and the actual formulation of American foreign policy. Ideological anxiety was a bridge which linked domestic politics and international politics as never before. A history of U.S. paternalism toward China made Communist success there more shocking than in Eastern Europe. The post-mortems on China policy, spurred by Republican resentment at the long Democratic dominance and by the anger of the China Lobby (Chiang Kai-shek's long right arm in the United States), were bitter and zealous. Partisanship on China policy began in earnest after the congressional elections of November 1946, which brought Republican majorities in both House and Senate. In January 1947, General Marshall's Mis-

sion to China, which had aimed at a peaceful settlement of the
civil war between Chiang and Mao, ended without success.
Meanwhile, as Chiang sank deeper into military and political
failure, there came in 1948 a string of Communist scares, including Fuchs's confession of atomic espionage and Chambers's
charges against Alger Hiss of the State Department. By early
1950, Senator Joseph McCarthy had pounced on China policy
as a natural weapon for his crusade against the U.S. foreign
policy establishment. When the North Koreans moved south in
June 1950, the time of troubles for U.S. Far Eastern policy
seemed complete. Since the Korean attack, which stimulated the
U.S. commitment to Chiang that exists to this day, relations between the U.S. and Peking have made little progress. In some respects they have gotten worse, as the United States has spread
900,000 men under arms in an arc close to China.

True, the wistful Dulles line that the Communist regime may
"pass away" has been abandoned. There have been occasional
Ambassadorial Talks between China and the United States. Mail
and literature flow between the two countries (though Washington will not permit Peking to settle the bill for Chinese materials bought by Americans). In July 1969 President Nixon eased
the travel restrictions on Americans visiting China and on the
importation of Chinese merchandise. Within the United States a
certain cut and thrust has returned to public discussion of China
policy. Yet the basic policy remains unchanged. Washington
maintains diplomatic ties with Chiang Kai-shek and his remnant,
who lost the Chinese civil war, not with Mao Tse-tung and his
government in Peking, who won it. A frozen China policy is an
echo of a rankling past, of an inability to reckon with it in
terms of facts rather than myths.

One myth about the loss of China was that "blame" lay largely
with the "China Hands." Just as Mao Tse-tung conjured up the
myth of Liu Shao-chi's apostasy to guard the image of his own
leadership as correct and wise, so certain mandarins in Washington conjured up a myth of the China Hands' apostasy in order to
guard their image of American leadership as omnicompetent and
innocent. Of the twenty-two officers who belonged to the elite

"China Service" in the State Department before World War II and who remained with the Department by mid-1952, *only two* still worked on Chinese affairs. The other twenty were by 1952 scattered in a variety of posts unconnected with China.[2] (One of them, John Paton Davies, fired by John Foster Dulles in 1953, subsequently became a resident of Lima, where he exchanged the making of China policy for the making of tables and chairs, finally receiving his security clearance in January 1969.)

The principal China Hand sacrificed upon the altar of American omnicompetence and innocence was John Carter Vincent. Born in Kansas in 1900, Vincent joined the Foreign Service at 24, choosing China because his "favorite Sunday School teacher [in Georgia] had gone to China as a missionary."[3] Beginning in 1925 as Vice-Consul in Changsha, he served in various China posts for a total of thirteen years, the last as Counselor of Embassy in Chungking (1941–43). In 1931 at Tsinan-fu, in Shantung Province, he married an attractive girl from Chicago named Elisabeth Thayer Slagle. She had come to China on the Trans-Siberian railroad as part of an adventurous world trip with Lucille Swan, the sculptress, who developed in China a remarkable correspondence with Père Teilhard de Chardin.

Rapidly promoted by several Secretaries of State, Vincent became Director of the Office of Far Eastern Affairs in 1945 (the equivalent position today is Assistant Secretary of State for Far Eastern Affairs), soon after attending, as China expert, the conferences at San Francisco (U.N.), Potsdam, and Moscow.

Vincent is a sharp, proud, elegant man, with piercing blue eyes and a straightforward manner. As a diplomat he was an independent, even obstinate spirit; the facts as he saw them were sovereign, ideas were not squeezed out by bureaucratic formality. He had no scholarly bent; skillful observation and judgment of men rather than organized erudition mark his reports.

Politically he had been a Wilsonian democrat; later he added a kind of social liberalism, or social democracy, as the depression, fascism, and the failure of the rich, corrupt, upper class Kuomintang government in China thrust the economic factor to the center of any consideration of political forms. He wrote from Chungking:

I am an advocate of no particular form of government. The state of development, education, and temperament of any social group determines what form of government is possible. But I do believe that the primary function of government is to insure, so far as possible, that the people shall live in security and freedom; as Spinoza says, that they shall "in security develop soul and body to make free use of their reason." The Kuomintang, as the governing party of China, has failed in this task.

Like other liberals, he came to believe that freedom, in the sense of absence of restraint, did not mean much unless the social and economic order was such as to give every man the opportunity to develop his capacities. He wrote from Shanghai in 1941:

Last night I listened to a line of thought which irritates me no end. The complaint (always from secure places) is that the people are getting soft; that they are willing to trade their freedom for security. And I say rot. An Indian hunting bison with a bow and arrow had a certain degree of freedom and I suppose little security. But the degree of freedom which the average man has in the modern social order, when elemental economic security is lacking, is negligible. Give [him] reasonable security and I'll vouch for freedom asserting itself.

Again he wrote, just after President Roosevelt announced the United States' entry into the war, mixing warm admiration for Roosevelt with criticism of some of Roosevelt's supporters, "I am not arguing against getting into the war. I am arguing against getting into the war in order to perpetuate the very system—no matter how beautifully it may be described—which basically brought about the war."

As the Cold War set in, Vincent was transferred from Director of Far Eastern Division (F.E.) to the remoter airs of Switzerland (1947–51), then Tangiers (1951–53), as U.S. Minister. The anti-Communist fever built up in Washington, not least over the issue of China, the Loyalty Program was started, and Vincent, to his amazement, found himself under challenge. In 1952, he returned from Tangiers to face a grueling week-long interrogation by the

(McCarran) Internal Security Subcommittee of the Senate Judiciary Committee.[4] The Subcommittee oscillated between trying to demonstrate Vincent knew nothing about communism and trying to insinuate that he was a Communist. Assisted by assorted ex-Communists, it indulged these "fanatics against their own past" to an amazing degree, fiddling scholastically with Communist myths and texts. Never once, however, did it turn the discussion to American ideals and traditions, about which Vincent knew and cared somewhat more than all McCarran's ex-Communists. Insults flew as Vincent evaded questions out of fear of committing perjury on some detail of time or place; counsel for the Subcommittee asked caustically, since Vincent had forgotten so much, whether he had perhaps forgotten that he had been a member of the Communist Party. It is hard to say which annoyed McCarran most: Vincent's prevarications and vagueness concerning doctrinal niceties or his gentlemanly bearing and individualistic spirit.

Though he was cleared by the State Department Loyalty Board, he then had to face a Loyalty Review Board, whose chairman, ex-Senator Hiram Bingham—evidently aware that two of its three members saw no case against Vincent—added two new members to the Board, which arrived at the conclusion, by a majority of three to two, that there was a "reasonable doubt as to Vincent's loyalty to the U.S." [5] In Tangiers, he read of this decision in the newspapers. Secretary of State Dean Acheson, outraged by Bingham's finding and convinced that the case against Vincent was nonexistent, consulted with President Truman, and the two of them agreed not to follow the Review Board's recommendation, but rather to set up a further group of five, chaired by Judge Learned Hand, to review the whole matter.

Before the new group finished its work, however, John Foster Dulles replaced Acheson as Secretary of State. Telling Judge Hand his services were no longer necessary, Dulles decided in March 1953 that although there was *no* "reasonable doubt as to the loyalty" of Vincent, "I do not believe that he can usefully continue to serve the U.S. as a Foreign Service officer." [6] Vincent had talked with Dulles in February and was given the choice of retiring or being fired. He "applied for retirement," returned from Tangiers, and settled down in Cambridge, Massachusetts, from where he views with a stoic eye the Far Eastern scene and the course of the U.S. foreign policy that he shared in making and executing for thirty years.[7]

A letter in his files tells him he was "completely cleared by the Department of State, on all the evidence, in regard to charges as to your loyalty to the United States and as to your security." [8] But it was a Pyrrhic victory, for though he was loyal, as even Dulles did not dispute, he had committed a more ultimate transgression. He had remained a diplomat, looking at the facts as he saw them, at a time of national hysteria when it became necessary to be an ideologue, looking at the facts as the ideology of anticommunism construed them.

PROBLEMS OF LENINISM—AND OF CHINA

Dulles once pulled down from his bookshelves Stalin's *Problems of Leninism* and asked Vincent if he had read it. Vincent had not. "If you had read it," mused Dulles, "you would not have advocated the policies you did in China." Since Stalin failed in China no less than Truman, one may wonder whether Stalin read his own book. Nevertheless, Vincent was weak on Communist theory. And he was not particularly informed on the U.S.S.R. and the American Communist Party. Weakness on Communist theory did not seem to be a serious obstacle to understanding and predicting Chinese-Russian Communist Party relations. Vincent was always skeptical of the durability of the Moscow-CCP alliance. From the earliest days of the Communist regime, he urged upon Washington a policy that would aim to drive a wedge between Moscow and Peking rather than to force Peking closer to the U.S.S.R. by refusing all dealings with Mao. Nor did Dean Rusk's knowledge of Communist theory lead him to understand Chinese-Russian relations notably better than Vincent. Two years after the founding of the People's Republic of China, the future Secretary of State could talk of the Peking government as a "colonial Russian government" that is "not Chinese." [9] Vincent was also one of the few to protest the folly of the concessions made to the Soviet Union—at Chiang Kai-shek's expense—during the Yalta Conference (which Vincent did not attend).

Nevertheless, if Vincent had understood more of Communist theory (as formulated by the Chinese rather than by Stalin) he might have understood the Nationalist (KMT)–Communist (CCP) relationship more subtly than he did. A better knowledge of the U.S.S.R., too, might have made him more wary of postwar Soviet foreign policy. American officials whose business it had been to deal with Moscow, such as Kennan and Harriman, saw the emerging outlines of Soviet toughness and expansionism —at least in Europe—sooner than China Hands like Vincent.

How deeply did the man who liked to show *Problems of Leninism* to visitors understand Communist theory himself? Certainly Dulles had read Stalin's book; he quoted from it thirty-four times within the space of twelve pages in his *War or Peace,* published in 1950.[10] And it was not only for those innocent of communism that he would pluck a text from Stalin. In 1947, he tells us, he was arguing with a "leading official of a communist country" about the reasons for the current strikes in France. "I had with me a copy of Stalin's *Problems of Leninism,* and took it from the shelf and read to him from page 12 a teaching on the use of 'the political general strike.' " [11]

But if Dulles had diligently read one book of Communist theory, one may doubt that he had stomached any more of these "not exactly amusing" books, still more that he understood communism well. He begins his analysis of communism, in a chapter of *War or Peace* entitled "Know Your Enemy": "Soviet Communism starts with an atheistic, Godless premise. Everything else flows from that premise." And he is able to believe it probable that even Stalin would not be able to "deviate from the Party line without signing his death warrant." [12] If ever there should be a kind of McCarran Subcommittee that bends its energies to investigating why the United States "lost Cuba" in the 1950s, perhaps Dulles may get a posthumous rap over the knuckles for—to use his words to Vincent—"failing to understand communism."

The strengths in Vincent's position are more concrete. He knew China intimately. Like John Davies, John Service, and many other China officers, he had built up the substantial perception of China that Kennan, Bohlen, Thompson, Kohler, and other "Russian" officers had built up of Russia, and that no one in the

State Department possessed after the "Chinese" purges took place. He knew China well enough to doubt that the Russians and the Chinese would get on well for long; to be sure that the United States could not possibly make a liberal democratic China in the present stage of history; to see in 1943 that a KMT–CCP civil war would break out after the defeat of Japan; and to grasp the truth that the peasantry was the indispensable base for political power in China (lacked by the KMT).

One sees the importance of these insights by a glance at the observations of those who destroyed the China Hands. "The Chinese," Dulles wrote, "through their religious and traditional habits of thought have become an individualistic people." [13] Not one China specialist in five hundred would agree with that. "There is little patriotism in China . . ." [14] he observed in 1950. Has failure to understand patriotism and nationalism been any less disastrous for U.S. China policy than failure to understand *Problems of Leninism*?

It is true that some of the China Hands became so immersed in China that they lost the perspective that the limitation of their work to "U.S. policy toward China" should have given them. Through long residence in that compelling, fascinating country, they came to feel, as Herbert Feis has put it, that "China was their cause." [15] But Vincent's papers, and the public record of what he said, reveal little sentimentality about China. His memoranda—whatever weaknesses they may have—are models of "national interest" thinking about Far Eastern affairs. He enjoyed the company of Chinese, but the naturalness of his relations with them excluded zealous Sinophilism. He wrote from Chungking in May 1942:

> Had dinner with Madame Sun Yat-sen. Dick Smith was the other foreigner present; the rest, about ten, were Chinese. Madame C[hiang] and Madame K[ung] were there. Also father H. H. K[ung]. Good Chinese food. I was literally encompassed by Soong sisters. Sitting opposite Madame Sun, in Chinese fashion, between Madame C and Madame K. We played bad bridge afterwards until very late. . . . [Dick and I] both like the Chinese and they recognise it. More than that: there is no conscious or subconscious feeling of

superiority and they recognise it. There is no question of "using" each other's company. We are simply enjoying each other's company. That is hardly normal in China. Even the missionaries "love" with a purpose.

He was neither arrogant nor effusive toward the Chinese. Another letter from Chungking reads: "I try to do my job and these Soong sisters are part of it; and a pleasant part. But my bones have not been reduced to jelly nor my sight beclouded. The Ambassador will admit that and he admits little, and so will the sisters, I think." Nor did Vincent build exaggerated Sinophilic myths when he returned to the United States. He remembers without enthusiasm the gatherings of old China Hands, "the sentimental cocktail parties at the Plaza in New York, where people wrapped themselves around each other who had hardly been acquaintances in Shanghai."

Vincent strove to look at China from the point of view of overall U.S. interests in the Far East. While he was its director, the Division of Far Eastern Affairs had some disagreement with the European Division over the attitude to adopt toward the nationalist movements then seeking an end to British, Dutch, and French colonial role in Asia. Far Eastern Affairs was generally sympathetic toward struggles such as that of Sukarno against the Dutch; the European Division (which enjoyed higher prestige in the Department than Far Eastern Affairs) was opposed. Vincent's argument was that it was foolish for the United States to get on the wrong side of the emerging Asian nationalist regimes. It was, characteristically, a "national interest" argument. He remembers George Kennan remarking: "John Carter, your views on Asian policy are quite sound from the traditional U.S. standpoint, but the immediate problem is to maintain the morale of Europe and its will to resist the communist challenge."

AMERICA'S INTERESTS AND CHINA'S SOVEREIGNTY

On one vital policy issue Vincent was prophetic. He urged the United States to oppose Japanese militarism in the mid-1930s, arguing that the sooner it was opposed the less terrible would be the consequences. When Japan attacked China in 1937, Tokyo probably considered Russia the only serious threat to Japanese plans. The United States, despite rich talk about China's integrity and nonaggression, had its arms firmly folded. Her interest was focused upon Europe, and she was unprepared, as the Chinese recall today, even to put an end to the supplies of U.S. fuel with which Japanese planes were devastating China. The Open Door was a splendid principle, but it did not seem to be much more.

Vincent had been the U.S. consul in Mukden when the Japanese went into Manchuria in 1931. He had pondered the nature and dynamics of Japanese expansionism. When consul at Dairen, in 1934, he attended a dinner given by the Japanese military and noticed on the wall a map that showed Japanese authority extending from Manchuria all the way down to the Yellow River. As he looked at it he wryly recalled the prevalent British view, which was "let the Japanese have Manchuria; it will keep them busy for at least ten years." From the time he returned to the Division of Far Eastern Affairs in 1935, after ten years in Changsha, Hankow, Peking, Tsinan, Mukden, Dairen, and Nanking, he came increasingly to favor strong support for Chiang against the Japanese threat. "From the long viewpoint," he argued in a memorandum of July 1938, "our involvement in the Far East may not be avoided unless Japanese militarism is defeated." He did not believe, nor did he think the Japanese themselves believed, that "Japanese aggression, if successful in China, will stop there." He saw Japanese militarism as an "aggressive force which should not be expected to become satiated on successful aggression or deterred from aggression by normal economic and political considerations." He judged that "American rights and interests may not be preserved unless China's sovereignty is preserved." He urged withholding loans, material credits, and trade that assisted Japan; a clear statement that the doctrine of nonrecognition applied to any regime Japan set up; financial aid to Chiang; and collective action with other interested governments to deter Japan.[16] All of these measures were eventually taken. Few would deny they were taken far too late.

Now Mr. Dulles was hardly in the vanguard of those urging support for Chiang against Japan. True, he thought it a glorious thing, in retrospect, that Chiang had resisted Japan, that Chiang decided to "base his policy on the historic friendship of the U.S. toward China." [17] True, he became a great champion of Chiang. True, he accused Vincent of insufficient support for Chiang. But in the 1930s, when the Generalissimo was in need and alone, Dulles had not yet begun to talk of "massive retaliation." In 1938 he went to China and urged Chiang to compromise with the Japanese.[18]

In 1939 he wrote *War, Peace and Change,* in which there is a truly astonishing absence of any advocacy of "massive retaliation" against either Germany or Japan. The major theme of its empirical sections is a call to appreciate the "interplay of cause and effect" behind German, Italian, and Japanese aggression. "There is room for much difference of opinion and of choice of emphasis." His emphasis fell this way: "The Japanese are a people of great energy. They possess to a marked degree those qualities which we have referred to as requiring an adequate national domain. Their own territory is meager in quantity and quality. Some enlargement of their national domain seemed called for." [19] Mr. Dulles was a great man for peace in 1939.

It is clear that Vincent was not absolutely opposed to American intervention in Asia. It was a question of whether U.S. interests were importantly at stake; whether the intervention could be effective; and whether the Asian elements the United States would intervene to support were stable, progressive, and actively helping themselves. He thought the case for intervention against Japan in the late 1930s strong (and believed that the earlier intervention came the less drastic it would need to be). He thought the case for direct U.S. intervention in the Chinese civil war a decade later weak. His criteria were the same. American interests were not importantly at stake in the KMT–CCP struggle; U.S. intervention could not be effective; and Chiang, by the late 1940s, was no longer strong, progressive, or an effective fighter for his own cause.

George Kennan has observed:

It was not . . . communist efforts which destroyed the old order in Europe itself in the thirties and forties and eventually delivered the eastern half of the continent into communist hands; it was Hitler who did this. And, similarly, in East Asia, it was not Moscow, and least of all Washington, which really delivered China into the hands of the communists; it was the Japanese.[20]

If Kennan is right, we confront a strange irony. Vincent was removed by Dulles for having helped lose China to the Communists. Yet it was Vincent, and not Dulles, who wanted the United States to try and stop Japan's thrust into China, at a time when stopping Japan might have saved Chiang from his rapid decline and prevented Mao from drawing the enormous political capital he did from the anti-Japanese struggle.

Vincent thought strategically about the Far East. He thought in terms not just of one country (China) but of the overall balance of power in the Far East. He saw the weakness of China as a fundamental evil for the Asian situation. In a lecture series named for Madame Chiang Kai-shek at Wellesley College in 1946, he stated, "The situation in China during the two decades prior to the last war, gave a strong encouragement to, if it did not actually make possible, Japan's war upon us in 1941." [21] Dulles, on the other hand, thought ideologically about the Far East. Before the war his theme might have been summarized as "moral fiber." After the war it was "opposition to communism." In neither period did his mind seem to work along strategic lines, as his views on Japan in 1939 and China in 1950 make all too plain.

Vincent was no more "anti-Japan," in any moralistic or absolute sense than he was "pro-China." That is clear from the views he gave on postwar Japan in off-the-record remarks at a Foreign Policy Association luncheon in December 1944.

> I am not a Japanese expert. I simply know them at their worst from four years in Manchuria. There is much serious thought being given to treatment of Japan after its defeat. There is the "stew in their own juice" school of thought; there is the "stability under the Emperor or anybody and get out quickly" school; there is the school that foresees a long and difficult period of military administration; and there is the school that believes the Japanese people

would support a liberal democratic government if given a chance. I belong to none of these schools but I have a leaning toward the latter. I recall that in 1936 the Japanese people voted decisively against the military adventurism of the Seiyukai and for the moderation of the Minseito. This vote caused the revolt of the young army officers and soon thereafter the parties were dissolved. My point is that the rank and file of the Japanese seem capable of making an intelligent choice through the ballot if given the opportunity.[22]

It is a judgment that does not look too bad twenty-five years later. It makes the attempt of the McCarran Subcommittee to prove that he had tried to get communism foisted upon Japan after the war seem foolish. It makes Mr. Dulles's judgment that Vincent had "failed to meet the standard" required for his work in the Foreign Service seem odd.

WAS THERE AN ALTERNATIVE?

What could the United States have done in China in the 1940s that was not done? Much criticism of the China Hands centered upon the Marshall Mission to China of 1945–47. Senator Joseph McCarthy, in his defense of an "uncontaminatedly American foreign policy," [23] claimed that the policy embodied in the Marshall Mission "turned 450,000,000 friends of America into 450,000,000 foes.[24] Dulles said to Vincent after the event, "I just don't see how you and Acheson and Truman could possibly have been so short-sighted as to send Marshall to China."

The argument against the Mission was that it was unreasonable, even suicidal, to insist that Chiang cooperate with the Communists, given his own weakness and given the abyss of convictions that separated them. The alternative was massive American intervention on the side of Chiang, without any attempt to bring about some kind of cooperation or coalition between the contending parties. But was massive U.S. intervention politically and militarily feasible?

Republicans offered no clear alternative policy at the time. H. B. Westerfield in his *Foreign Policy and Party Politics*—a work not very sympathetic to the senior China Hands—concludes: "Marshall went to China with no serious congressional opposition to his mission from either party." [25] The basic reason was that people were sick of war. And influential opinion thought European affairs more important than Far Eastern affairs (hence the emergency in Greece and Turkey was allowed to put an end to plans to spend half a billion dollars in Korea). As Truman points out in his memoirs, the public as a whole were in no mood at all to have hundreds of thousands of Americans go and fight in China.[26] Contrary to a view widely held, General Wedemeyer did not oppose the United States' policy of promoting a coalition in China; he shared the American consensus on this point, and in his famous Report—which is scathingly critical of Chiang —offered no alternative to it.

Accusers of the China Hands claimed that "pro-Communists" in the State Department drew up a directive to Marshall which put impossible demands upon Chiang. Yet a detailed study by Herbert Feis in *The China Tangle* uncovered no dissension within the various arms of the government over the directive.[27] Vincent prepared an early draft. The Pentagon prepared its own draft. The final version of the directive shows little change from the basic lines of Vincent's draft. Vincent had placed slightly more emphasis upon the attainment of a further degree of unity in China as a precondition of U.S. economic aid. But the differences were small, and they were resolved to the satisfaction of all parties.

The conclusion of Dean Acheson, in his "Letter of Transmittal" of the *China White Paper,* has not been overturned by twenty years of further digestion of the evidence: Chiang could have been saved from defeat only by American intervention beyond the "reasonable limits of its capabilities." [28] Whether Chiang could ever have won, in the full political sense, was doubtful even then. He was not short of arms (in the sense that he could have effectively used more) as he and the China Lobby claimed; and much of what he was given was captured by the Communists. When Colonel McCann of the CIA was sent to brief a private discussion on China at the State Department in October 1949, he reported: "The Communist forces that took over Tientsin were so completely equipped with American equipment that they appeared to be American equipped units." [29] The Vietnam experience of the United States raises a further doubt. If U.S. intervention to aid Saigon against the NLF and Hanoi brought such loss, escalation, frustration, and so many incalculable twists and turns, could an effective intervention in China, thirty times as big as Vietnam, with twenty-five times the population, have been made without precipitating the hell of World War Three?

In a devilish moment, Vincent observed years later: "What a pity Dewey was not elected in 1944, so that Dulles could have had a chance to 'save China.' " Actually, there was a weakness in Vincent's own position as an architect of the Marshall Mission which has seldom been focused upon (perhaps only by Walter Lippmann, reviewing the *China White Paper* in 1949). If it was true that nothing the United States could have done would have determined the outcome of the Chinese civil war, why did Vincent continue for so long to back Chiang, whom he had known could not win against the Communists?

LOSS OF AN IDEAL

The American ideal of self-determination, and with it the American awareness of the potency of nationalism, all but disappeared after the "Loss of China." The stampede of ideology trod it underfoot. On NBC Radio in May 1946 the following exchange took place between Vincent and Representative Walter Judd:

> JUDD: In my opinion, the Generalissimo's greatest mistake may have been in not liquidating the Communists in 1937, when he had the chance.
>
> CHAIRMAN: But that was when Japan was opening her attack on China.
>
> JUDD: Exactly. The Communists were right in the path of the Japanese attack. They would have been caught in the middle.
>
> VINCENT: But Dr. Judd, that would have meant turning China over to the Japanese in order to get rid of the Chinese Communists. . . .

Down the corridors of postwar U.S. Far Eastern policy, Judd's line has echoed dominantly. Vincent's line, remonstrating that nationalist feeling does matter and should matter, and that it generally outweighs ideology, hardly won a battle for the next twenty years.

Vincent recalls that when he headed the Division of Far Eastern Affairs, one of his toughest tasks was to allay congressional, press, and public fear that U.S. ground troops might be sent to China. "People forget," he says today, "that there was a time when you simply did not go into an Asian country and take over." Today, intervention to the point of throttling an Asian nation's sovereignty is taken for granted. It is justified by ideological fear and zeal, but it has pecked away at the classical U.S. moral commitment to the self-determination of peoples, and has blunted U.S. alertness to nationalist feeling in Asia.

A depressing moral and political confusion has resulted. Former Ambassador to Thailand, Kenneth Young, in most respects a reasonable observer of U.S.-China relations, has lamented about China: "Kindergarten children have even been reported singing about their determination to shoot down American planes!" [30] Now those kindergarten schools are in China, not in the United States, or Mexico, or even in Vietnam. If they shoot down American planes—and no one suggests it is pleasant for tiny tots to use guns any more than for B-52s to bomb their kindergartens—they will be planes that are violating Chinese territorial integrity. In the years of "interventionism" it has been forgotten that aggression basically means interference, not some kind of political sin against democracy; that if the principle of self-determination is accepted, there will be many things in the world that will not please democrats; that it may be more just to allow a people to become dominated by Communists (of their own nationality) than to force them from outside to be governed by anti-Communists.

Few issues receive more stress in Vincent's papers of the 1940s than self-determination. Few issues were more totally disregarded by his accusers. In 1952, the House Un-American Activities Committee interrogated former Ambassador to China,

Clarence Gauss, and Vincent during a session on "The Role of the Communist Press in the Communist Conspiracy." The Committee's concern was that a leftish paper called *The Voice of China* had been published in Shanghai by an American at a time when Gauss was U.S. Consul-General there and Vincent was working on China affairs in Washington. Gauss and Vincent tried to suggest that the reason why they did not banish *The Voice of China* was that the wretched paper was being published not in the United States but in China, and that the State Department had no *power* to banish it. The Committee was utterly unimpressed by such a petty jurisdictional quibble. Representative Harold Velde pinpointed its concern:

. . . if American authorities operating in foreign countries, apparently diplomats, do not have any legal way of stopping the circulation of subversive material, I think it is high time that the Congress made available some way to our American diplomats operating in foreign countries to do just that.[31]

Such was the Committee's respect for the sovereignty of other nations, and such was the "logic" which swept Vincent into retirement.

BALANCE OF POWER VS. IDEOLOGY

We have seen that Vincent had urged the United States to back Nationalist China against Japan. He had become depressed in Washington in the middle and late 1930s because the United States was twiddling its thumbs while Japan ate into China. He saw a strong, united China as a key to stability in Asia and consonant with U.S. interests. But the stampede of ideology after the war trod under any serious consideration of the notion that a strong China might further overall stability in the East. Of what account is mere stability when an ideologue gets the sniff of communism in his nostrils? Dulles, lawyer though he was, did not blush to don the feathers and war paint of rebellion and subversion; as late as 1957 he said of the Government of China: "We will do all that we can to contribute to the passing away of this regime." [32] Dulles wanted a weak, disunited China; indeed, he wanted chaos, if he wanted to get rid of the settled regime of a nation of 650 million people. It is hard to resist the impression that he was not thinking in strategic terms at all.

"If Chiang Kai-shek is overthown," General Douglas MacArthur said in 1944, "China will be thrown into utter confusion." [33] This is an interesting halfway house between the thinking of Vincent and Dulles. MacArthur wanted America to evolve an overall strategy for Asia, and he knew that a China in "utter confusion" would make Asian stability about as durable as a block of ice in a furnace. Here Vincent agreed with him. But MacArthur could not see that Chiang was not going to be able to stabilize China. Nor did it seem conceivable to him that Mao might accomplish that task, and might, in doing so, actually serve the cause of an overall pattern of stability in Asia. Vincent believed that the role of China in Asia was a more fundamental consideration than the political philosophy of the men who governed China. And before leaving Chungking in 1943, he had come to the conclusion that Chiang would not succeed in creating a strong and united China.

Dulles seemed to be a step further from reality than MacArthur. Even when he saw the evidence of a decade of stable rule by the CCP, he could not contemplate recognition of Peking, let alone weigh the possible usefulness of including China in overall arrangements for Asian stability. Rusk was faithful to the moralism of Dulles, applying Dullesian China doctrine to other parts of Asia. Talking of the need for Asian countries to be "independent" and "stable" and to "develop," he evidently did not see that North Vietnam and North Korea fulfilled those three desiderata. Indeed, he pursued a Vietnam policy that historians from Mars could be excused for thinking was designed to hinder the development and stability of North Vietnam (by bombing it) and to compromise its independence (by making it necessary for Ho to receive massive aid from China and the USSR).

The China scholars, no less than the State Department, have in their vast majority upheld the desirability of Maoist collapse. What should the United States desire of China? Of course Americans may naturally desire a relaxation in the rigor of the dictatorship in Peking for the sake of the Chinese people; and some of them desire a new opportunity for Christian ideas in the land that a famous missionary, 100 years ago, characterized as a "Niagara of souls, crashing down to perdition." But politics is not religion, and diplomacy is not character-building. What is it in the U.S. *interest* to expect and desire of China?

Perhaps a strong and united China is still in the U.S. interest. Leaving aside for a moment the moral pleasure that the collapse of Maoist China would bring to those who sought a China in their own image, who would benefit most from such a collapse? The USSR might. China and the Soviet Union are perhaps closer rivals than China and the United States. In terms of the power vacuum that a Maoist collapse would bring about, Moscow is better placed geographically to extend her influence (once more) into China. In terms of the power of communism in the world, a collapse of Chinese communism would find Moscow preening itself as *the* center and *the* successful model for communism, thus removing the sharpest thorn in the side of Soviet foreign policy during the 1960s. By and large, it is hard to see that the United States would find a weak and disunited China any more helpful to the Far Eastern situation than it was in the two wretched decades between Versailles and Pearl Harbor.

This, too, is not to speak of the setback that chaos in China would administer to efforts to close the "development gap." A chronically poor Asia is unlikely to be a peaceful Asia (not that there are lacking reasons other than poverty why violence and war are likely). But the possible contribution of Communist regimes such as North Korea and China to closing the development gap is seldom pondered. Under certain conditions, Communist power, achieving by compulsion the maximum use of the great resource of Asia—manpower—and dissolving the unprogressive traditionalism of Asian society with the acids of its Western-derived rationality and organizational capacity, may be the best available vehicle for development. When this is true, and when, as with China, the developmental effort diverts the regime from foreign adventures, the strength and unity of a Communist power may be more in the interests of the United States than its disintegration. Chaos in China proved disastrous enough forty years ago when it set Japan whoring through Asia. It might be even worse today: for the Chinese, for America, for mankind. But such possibilities were swept aside during the stampede of ideology.

A further speculation suggests itself. Enduring stability in the region over the coming decades is probable only if some kind of balance of power emerges between the United States and China comparable to that between the United States and the Soviet Union in the northern hemisphere. That balance requires a strong China. General Wheeler, when Chairman of the Joint Chiefs of Staff, remarked: "We would not like to see one nation dominate all of Europe or all of Asia." [34] The General did not mention Latin America, which showed a healthy prudence, but his point is a crucial one. The trouble in Asia, ever since the Bandung Era faded, has been in no small measure due to an overall power imbalance. With China inwardly preoccupied, Japan still too diffident, India and Indonesia too weak, poor, and disunited, there has been no effective counterbalance to U.S. power. The United States has some 900 thousand men under arms in Asia; China has practically none outside her own borders; the USSR has none outside her own borders in Asia. Thoughtful Asians, including leaders like Prime Minister Lee Kuan Yew of Singapore who must dance nimbly to whatever music blares loudest at any point of time, understandably see China as the natural counterweight to the United States. True, they fear China. True, they sometimes dislike Peking's policies. But they did not like Vietnam either. And they believe that Vietnam could never have become such a horrific slaughter if there had been a *major* counterweight to the United States in Asia; the way, for example, the United States and the Soviet Union provide a counterweight to each other in Berlin.

THE POLICYLESS POLICY

We can see in the story of Vincent how interests and desires (even fantasies) came to be confused in U.S. China-policy. It is easier to indulge in dreams when you have few responsibilities. That was true of America's first perceptions of China. For almost a century after the Opium Wars, it was Britain that did the necessary military dirty work and established, with whatever fragments of cooperation she could induce from the Chinese, the institutions indispensable to trade and religion on the China coast. America was free to be idealistic about China. The legacy of idealism continued into the period of heavy U.S. responsibility in China, which reached its climax in the 1940s. It continues now, even more confusedly, into a period when the United States has no possibility of exercising moral influence upon China, but has a profound interest in coming to certain businesslike understandings with China. The problem is that U.S. policy is still built too much on *desires for* China, and too little on U.S. *interests in relation to* China.

Some of the China Hands may have contributed to this confusion. Certainly, the ideologues who attacked them found it useful to confuse U.S. desires for China with U.S. interests toward China. In the late 1940s the air was thick with apprehension about Russian intentions. The appearance of a Russian A-bomb in 1949, and soon after of an H-bomb, intensified it, as did the uncovering of some nuclear spies. There seemed to be a historical creedal struggle unfolding comparable to the one that brought on the religious wars of the sixteenth century. This made it easy for the ideologues to portray the Chinese civil war as one act in a global creedal drama. Party and political considerations reinforced this temptation. Governor Dewey in 1948, Eisenhower in 1952, and congressional Republicans from 1946 onwards sought to dramatize the failures of Democratic policy in China. Instead of analyzing U.S. interests, they bewailed the shattering of an American dream. It proved easier to blur the issues than to admit that a Communist regime had come to power after its opponents had failed to govern China with strength and justice. It proved more satisfying to say that the United States *could* have stopped Mao if the China Hands had not betrayed their country— and thus sustain the image of an omnicompetent and innocent America—than to admit that the world was a very complicated place, diverse in culture, polycentric in power, in which prudence and tolerance might be worth as much as zeal.

The Vincents had met Henry Luce of *Time* and *Life* at dinner parties in Georgetown. After China became Communist, Luce's magazines attacked Vincent and others responsible for the State Department's "pro-Communist" line. From Tangiers, where Vincent was U.S. Minister, Mrs. Vincent wrote to Luce in February 1953, remonstrating with *Time*'s coverage and trying to "enlist your talents and power . . . to make the end a happier one than sometimes my nightmares permit me to believe possible." Luce wrote back to Mrs. Vincent and included an analysis of the China tragedy as he saw it:

The China business has been in every sense a tragedy—especially for the millions and millions of Chinese who have been killed, brutalized and brainwashed. As to America's relation to this problem, opinions and judgments differ. That America *had* an important relation cannot be disputed: the most eminent presence of the most eminent George Marshall attested to our involvement. Marshall failed. He, of course, will say it wasn't his fault—it was Chiang Kai-shek's or somebody else's or "fate." In any case Marshall, and the strategy he pursued, failed. I was astounded that Marshall, when he got to China, pursued the strategy he did. I believed it was a hopeless strategy based on a hideous error in evaluation of all the factors.[35]

Luce evidently had a deep humanitarian concern for China. But neither in this long letter nor in *Time* does he say upon what conception of U.S. interests in the Far East his attack on the "hideous error in evaluation of all the factors" is based. He had clear *desires* for China, but there is no clue as to what he thought U.S. *interests* toward China were.

It is curious how *policyless* was the policy of Dulles himself toward China. His book *War or Peace,* which begins with a chapter on "The Danger" and ends with one entitled "Our Spiritual Need," is more like Bunyan's *Pilgrim's Progress* than a book on foreign policy. The idea of an "ever-tightening noose" [36] runs through its pages. Biblical texts are jerked directly into a political application. Thus St. Paul is pitted against Mao and Stalin: "Under the pressure of faith and hope and peaceful works, the rigid, top-heavy and overextended structure of Communist rule could readily come into a state of collapse." [37] Policy and missionary activity seem to be one and the same thing. But is "policy" the right word? Is it a policy to hope that fate or God or Chiang Kai-shek will bring down the government in Peking? Is the "quest for liberty" a valid aim for a foreign policy, as Dulles declared in his 1953 speech, "The Moral Initiative"?

Dulles rejected nonideological policies and banished many of those who formulated policy by reference to facts rather than to ideologies. The consequences were grave. At a closed discussion in the State Department in October 1949, many participants— Kennan was one of them—urged that the question of China having a Communist government be distinguished from the question of the prospects of a durable Soviet tutelage over the Chinese Communists. The latter was the real problem, said Kennan, and he doubted that Russia and China would "combine" well together.[38] Such an approach to policy-thinking got short shrift in the 1950s. Marshall pointed to a second factor that ideologues took little cognizance of. Testifying on the China issue before the MacArthur Hearings (combined Senate committees on Armed Services and Foreign Relations), he said: "The issue in my mind, as Secretary of State, was to what extent this government could commit itself to a possible involvement of a very heavy nature in regard to operations in China itself." [39] He contrasted this to the spurious nonissue of whether to "support" the CCP way or the KMT way.

Vincent's accusers had presented the controversy in this latter form. In its January 1953 story on the "Vincent Case," *Time* magazine spoke of "State's pro-Communist, anti-Nationalist line." In her letter to Henry Luce, Mrs. Vincent criticized this "pro-Chiang or pro-Mao" approach. "That to me is a contrived issue," she wrote. "The real one is what was pro-American and what was anti-American." From the point of view of American interests, it was vital to be clear under what conditions the United States could intervene effectively. To have desires or political preferences which could not be furthered by effective intervention was pipe-dreaming. By contrast, Marshall, having seen a lot of China, knew there were limits to what the United States could accomplish there. And he tried to keep policy proportionate to capacities.

In the subsequent evolution of China policy, the legacy of this confusion between desires and interests has made itself felt. The Kennedy and Johnson administrations took a few timid steps toward greater realism, yet the old myths have mostly remained. Roger Hilsman, Assistant Secretary of State for Far Eastern Affairs, 1963–64, in his book, *To Move a Nation,* treats "hostility" toward the United States as if it is the same as "aggression" against the United States. He says, as do most China specialists now, that Peking has been "essentially cautious" in its policies, "especially in confronting American power." [40] A few pages later, however, he refers to the "coldly aggressive policies" of Peking. The facts are no longer denied or neglected: China has been prudent. But she is still aggressive in some spiritual sense that is over and above the facts. The moralistic hangover persists. It is not only Chinese behavior that determines whether or not we can live with her. It is, as it used to be of old, the state of her soul that gets under Hilsman's skin. So long as Peking is hostile to the United States, somehow she is being aggressive, even though the *Peking Review* is the nearest thing to a missile she ever despatches to the outer world.

President Nixon's first statement on China, in January 1969,[41] did not entirely escape from the moralistic hangover. On the U.N. question, for example, he asked whether China was *worthy* of a seat, not whether it would be in U.S. interests to have China sitting in the U.N. It is quite possible that, even if China is unworthy of a seat (maybe one or two other nations are too?), her participation in international arrangements is so important that any moral niceties should, in this case as in others, take second place. Lord Palmerston had a useful word for U.S. China-policy in his famous remark: "We have no eternal enemies, only eternal interests."

The moral tone of Palmerston's remark seems sadly lacking alongside the breathless spiritual athleticism of Dulles. Yet it is a large question whether morality touches foreign policy primarily at the level of aspiration or primarily at the level of concrete action. Vincent had views on this matter. Like Dulles, he came from a Christian background; his mother, he recalls, wanted him to become a "minister of the Gospel" but he became instead a "minister of diplomacy." On first entering the Foreign Service, his intention was to remain only long enough to get money to do graduate work in aesthetics or ethics.

If the Presbyterianism of Dulles had in it a streak of Calvinist authoritarianism—sins could easily be viewed also as crimes—the Baptist polity that influenced Vincent had liberty at its center —the rule of virtue in the world could only be indirect, expressed through the convictions of individuals. Dulles applied Christian morality directly to the world of nations. He thought governments should carry out scriptural injunctions. And he analyzed U.S. foreign policy toward the USSR from the starting point that Soviet communism is godless. Vincent, however, saw morality entering foreign policy indirectly, mediated through the choices made by a democratic people. It is not for Washington to carry out God's will for China. Such an imperative, if it is to exist at all, enters the sphere of government only in the form of concrete, secular goals that express the will of the American people. Also, he did not consider any foreign policy course moral unless it was also possible. A noble dream, if pursued by state power when the chances of success were small, could turn into a very immoral business. A foreign policy based upon interests could yet be moral, if it strove to bring into its definition of interests all the enlightened understanding of a free people.

We now confront the heart of the story of John Carter Vincent. His weakness lay in being an unideological man in a period which called for ideological swagger. After World War II there came a period of panic. America had been rather suddenly thrust from isolationism into world leadership. The transition was accompanied by intense ideological self-consciousness. Perhaps ideological swagger helped conceal self-doubts in the face of enormous responsibilities.

There seemed to be a momentary loss of confidence in the real traditions of America. "The only ones we can believe are those who were in the know," observed Senator Ferguson at the McCarran Subcommittee Hearings, "the ex-Party boys." It was no longer enough to be an ordinary American; one had to have ideological swagger. Best of all was to be an ex-Communist. In her letter to Henry Luce Mrs. Vincent accurately observed:

"To the McCarran Committee, honor lies only with ex-communists." And she added these poignant, bewildered words: "I find at this moment in our career our greatest difficulty is that we are not ex-anything, still Christians, still diplomats, still loyal Americans."

THE FALLACY OF "POSITIVE LOYALTY"

A further issue reflected into the present by the mirror of the past is that of loyalty in the Foreign Service. Vincent paid a price for being an unideological man in an ideological period; in this way the State Department lost its best China men. But it also lost morale. When William Rogers became Secretary of State in 1969, he greeted the Foreign Service with a message that had a deep impact: "I hope to lead a receptive and open establishment, where men speak their minds and are listened to on merit, and where divergent views are fully and promptly passed on for decision." [42] It was contrasted in the Department with the comparable message of Dulles on his first day as Secretary of State, when he called for his famous "positive loyalty."

One day toward the end of the war, when Vincent was back in Washington from Chungking, he chanced upon a friend who was about to return to China. He "sent his regards"—orally—through this colleague to Madame Sun Yat-sen. Madame Sun was later to be a high, if largely honorary, official in Peking. However, she was at this time still in the circle of her sisters in Chungking. One of those sisters was none other than Madame Chiang Kai-shek; the other was the wife of H. H. Kung, one of Chiang's highest aides. The McCarran Subcommittee found it worthwhile to spend thirty minutes trying to draw out the sinister inner meaning of this trifling social amenity. [43] Their stick was guilt by association. Its special twist was a kind of retroactive ideological responsibility in reverse; one is responsible not only for the views of everyone one encounters, but for their future views as well. (Actually, Vincent saw all three of the beautiful Soong sisters socially in Chungking. Together with the U.S. Naval Attache, he played bridge with Madame Chiang and Madame Kung. Madame Sun herself did not play bridge, nor did Vincent address her by her first name, as he addressed Madame Chiang. The McCarran Subcommittee might have boggled had they known that when Vincent left Chungking in May 1943, Madame Sun gave him a carved bamboo brush holder, inscribed with a charming poem in Chinese characters.)

Vincent observed years later: "Any young Foreign Service Officer who read through the McCarran Hearings may not be edified but he would certainly be troubled." [44] Young men considering the Foreign Service as a career would also be deterred. (In 1949, 1,128 candidates took the Foreign Service examinations; in 1950 only 807 did; and in 1951 only 760.) [45] Good reporting from the field depends heavily upon their being, in Washington, what Rogers called a "receptive and open establishment," an establishment that does not equate "error" with "disloyalty." It depends also upon the richness of the contacts the officer is able to cultivate at his post. Vincent's bitter experience of the consequences of being an acquaintance of Madame Sun was small encouragement to the cultivation of contacts. Truman made this point forcefully when he refused to allow the State Department to turn over Vincent's loyalty file and other papers to the McCarran Subcommittee. To surrender these documents, said Truman, "would create a serious danger of intimidation and demoralization of Foreign Service personnel."

In Vincent's case, it was not only actual contacts that brought recrimination, but imagined contacts, too. One day in 1950, when he was U.S. Minister in Switzerland and the Tydings Committee Hearings were proceeding, the State Department phoned him in Bern to ask whether he had been at a dinner party given by the mother of a Mr. Frederick Field in New York on a certain date. Vincent assured the Department that he had never dined with Mrs. Field, or in her house, and did not know the lady. But that was not the end of the matter. The transatlantic cables tingled once more and the question this time was: Did Vincent know who *were* the guests present at this infamous dinner party? There were scores of such tragicomic operations.

Within the Department of State, distrust grew as Senator Joseph McCarthy and his helpers sought to "discover" damaging information, sometimes setting officer against officer in the process.

While Minister in Switzerland, Vincent discovered that McCarthy had sent a man there to try and get "evidence" against him. He received a telegram, sent from within Switzerland, above a signature he did not recognize, requesting him to meet at such and such a place "concerning a matter of interest to us both." Presumably the plan was to produce a copy of this telegram at a later date as proof of the subversive contacts Vincent maintained in Switzerland, for the signature on the telegram was that of a Swiss Communist official. McCarthy's man in Europe had sent the telegram, signing it with the name of the Swiss Communist, as the diligent Swiss police quickly discovered. He was imprisoned, and from prison wrote to Vincent admitting and apologizing for his treachery.

The "China Lobby" group, partisans of Chiang Kai-shek in the United States and bitter foes of Vincent and other China Hands, upon whom they blamed the Communist victory in China, did much to undermine morale in the State Department. These were years when, to quote a former Foreign Service officer, "desks were periodically searched, private correspondence was opened and read, telephones were tapped, secretaries were asked to report on the men for whom they worked." [46] From the "China Lobby" point of view, Alfred Kohlberg, a rotund little importer of Chinese embroidery with a vivid perception of the Communist danger within America, who supplied part of McCarthy's "case" against the China Hands, had this to say about the informers within the State Department who ferreted out "evidence" for him:

> I don't consider all the $250 million we spend on the State Department as waste. There is a little of it I consider not waste. That is the small part of it that goes to pay the salaries of the good Americans in there, whom I call the pro-American underground, who pass on information of what is going on. [47]

What did Dulles mean by "positive loyalty"? No one seemed to know, and therein lay part of the problem. "Disloyalty" can readily be defined. But loyalty and disloyalty are perhaps not opposite sides of the same coin. If loyalty means the absence of disloyalty, its meaning is also clear. But "positive loyalty"? Peter Berger has observed of freedom that it is "not empirically available." [48] One might say the same of loyalty. Vincent has put it this way: "True loyalty, like true love, cannot be had on demand." If it means something more than the absence of disloyalty, it is probably a product of high morale, of the kind of openness, dynamism, and trust that Rogers spoke of in his striking message of January 21, 1969. But Dulles did not conceive "positive loyalty" in this fashion; he meant by it a kind of "right-thinking." Vincent considered that loyalty in the Foreign Service should mean loyalty in carrying out government policy. That may not mean one agrees with all of it, nor that reports from the field may not, at any point of time, present views that cast doubt on it. [49] The other view is that loyalty is not just a matter of conduct. In addition to carrying out its policy, you must think the way the government seems to think, and certainly not reveal any contrary thoughts—or facts which question the government view—in a field report. Mr. Rogers appears to have proclaimed the obsolescence of positive loyalty.

THE BEST TRADITIONS OF AMERICA

Vincent sees the McCarthy hysteria, and the Dulles policies which arose out of it, as the start of two decades of awful mistakes in China-policy and Asia-policy. The issues over which he was attacked have remained pivotal: the distinction between national interests and ideological desires; the importance of self-determination in Asia; realistic assessment of what the United States can and cannot achieve, especially by force, in Asia; and a Foreign Service in which officers are encouraged to report what they see and believe.

Over and above the issues, the man himself stands as testimony of the points he makes about U.S. policy. He embodies the traditions of American diplomacy; alongside him, his "conservative" accusers seem not "conservers" of anything, but rootless iconoclasts, who tore down not subversive outgrowths, but some of the central fabric of the American diplomatic edifice. The scores of moving tributes Vincent received, especially during 1952 and

1953, from people of many nations who knew him as an American diplomat, insistently stress his effective stewardship of American traditions and ideals. "Those of us who have closely observed your conduct as our American Minister," wrote the president of the *Moroccan Courier* in Tangiers, "say it has exemplified the best tradition of what we citizens of the U.S. like to think our representation abroad should be."

One notable feature of the Vincent case is how orthodox Vincent is. Yet in one respect Vincent was exceptional: he was a diplomat with a strong social conscience. Vincent in fact was a social liberal—a non-Communist rather than an anti-Communist. His social philosophy, unlike that of the next generation of liberals, was not oriented around an attitude toward communism. In a sense, communism did not come into the picture of his social philosophy at all; he thought the hill of social injustice could be breasted by another path entirely, which broadly speaking could be called social democratic.

When that is said, it remains true that it was Vincent the forthright diplomat, rather than Vincent the social liberal, who infuriated the McCarthyites and attracted their poisoned darts. The fatal charge against John Carter Vincent was that he did not, and could not, become an ideologue to fit the fashion of crusading anticommunism.

NOTES

1. Robert L. Heilbroner, *The Future as History* (New York: Grove Press, 1961), p. 58.

2. "The China Lobby," part II, *The Reporter*, April 29, 1952.

3. Throughout this essay there are references to statements by Vincent that are drawn either from interviews that Mr. Vincent granted me in the spring and summer of 1969 or from papers in Mr. Vincent's possession. These papers consist mainly of letters written from his various posts in China, memoranda prepared while in office, and notes for speeches delivered while in office or in retirement. I am deeply grateful for the kind help both Mr. and Mrs. Vincent have given me.

4. The full record of the questioning of Vincent may be found in *Hearings: Institute of Pacific Relations* (Internal Security Subcommittee of the U.S. Senate Judiciary Committee), 1952.

5. *Department of State Bulletin*, January 19, 1953, p. 121.

6. *Department of State Bulletin,* March 23, 1953, p. 455.

7. Mr. Dean Acheson, in a book of memoirs, *Present at the Creation* (New York: W. W. Norton, 1969), recalls the Vincent case. Of the findings of the Loyalty Review Board, which reversed the State Department's own judgment and found Vincent's loyalty suspect:

I knew John Carter and the charges against him well enough to know the imputation of disloyalty was unfounded and that the charges were in reality based upon the policies he had recommended and the valuations of situations he had made and that I had largely accepted. I also had high regard for our Board and its Chairman, and none for the Review Board and its Chairman, Senator Hiram Bingham of Connecticut. . . . I could disregard its advice and restore Vincent to active duty. This, however, would do him little good since Senator McCarthy would delight in renewing charges against him and demand that my successor act upon the Review Board's decision. After consulting with the President, we decided that the better course would be to appoint a group of unimpeachable authority and reputation to review the record and the two conflicting recommendations. . . . I had no doubt what a fair and judicial decision would be.

On Dulles's final condemnation of Vincent:

Mr. Dulles's six predecessors, under all of whom Mr. Vincent had served in the China field, did not find his judgment or services defective or sub-standard. On the contrary, they relied upon him and promoted him. Mr. Dulles's administration was later to find the morale of the State Department personnel in need of improvement.

Of his farewell at the State Department in 1953:

Few experiences have so moved me. I told them they had been through three years of bitter persecution and vilification, largely at the hands of fools and self-seeking blackguards, touted by the press. The worst, I feared, was still ahead of them, when what protection the President and I have been able to interpose against abuse would be withdrawn.

8. The Deputy Under Secretary of State to John Carter Vincent, February 18, 1952.

9. Dean Rusk, from a 1951 speech cited in *The New Republic,* March 19, 1966. Rusk was then Assistant Secretary of State.

10. John Foster Dulles, *War or Peace* (New York: Macmillan, 1950), pp. 7ff.

11. *Ibid.,* p. 15.

12. *Ibid.,* pp. 15–16.

13. *Ibid.,* p. 245.

14. *Ibid.*

15. Herbert Feis, *The China Tangle* (New York: Atheneum Books, 1965), p. 90.

16. The memorandum cited in this paragraph, an especially important and prophetic one, was in the form of a letter to Dr. Stanley Hornbeck (Vincent's superior) dated July 23, 1938.

17. Dulles, *op. cit.,* p. 225.

18. Cf. *Foreign Relations of the United States, 1938,* vol. III, The Far East, pp. 119–20. In *War or Peace,* Dulles refers to his visit to China and his talk with Chiang, but omits to mention that he urged upon Chiang a compromise with Japan (p. 225).

19. John Foster Dulles, *War, Peace, and Change* (New York: Harper & Bros., 1939), pp. 144, 149.

20. George F. Kennan, *Russia and the West under Lenin and Stalin* (Boston: Little, Brown & Co., 1961), p. 275.

21. John Carter Vincent et al., *America's Future in the Pacific* (New Brunswick: Rutgers University Press, 1947), p. 9.

22. These remarks were made in an "off the record" address at a luncheon of the Foreign Policy Association in New York, December 13, 1944.

23. Joseph R. McCarthy, *America's Retreat from Victory* (New York: Western Islands, 1952), p. 77.

24. *Ibid.,* p. 66.

25. H. B. Westerfield, *Foreign Policy and Party Politics* (New Haven: Yale University Press, 1955), p. 254.

26. Harry S Truman, *Years of Trial and Hope* (New York: Doubleday, 1958), p. 82.

27. Feis, *op. cit.,* pp. 413ff.

28. *United States Relations with China,* with special reference to the period 1944–49, republished as *China White Paper,* 2 vols. (Stanford: Stanford University Press, 1967), p. xvi.

29. Department of State, *Round Table Discussion on American Policy Toward China* (October 1949), p. 117.

30. Kenneth T. Young, *Negotiating with the Chinese Communists* (New York: for the Council on Foreign Relations by McGraw-Hill, 1968), p. 357.

31. *Hearings* on "The Role of the Communist Press in the Communist Conspiracy," House Un-American Activities Committee, January 1952, p. 2156.

32. John Foster Dulles, in the *New York Times,* August 12, 1958.

33. Douglas MacArthur, in Walter Millis, ed., *The Forrestal Diaries* (New York: Viking Press, 1951), p. 18.

34. Earl Wheeler, in *Look* magazine, May 30, 1967.

35. Mrs. Vincent's letter is undated; Luce's reply is dated March 5, 1953.

36. Dulles, *War or Peace, op. cit.,* p. 251.

37. *Ibid.,* p. 252.

38. Department of State, *op. cit.,* p. 24.

39. *Hearings* on Far East military situation, U.S. Senate Armed Services and Foreign Relations Committees, May 1951, p. 465.

40. Roger Hilsman, *To Move a Nation: The politics of foreign policy in the administration of John F. Kennedy* (New York: Doubleday Anchor Books, 1967), pp. 326, 346, 349.

41. *New York Times,* January 28, 1969.

42. William Rogers, in the *New York Times,* January 23, 1969.

43. I.P.R. *Hearings,* p. 1803. (Among other references; the Subcommittee returned repeatedly, like a dog to its favorite bone, to this incident.)

44. John Carter Vincent, "Loyalty and the Foreign Service," speech delivered to the Massachusetts Chapter of Americans for Democratic Action, May 10, 1955.

45. *The Reporter,* April 29, 1952, p. 19.

46. Remarks cited in O. Edmund Clubb, "McCarthyism and Our Asia Policy," a memorandum prepared for a conference of the Association of Asian Studies in Boston, March 1969.

47. Alfred Kohlberg, in *The Reporter,* April 29, 1952, p. 18.

48. Peter L. Berger, *Invitation to Sociology* (New York: Doubleday Anchor Books, 1963), p. 122.

49. Nor that officers may not err. Benjamin Schwartz, then assistant professor at Harvard University, wrote a fine letter to the *New York Times* during the Vincent case (December 30, 1952) pointing out the difference between error and disloyalty.

Peking and Washington: is Taiwan the obstacle?

EDWARD FRIEDMAN

Hope for better relations with China "founders on the fundamental issue of Peking's demand for Taiwan. . . ." Most informed people would agree with this assessment by former Assistant Secretary of State for Far Eastern Affairs William Bundy.[1] Although relations between the United States of America and the People's Republic of China is an explosively controversial subject, few would dispute the notion put forward by former White House adviser James Thomson, Jr., that "the paramount obstacle to progress" in improving relations between Washington and Peking is Formosa.[2] This essay argues, however, that this view, agreed upon by people ranging from solid liberals such as Doug Mendel [3] to extreme conservatives such as David Nelson Rowe[4] is actually mistaken. It should be reconsidered carefully—and then rejected.

THWARTING RAPPROCHEMENT

In the spring of 1955, China offered to negotiate with the United States to reduce tensions in the Formosa area. Talks between the two parties had begun in Geneva in mid-1954. Washington wanted the more than thirty-two Americans imprisoned in China returned to the United States. Peking wanted the thousands of Chinese students in America to be returned to China. To succeed in the former issue would be a feather in the political cap of the Eisenhower-Dulles administration. To succeed in the latter issue would increase the pool of skilled personnel China needed for its first five-year plan. But much more was at stake than the particular issue.

In 1954, China had helped impose an unhappy and temporary

solution on the war for independence then in progress in Indochina. Chou En-lai flew to India to get Nehru to agree to head up an International Control Commission. He went to persuade Ho Chi Minh to settle for a temporary division at the 17th parallel, national elections in two years, and independence and neutrality for Cambodia and Laos. He put Chinese offices in Switzerland at the private disposal of the negotiators. To help get the military power of the West out of China's border areas and to reduce the likelihood of China's getting involved in a war, Chou En-lai worked for a solution that was much less than that which the arms of the Vietminh could have demanded. China's security and development came before revolution in Southeast Asia. As former Assistant Secretary of State for Far Eastern Affairs Walter Robertson (exaggerating a bit) put it: "the 1954 Geneva agreement . . . represented a deal between Chou En-lai and Mendes-France, negotiated privately in Berne and brought to the conference as a fait accompli." [5]

The question before the Chinese government, then, was how far this line of peaceful coexistence, of negotiation and compromise, could be carried. Could China coexist peacefully with the United States? There was much evidence that argued against peaceful coexistence. Soon after Eisenhower took office, Washington threatened Peking with nuclear destruction for its involvement in wars in Korea and Vietnam. Larger contingents of Chiang Kai-shek's army were sent to the offshore islands of Quemoy and Matsu. Their equipment was modernized. American advisers to Chiang's military donned military uniforms—a significant symbolic escalation representing a joint commitment, if one can judge from John Kennedy's actions in Laos in 1961. Chiang Kai-shek urged an immediate reconquest of China. Attacks on the China coast were stepped up. Syngman Rhee in Korea threatened to march north. Thus, before the Geneva settlement of mid-1954, China was confronted by direct military attacks and threats by America and its allies from the north, east, and south. All this pressure was put on Peking at a time when China would probably have preferred to disengage from international entanglements so that she could devote her resources to internal development.

Foreign ministers in China, just like Secretaries of State in America, tend to believe that aggressors feed on aggression, that bullies only understand force. China therefore counterattacked in September 1954 and tried to knock the threatening and thrusting Chiang Kai-shek forces out of China's offshore islands. Chiang Kai-shek responded with air attacks against the mainland, hoping a larger war might be imminent.

IN THE INTERESTS OF CHIANG KAI-SHEK

And then suddenly things began to change for the better. In October, under American pressure, Chiang Kai-shek stopped the air attacks. The Chinese deployments had been seen in Washington as essentially defensive. Some of the more exposed offshore islands were abandoned by Chiang Kai-shek's troops and returned to China. Dag Hammarskjold went to China to persuade Peking that Formosa and the return of nationals were negotiable. In January 1955, Congress insisted that America should only defend the offshore islands if an attack on them were a prelude to an attack on Formosa. By April 1955, Admiral Radford, Chairman of the Joint Chiefs of Staff, and Assistant Secretary of State for Far Eastern Affairs Robertson were dispatched to Formosa to ask Chiang to evacuate Quemoy and Matsu. After all, the tiny islands did not help to defend Formosa. Instead, they blockaded Chinese ports and were a constant provocation to China. Since Washington was increasingly persuaded that only revolution from within China could unseat the Communist government, the islands served no American interest. In fact they hurt American interests, as Robert Scalapino and many others have pointed out. They made America a party to Chiang Kai-shek's ridiculous military threats, which placed China in the position of the injured party, won China international sympathy, and rallied the fervent support of patriotic Chinese citizens to the Peking government. They also put America in a position where China or Formosa might involve America in a big war that America did not want.

Chiang Kai-shek, however, refused to abandon the provocative island fortresses. And Washington did not press the issue. Here is the crux of the matter. American foreign policy makers seemingly could not act in America's own interest or in the larger interests of peace in Asia. An ideology which assumed that accommodation with Communist countries is equivalent to a "Munich" had become dominant. Consequently American politicians would not put themselves in a position where they could be attacked by opponents, led by Chiang Kai-shek's powerful friends, with charges of softness on communism. As the *New York Times* editorialized against a deal in "The Ambassadorial Talks" with China: "we can have peace whenever we are ready to surrender." [6]

Peking apparently took the few straws in the wind—negotiated compromise on Korea and Indochina, U.N. intercession, Afro-Asian desires for a peaceful solution, America's restraint of Formosa—as evidence that it was worth trying to achieve some modicum of peaceful coexistence with Washington. The Chinese strategy was to begin negotiations with an easy issue. One would build on the solution of that matter and move on to more difficult issues. The first issue was the already mentioned voluntary repatriation of nationals who wanted to return home. Although an agreement was signed and virtually all Americans imprisoned in China were released, Washington undermined the agreement.

About 5,000 Chinese had hastened to America as students in the late 1940s as a popular revolution toppled Chiang Kai-shek's regime. Subsequently, war with China in Korea convinced Washington that Peking was a dangerous enemy. Consequently, Chinese students in the United States who had technical training were restrained, then detained, and prevented from returning to China with their knowledge. Their brainpower was considered dangerous to the security of the United States.

At the Ambassadorial Talks Peking asked that Chinese students be permitted to return home. Washington replied that no Chinese who wanted to leave this country was prevented from doing so. Peking knew that was not true. Many young Chinese feared to declare their allegiance because they could then be deported to Chiang Kai-shek's Formosa which, Washington insisted, represented China. On Formosa they could be greeted by imprisonment or death. The notoriously extreme right wing Immigration and Naturalization Service presided over by J. M. Swing did deport a number of Chinese students.

Washington even declined to give Peking or an intermediary a list of Chinese young people in the United States. With such a list these people could be approached without stigma and declare their intentions secretly without fear of reprisal. Instead, some regional offices of the Immigration and Naturalization Service called in, questioned, and intimidated "almost any Chinese student who had sometime in the past indicated a liberal attitude. . . ." [7] In April 1955, Secretary of State Dulles permitted some of these students to return home. Although it is difficult to peek through America's plastic curtain, it is probably true that some 1,400 young Chinese men and women eventually went back to China. There has been precious little understanding of what Ralph Lapp has called "this brain drain from the free world." Yet it only takes a simple act of empathy to understand why these well-educated, middle class students might want to help their own people, who were engaged, as they saw it, in building a new, wealthy, and strong China, and in protecting it from armed and hostile powers. Lapp has written,

> The exodus of Chinese scientists to their homeland was the Asian counterpart of the flow of refugee scientists from Europe to America before World War II. Men like Enrico Fermi, Leo Szilard, Eugene Wigner and Edward Teller played heroic roles in the U.S. atomic project. Their Chinese equivalents are Ch'ien San-ch'iang, Wang Kan-ch'ang, P'eng Huan-wu and Chang Chia-hua. [8]

Allied to Chiang Kai-shek, Washington took the position of an aggressor out to undermine the Peking government. It may be shocking, but it should not seem surprising, that America thereby became the enemy not only of people in China but even the enemy of many Chinese students in America.

Nonetheless America never could properly carry through the agreement to repatriate Chinese nationals out of fear that passports or other official dealings with China would undermine the legitimacy of Chiang Kai-shek's claim to represent China. In short, America erected a Berlin Wall so as not to injure the parochial and aggressive interests of Chiang Kai-shek rather than amicably remove an unnecessary cause of bad feelings between America and China. Former Ambassador Kenneth Young concludes that as a result of the Talks "most of the American prisoners were released and that no concessions were extracted from the United States in return." [9]

The Chinese would be justified in believing that they were swindled by the Yankee horse traders. Yet the Chinese were so interested in pursuing the possibility of coexisting peacefully that rather than breaking them off, they suggested that the Ambassadorial Talks move on in 1955 and 1956 to discuss a renunciation of force in the Formosa area.

It again became clear that Dulles could not comply with reasonable requests from Peking because of the power of anti-communism and pro–Chiang Kai-shek forces in the United States. China's offer, in sum, was to renounce force in the Formosa area in return for a U.S. military withdrawal. This peace-directed Chinese initiative could have served as a basis for solid negotiations that could have protected the independence of Formosa and diminished military tensions in the area. But the American government chose instead to keep the Talks away from practical issues, thinking up extraneous issues that Peking hopefully would not agree to and preserving the military status quo. The Chinese side, in January 1956, then chose to make the various drafts on the Formosa area public so that the world could see that it was America who was blocking agreement. Dulles, after all, was going through empty motions to keep domestic and foreign critics off his back. Despite Chinese concessions, Kenneth Young writes,

the United States did not intend to make any concessions by trading its relations with Taipei, particularly since the United States government did not want diplomatic relations or continuing negotiations with Peking. Washington wanted to isolate, not enhance, Peking.[10]

By the end of 1957 the United States broke off the Talks. Liberal critics of this policy of trying to isolate China have suggested that America should only try to contain China. But few people have been willing to propose that Washington might do best by responding to Peking's overtures for a general reduction of tension through a disengagement of the forces of both powers from Indochina, Korea, Formosa, and other areas. This mutual interest of China and America in damping out sparks that might otherwise explode in wars has been largely overlooked.

GOING TO THE BRINK

China saw by 1957 that the United States had abandoned efforts to overthrow the government of China and was content to surround it and isolate it with armed and hostile bases. That was not an excessively happy prospect for Peking. She was fearful of what a Douglas MacArthur out of control, an aggressive Rhee in Korea, a hawkish Chiang in Formosa, a militant Diem in Vietnam or, most fearful of all, a powerful rightwing Japanese government might one day do with such American arms. China's basic interest was to defend and secure her borders by working for neutral states around her periphery. This goal was as valid and compelling in Nepal and Indochina as in Japan and Formosa.

Peking wanted American military might out of Formosa but (as the Chinese pointed out) "the U.S.A. refused to withdraw its troops from Taiwan and at the same time insisted that China renounce the use of force in that region." Peking's assessment was that Washington now saw the insanity of Chiang succeeding in "a counter-offensive against the mainland" and therefore in effect accepted the notion of a de facto state of Formosa. And the idea appealed to other countries who saw that mutual acceptance of one China and one Formosa would decrease world tensions. Peking warned that people who thereby approved the inclusion of Formosa in America's military empire "forget the lessons of Munich . . . any toleration of the aggressor only serves to whet his appetite. . . ." [11]

American obdurateness had prevented the Ambassadorial Talks from eliminating the continued American military threat on China's periphery in Formosa. Then, in mid-1958, Peking, with Moscow's approval, attacked Chiang Kai-shek's troops on the neighboring offshore islands. Peking may have hoped that the contradiction between Chiang Kai-shek's need for legitimacy through a forward position and engagement in a continuing war against China and America's need merely to maintain pressure on China, the better to isolate her, would explode if ignited by "the military operations in the Chinmen Islands area [that] are no more than mopping-up operations." [12] Peking's hope for this split between America and Chiang Kai-shek was probably based in part on the publicly known deterioration in relations between the two in 1957. The American Embassy on Formosa had even been stormed by Chiang Kai-shek's youth corps.

Neither Russia nor China would risk anything. Chiang Kai-shek hopefully would try to force America to risk war to protect his prestige. America, not wanting war over Quemoy, would resist. America's allies had restrained it in Indochina. They would restrain America again with regard to Quemoy, which would result in a crisis in Formosa. "There is just one way out of the painful situation into which the United States has rushed in the Far East," Moscow declared, "and that is to withdraw American armed forces from Taiwan and the Taiwan Straits and end America's interference in China's domestic affairs." [13]

Instead, America backed Chiang Kai-shek to the hilt. The Eisenhower administration fancifully declared that it was not Chiang Kai-shek's armed provocation on the island of Quemoy that was at stake but "at least the western half of the now friendly Pacific Ocean." [14] The *New York Times* imaginatively agreed that the issue was "freedom in the Far East." [15] Actually, little was at stake but Chiang's armed madness, a myth that propped up his ego if not his regime.

As soon as China agreed to negotiate, America agreed to resume the Ambassadorial Talks and Secretary of State Dulles pressured Chiang Kai-shek to abandon his "civil war complex" and to begin thinking about an armistice along existing lines. Notwithstanding this millstone around her neck, Washington went to the brink of war and escorted ships from Formosa to within three miles of the tiny islands despite China's claim to the islands and a twelve-mile territorial limit. Peking fortunately did not call America's "bluff," and we were saved from going a step closer to the brink over an issue that, according to America's own prior intentions and subsequent actions, had no place in America's national interest.

CONCESSION TO THE RIGHT

Dulles did subsequently get Chiang Kai-shek to remove some of his troops from the islands. Immediately thereafter, in 1960, as a presidential candidate John Kennedy called for the evacuation of all troops from the occupied islands, a conservative proposal backed by most moderates from Edwin O. Reischauer (soon to become Ambassador to Japan) to University of California professor Robert Scalapino. Yet so much was the American scene mesmerized by Chiang Kai-shek's supporters that even this modest step in America's most immediate interests has not been carried out. In fact its advocates have come under attack as following in the path of "Munich."

After he was elected President, Kennedy never carried out his new China policies. Following his defeat at the Bay of Pigs in April 1961, he would not change America's policy toward the islands of Quemoy and Matsu (or even recognize the government of Mongolia). Such moves would risk charges of softness on communism. There was little reason to make domestic enemies just for a more rational policy toward China. Also, such initiatives would win the wrath of Chiang Kai-shek and his American friends. Chiang Kai-shek claimed that Mongolia was part of China. Since Kennedy was concerned principally about his relations with Khrushchev and the Soviet Union, he had no desire to alienate support in that area because of moves with regard to China. Precisely because the China question was not considered a primary one by the Democratic administration, the rightwing, pro–Chiang Kai-shek warriors had their way.

In fact it is by this same logic that the Democratic administration of Harry Truman got involved with Chiang Kai-shek on Formosa in the first place. In the late spring of 1950, Chiang Kai-shek's defeated remnant was holding out on Formosa. The army of China was preparing to attack him there, end China's revolutionary civil war, and unite China for the first time in half a century. In Washington the Joint Chiefs of Staff agreed that

America had little interest in preventing that occurrence. It seemed silly to go out of one's way to unnecessarily antagonize the new government of China. Secretary of State Acheson pointed out that "anyone who violates the [territorial] integrity of China is the enemy of China." [16]

But the growth of the power of rightwing forces in America at that time included a growth in support for Chiang Kai-shek and attacks on Truman, Marshall, and Acheson for "selling out" Chiang Kai-shek. The voice of pro–Chiang Kai-shek people grew even within the Democratic administration in the spring of 1950. Consequently Truman used the pretext of the Korean War to intervene with American armed forces on Chiang Kai-shek's behalf on June 27, 1950. Richard Rovere was told by people in the White House of this commitment:

> At the time it was made, it was judged in most critical circles to be a crafty political move, since it seemed apt to neutralize not only Formosa . . . but also Chiang Kai-shek and that confederation of his admirers that has come to be known as the China lobby. . . . Uneasiness over [the policy] is apparent in both the State and Defense Departments. . . .[17]

Nothing was said about enhancing American security. Rather it was the security of Truman's administration against McCarthyite attacks that was at stake. To free himself for what he considered more important matters, Truman conceded to the rightwingers on Chiang Kai-shek, thus making the United States, in Acheson's prescient words, "the enemy of China." Since that time, the policies of liberals such as Kennedy have been hardly distinguishable from those of conservatives such as Dulles. America simply has not been able to carry through an intelligent foreign policy with regard to China because, among other reasons, she has bound herself to the hostile forces of Chiang Kai-shek. Vested rightwing interests and a Cold War climate have tied the hands of Kennedy as well as Dulles. And from the beginning China's major demand has been the withdrawal "of all the United States armed invading forces from Taiwan and from other territories belonging to China." [18]

Incapable of intelligent action, in need of illusions to obscure the origins of America's China policy, Washington again, between 1959 and 1962, missed a great opportunity to better relations with China. In about 1960 Peking was worried about its deteriorating relations with Moscow, and she put out trial balloons for improved relations with the United States. Whether conveyed through intermediaries such as Edgar Snow or in open statements by China's Foreign Minister that removal of the U.S. Seventh Fleet from the Formosa Straits could lead to a settlement with the United States,[19] Peking made clear in this period, if it hadn't been clear already, that she was not simply asking America to hand Formosa over to China. This is confirmed by secret Chinese military documents captured in 1961.[20] As with Vietnam in 1954 and Laos in 1962, so with Formosa throughout this period: Peking's primary interest was not territory or revolution but the removal of the military might of hostile powers from her periphery as part of a general settlement of outstanding difficulties. Given the willingness of America to risk nuclear war in 1962 over Russian missiles in Cuba, China's anxieties over relatively far greater American, Russian, or Japanese might in potentially aggressive border areas should not seem unreasonable. America reasonably traded a promise not to invade Cuba for the removal of the Russian missiles.

America, however, was not interested in looking for reasonableness in China in the 1960s, after she committed herself to counterinsurgency and then to limited war in Southeast Asia, supposedly to contain the expansion of Chinese influence in the guise of a Maoist revolutionary model. Chiang Kai-shek did his best to undercut the opportunity early in the 1960s for improving U.S.–China relations by claiming that China's peace initiatives proved Peking was about to be overthrown by a starving, enraged people and that 1962 was the perfect time to launch an all-out attack on the Chinese mainland. Chiang Kai-shek made actual moves in that direction. Attacks on the China coast were launched from the offshore islands. Chiang Kai-shek's troops in Burma moved into Laos to join with rightwing forces there trying to upset peace talks in Geneva. Peking became suspicious. Washington had to reassure Peking. Yet Mao Tse-tung was open to further concessions and compromise until after America began its massive escalation in Vietnam in 1965. A diplomatic settlement in Vietnam reopens the possibility of serious negotiations between China and the United States.

LEAVING IT UP TO PEKING

Chinese leaders seem convinced that America cannot do all it wants in Asia. They have watched Lyndon Johnson forced out, watched foreign aid cut, and have watched Americans more and more insist on the need to concern themselves with domestic problems. In India, which concerns China very much, the United States has not come through with the financial aid New Delhi desired. One Chinese commentator noted in this regard that "the United States does not have the strength equal to its will." [21] Richard Nixon's election was explained in the same way.

Nixon was "elected" after he called for the necessity to "reduce our commitments around the world in the areas where we are overextended" and to "put more emphasis on the priority areas," namely Europe and other areas.[22]

If America is going to reduce its military commitments in South and Southeast Asia, China would appreciate an opportunity to work out a way to maintain the independence and neutrality of that area rather than have another major power such as Russia or Japan move in, encircle China, and press forward against her. There is much for Peking and Washington to talk about.

After Nixon's election China offered to resume talks with America on a treaty of peaceful coexistence and on the solution of problems in the Formosa area. In January 1969, Chinese papers seemed to indicate that the latter issue mainly referred to a facesaving removal of the (nonpresent) Seventh Fleet. But in February, after Nixon showed no willingness to change his policy on China, escalated in Vietnam, and made detente with Moscow his first priority, Peking backed out of the talks. Apparently Chinese politicians, who have been burned too often by America, will not readily risk their political necks on talks with the United States unless Washington offers some reason for them to believe that the talks will prove fruitful.

One must wonder, however, if Washington believes it should give any signals to Peking. U.S. government specialists on China explained China's decision in November 1968 to resume talks with Washington and China's subsequent decision in February 1969 temporarily to delay those talks as proof that the initiative lies with Peking. If the alleged good guys win in Peking, as in November 1968, then there is hope. If the alleged bad guys win, as in February 1969, then there is nothing Washington can do. No mention is made in such analyses of real American actions that might lead men in Peking to change their minds. Actually a new faction didn't rise in November and fall in February. The same men were making China's foreign policy both times. But an American preference to see itself as blameless in its difficulties with China also unrealistically makes America blind to how much a minor change in American policy could do, at the right time, to improve relations with China.

Even after the talks were called off, Peking did not change its basic position. It still believes America is in an "embarrassing predicament . . . hard pressed by internal and external difficulties" brought on by the need to face "difficult decisions about how to allocate available resources against many claims." [23] And Peking remains open to a peaceful solution in Formosa as part of a larger arrangement that will provide her with neutral and independent buffer regions.

When a contingent of Harvard University's Committee of Concerned Asian Scholars visited Chinese diplomats in Paris in 1969, they told the Chinese that they supported China's claim to Formosa.[24] The Chinese diplomats, however, did not put forth such a claim. Instead they thanked these Americans for their support of China's just stand that the American military must leave the Formosa area. In short, aside from "October First" rhetoric, there seems to be little evidence that China is demanding Formosa as the price of better relations with the United States. China's rational fear is armed, hostile powers at its door. It has compromised and will compromise much else to try to remove that danger.

THE CONTINUING POWER OF TAIPEI

Many people in the free world would cringe at the prospect of placing the people of Formosa under a dictatorship they do not want. Of course the people of Formosa already live under such a dictatorship, that of Chiang Kai-shek. But for power politics specialists, the fate of Formosa itself has never been viewed as a vital American concern. Therefore many foreign relations specialists in and out of the government are quite willing to sacrifice the Formosan people to America's broad interests or the administration's narrow political interests. Ambassador Reischauer, for example, "would not oppose reconciliation between Taiwan and the mainland if it should come." As Reischauer sees America's interests in the Formosa area, "we can accommodate ourselves to almost any outcome without great menace to our own vital national interests." [25]

Peking is not suggesting that it favors an independent Formosa. Yet Peking certainly knows that Formosa, even without American military bases, would stay within America's or Japan's economic orbit. Peking seems to have been suggesting for fifteen years now that she is willing to risk that outcome in order to move America's military threat further from her borders. Is America willing to risk a Formosa open to economic and cultural relations, better able to decide her own fate, and free of American backing, for an aggressive Chiang Kai-shek? American politics would first have to free itself from Chiang Kai-shek before it could consider that alternative and open itself to a new relationship with China.

It is easy to believe that the days of McCarthyism are past and that America can now act rationally in its own interests and in the larger interests of peace in Asia. Unfortunately the evidence does not quite support such an optimistic assessment. In June 1969, when Secretary of State Rogers suggested that America recognize Mongolia and win for Washington "a valuable listening post," President Nixon reportedly resisted the proposal "primarily because of strong objections from the Chinese Nationalist Government in Taiwan—the same reason that made Washington back away from recognizing Mongolia in 1961." [26] Chiang Kai-shek still seems to have veto power over American policy. Perhaps he will change his mind on Mongolia as he moves closer to Moscow; he did that once before in 1946. Either way, Washington still does not seem able to decide America's China policy on any rational or national-interest basis. Chiang Kai-shek's view of Mongolia changes with his international political position. China's policy similarly is flexible with regard to Formosa. Only American policy remains frozen.

PEKING'S ERRORS AND TAIPEI'S PLOTS

This is not to suggest that China's policy has been all wise or entirely open. Peking's 1958 judgment on the state of relations between Chiang Kai-shek and America was in error. The policy of attacking the offshore islands based on that misjudgment was a serious blunder. In addition, China would do much better in the international arena if she openly said that she recognizes that twenty years of de facto independence of Formosa—or 75 years counting from the Japanese takeover—makes some difference. She could then say she sympathizes with the desire of the Formosan people to overthrow the military dictatorship of Chiang Kai-shek that rests on American military backing. She could say that while she hopes that in the long run that the people on Formosa will naturally choose to be one with their brothers on the mainland, their mainland brothers now support the people of Formosa in their immediate struggle against Chiang Kai-shek and the American military. Such a policy statement would place full blame for continuing armed hostilities against China on Chiang Kai-shek and the United States, and still not foreclose the nationalist aspirations of the leaders and people of China for a single, united Chinese nation.

Of course Chiang Kai-shek and his colleagues will do everything they can to prevent a smoothing of troubled waters between China and America. They will continue by armed acts to try to make the Formosa Straits a turbulent sea of war. They had Douglas MacArthur's backing and came close to succeeding in obtaining American support for attacking China late in 1950. They offered their troops for use in the Vietnam War, hoping that would induce a reaction from China and thus escalate the Peking-Washington confrontation. They urge Washington to bomb Peking's nuclear installations. They are happy to have Formosa used for U–2 spy flights over China and for training, supplying, and storing for wars in South and Southeast Asia, everywhere from Tibet, to Burma, to Vietnam, to Indonesia. Consequently, one can expect Chiang Kai-shek to try to get America to move missiles or atomic weapons or military bases and troops to Formosa—anything to keep Formosa a somewhat viable and threatening military worry for Peking so that China's relations with the United States cannot easily improve. Since there seems to be little organized opposition to Chiang Kai-shek's plans, he may yet succeed in further embroiling America against its own interests.

Silence seems to be the American stance with regard to its interests in the Formosa area. There was no public discussion of Washington's decision to approve Chiang Kai-shek's son as his successor on Formosa. There does not seem to be any move afoot to withdraw American backing for the military deployments on the islands of Quemoy and Matsu. Formosans in Japan deemed dangerous by Chiang Kai-shek's regime have been kidnaped, jailed, and deported. Formosans returning from America have been barbarously punished by Chiang Kai-shek for exercising American political rights while in the United States. There is no loud, sustained, and organized outcry from American academics (myself included). After all, why antagonize Chiang Kai-shek and lose access to research materials on Formosa, as a few courageous American scholars have done? And more important, why antagonize Chiang Kai-shek and endanger innocent and apolitical Chinese acquaintances on Formosa?

Elements in the Department of Justice continue to serve Chiang Kai-shek's interests. In the early 1950s they pressured Chinese students in America. In the late 1950s they successfully scared the Macmillan Publishing Company from distributing Ross Koen's book on the China lobby in American politics.[27] In the last days of the Johnson administration and again in the first days of the Nixon administration, the Internal Security Division of the Justice Department ordered the United Formosans in America for [Formosan] Independence to register as a foreign agent. Such registration could invite reprisals to the Formosans and their families still in Formosa. Has the political atmosphere which forced Harry Truman's hand in 1950 changed so very much? While it may well be true that Chiang Kai-shek and his people "have an ever diminishing potential to influence Washington's China policy," [28] that influence does not seem yet to have diminished to a point that is safe for America, China, or peace in Asia.

THE FORMOSA MYTH

The point is not that Formosa *cannot* be an obstacle to better relations between China and America. Mao Tse-tung's successors who have been brought up on the rhetoric of "liberate Formosa" may come to believe and act on the slogan as he has not. The issue may get entangled in domestic Chinese politics, and men in Peking may find it no easier to seem soft on American imperialism than American politicians can readily afford to seem soft on communism.

Yet one point stands out clearly. The accepted belief about "the same old roadblock in the way: the fate of the island of Taiwan," [29] is a myth. I would suggest that there is no cluster of fundamental, vital, irreconcilable interests separating the People's Republic of China from the United States of America. Rather, the prior concerns of moderate liberals for other areas has permitted extreme conservatives to win their way with regard to China because the liberals thought the sacrifice there would be worth the gain elsewhere. In a Cold War, anti-Communist climate that fears all revolution, the moderates have been forced out.

In the mid-1950s, in the early 1960s, and probably again today, China has been willing to discuss a settlement with America. Not once yet has America sat down seriously at the negotiating table with China to test the character of such a settlement. Meanwhile Chiang Kai-shek has done and continues to do all in his power to create situations that will prevent a settlement. The crux of the problem then is not an unproved and untested Chinese demand for Formosa but a weakness in the political system of the United

States that permits America's foreign policy toward China to reflect the whims of a discredited general on Formosa more than the interests of the people of the United States and the conditions for a stable peace in Asia.

NOTES

1. William Bundy, speech at Pomona College, Claremont, California, February 12, 1966.

2. James Thomson, Jr., "How to Wink at China," *The New Republic,* March 1, 1969, p. 12.

3. Doug Mendel, in *The Journal of Asian Studies,* May 1969, p. 514.

4. David Nelson Rowe, in Anthony Bouscaren, ed., *The Case for Free China* (Arlington, 1967), p. 128.

5. Walter Robertson, in Bouscaren, ed., *op. cit.,* pp. 112–13. Cf. Philippe Devillers and Jean Lacouture, *End of a War: Indo-China 1954* (New York: Praeger, 1969), pp. 238–94.

6. *New York Times,* August 1, 1955.

7. Harrison E. Salisbury, "U.S. Is Criticized on Chinese Students," *Congressional Record,* vol. 101, part 9, 1955, pp. 11670–71. This quotation, and also much of the material for the preceding three paragraphs, is based on an unpublished paper by Paul David Schumaker, "Repatriating Chinese Students," Madison, Wisconsin, January 1969.

8. Ralph Lapp, *New York Times,* July 14, 1968.

9. Kenneth Young, *Negotiating with the Chinese Communists* (New York, 1968), p. 90.

10. *Ibid.,* p. 113.

11. Kung Pu-sheng, "A Conspiracy Against the Chinese People: Imperialist Plans for the Formation of 'Two Chinas,' " *International Affairs,* January 1958, pp. 15–22. Edgar Faure, *The Serpent and the Tortoise* (New York, 1958), p. 19, also shows Peking worried about the two-China plot rather than invasion.

12. M. Ukraintsev, "American Adventurism in the Far East," *International Affairs,* November 1958, pp. 29–30. Cf. *ibid.,* December 1958, p. 27.

13. *Ibid.*

14. Cited in George Quester, "The American Attitude," in Morton Halperin, ed., *Sino-Soviet Relations and Arms Control* (Cambridge: MIT Press, 1967), p. 241.

15. *New York Times,* September 2, 1958, editorial.

16. Quoted in Joseph Ballantine, *Formosa* (Washington, D.C.: The Brookings Institution, 1952), p. 124.

17. Richard H. Rovere and Arthur Schlesinger, Jr., *The MacArthur Controversy and American Foreign Policy* (New York: Farrar, Straus,

1951), p. 152. Cf. James Reston, *New York Times,* July 28, 1950, who tells the same story.

18. Ballantine, *op. cit.,* p. 152.

19. Gregory Clark, *In Fear of China* (Melbourne, 1967), p. 87. Cf. Han Suyin, *China in the Year 2001* (New York: Basic Books, 1967), pp. 211–13; Frederick Nossal, *Dateline Peking* (London: Macdonald, 1962), pp. 183–84; *Communist China 1962* (Hong Kong, 1963), p. 76.

20. Young, *op. cit.,* p. 369.

21. *Peking Review,* November 8, 1968.

22. *Peking Review,* November 15, 1968.

23. *Peking Review,* June 6, 1969.

24. A report of the visit appears in *Far Eastern Economic Review,* May 22, 1969. The contingent's "Position Paper" appeared in the *Newsletter* of the CCAS, May 1969.

25. Edwin O. Reischauer, "Transpacific Relations," in *Agenda for the Nation* (New York, 1968), pp. 423–24.

26. *New York Times,* June 15, 1969.

27. See *Bulletin of Concerned Asian Scholars,* May 1969, pp. 27–31.

28. Louis Halasz, *Far Eastern Economic Review,* May 22, 1969, p. 445.

29. *Ibid.,* p. 444.

The good earth and the good society

NEALE HUNTER

The physical center of colonial Shanghai was the British race-course. This spacious oval of green grass acted as a lung in the middle of the grimy metropolis. The racecourse was also a symbol. It was the only place, for example, where the Chinese were encouraged to gather in large numbers. Like the Roman Colosseum, it was a substitute for political action, an application, perhaps, of the principle: "Divert and rule."

More important, it was a microcosm of the colonial economic system. I realized this while teaching in Shanghai in 1966. When I needed books I would go to the racecourse, for the Communists, with a touch of irony, had converted one of the grandstands into a public library. I would sit and read in the former clubrooms, where Englishmen had presumably discussed the White Man's Burden over gin and tonic. Outside the windows the tiers of seats were still there, and I would picture great crowds assembled for the "sport of kings," or perhaps a more select audience for the cricket that was played on the oval circumscribed by the track.

That was how Shanghai was: the master race, center stage, playing a game which it alone understood; and the "natives" unable to advance beyond the magic circle of the racetrack, where they were offered the tantalizing but remote specter of wealth. As I tried to understand the mentality behind such a system, the spirituality which had driven the merchants of Europe to build their empires, the racecourse seemed to provide a clue: the *sporting* instinct, the idea that life is a *game,* that the goods of the earth are for *playing* with, lies close to the heart of capitalism. All its main institutions—the stock exchange, banking, commerce, real estate, and so on—smack of the assumption that the world is one vast racetrack, a game of chance in which some are destined to win and others (most, as it turns out) are fated to lose.

With all due respect to the concept of *homo ludens,* life for the Chinese in old Shanghai cannot have been much fun. The Communists, swept into power by an army of paupers, certainly failed to appreciate the sporting mentality of Western business. With the zeal of angels, they set about suppressing opium, prostitution, child labor, gangsters, and other not-so-picturesque byproducts of the colonial economy.

The racecourse came in for special treatment, a sign that the Communists were not unaware of its symbolic importance. It was summarily ripped up and made into a "People's Square," with a circular park to replace the old track, and the members' grandstand became Shankhai's public library.

Old China Hands were appalled! Of all the changes, these were the most sinister. Governments may come and go, but the elimination of a racecourse was no joke. At a single stroke the light heart of the city had been plucked out, to be replaced by an open space for the purpose of "politics."

It is doubtful whether many of today's Shanghai residents feel this way. The People's Square represents for them their own strength, their new unity, their independence from foreign rule. It symbolizes the birth of a Chinese "body politic." Few regret the conversion of the Roman Colosseum into the Roman Forum.

THE ABUSE OF MATTER

Let us pursue the notion that capitalism perceives the world as a plaything. We shall not be able to understand the Chinese Communists until we know why the bourgeois ethic disgusts them, why they look on it as something *pornographic.*

Here is a passage from a book on tourism, put out by a Madison Avenue consulting firm in the early 1960s. The book advises Asian governments how best to increase their income from the tourist industry. Whether this is typical of the capitalist worldview is for the reader to judge; the point here is that the

Chinese Communists see this sort of thing and draw their own conclusions:

> International travelers are interested in and can be lured by jungles and wild-life reserves. They like to see and take pictures of natural flora and fauna, such as exotic flowers, magnificent trees, beautifully colored birds, monkeys and other forms of wild-life. We believe it should be possible for Vietnam to develop in its interior an important tourist attraction of this kind, one that would depend on seeing and photographing wild-life rather than shooting it. In any case, tourism built around such sanctuaries pays off more handsomely than do hunting expeditions, which appeal to a minority.

The irony needs no emphasis in 1970. The underlying assumption of this paragraph—that in the universal game of business, everything under the sun, animal, vegetable, or mineral, can be manipulated by certain players for profit—has become obscene in the light of what has happened in Vietnam in the past decade.

From what philosophical and theological sources does this assumption derive? I want to argue that it originated in an attitude toward *material* things, which then evolved into a like attitude toward *people*. For capitalism, matter is only of value as a means to an end. Used to generate wealth and power, it is good; in itself, it is not only meaningless but even threatening.

Critics of capitalism have often attacked its "crass materialism" because it results in neglect of the "things of the spirit" in favor of "treasures on earth." This represents a faulty analysis. A materialist is not someone who uses material things and values them in that regard, but someone who *believes* in matter, who *respects* it as the source of life, ideas, and spirit. Capitalism is the opposite of materialism in this sense; it even *abuses* and *despises* matter. America, which in some respects can be said to have taken capitalism to its logical conclusions, is choking on its own garbage and waste precisely because it is *not* materialistic. People who pollute their own water and air can hardly be called materialistic.

In Western philosophy, there are diverse and contradictory traditions on the status of matter. Those that have been characterized as materialist see matter as the ultimate reality from which all phenomena, no matter how intangible, are derived. Those that have been characterized as idealist hold that *ideas* have primacy over things, that matter is derivative, or "epiphenomenal." Both the social and the intellectual history of Europe has been influenced by these competing streams of thought. But it is idealism, I believe, particularly in the Platonic form, that has had the most decisive influence on Western thinking. Since the Renaissance, it is neo-Platonist idealism in one form or another that has enjoyed the position of orthodoxy.

The Renaissance saw not only a revival of Platonist idealism but also the development of capitalism. It was the emerging bourgeoisie who found idealism so attractive. Any theory that made abstraction primary was clearly useful to men engaged in business: if ideas were the ultimate reality, then man was free—indeed, "called"—to treat matter as the servant of ideas. The world could and should be completely rearranged—mountains moved, wars fought, and cities built without much regard for the givens with which man is confronted.

The Industrial Revolution greatly accelerated this trend, but only today are we beginning to see its full implications. What man can do to the material world through the increasingly efficient technologies he devises seems to know no bounds. And all of this—"modern civilization," as we call it—is justified by faith in the primacy and goodness of ideas.

THE ECLIPSE OF MATERIALIST CHRISTIANITY

One of the few effective opponents of this idealism was Christianity. In its original form Christianity was a religion grounded in the nonidealist thesis that God—the ground of reality—could not be identified with ideas any more than with material things. The significance of the birth of the God-man Jesus was precisely that God could no longer be conceived as over against the material world. He "leant to one side" in the dramatic sense that he took upon himself fully the form and substance of human life. He took upon himself not simply a *part* of human existence—some spiritual essence that could be dissociated from the material features—but the *whole,* body as well as soul. Thus he identified himself not simply with man but with the environment from which men has emerged.

The fact of the Incarnation should have settled once and for all the question of the Christian stance toward idealism. The theology of Platonism should once and for all have been identified as alien to the spirit of Christianity. But of course it was not.

Platonism was read back into the Incarnation in the early stages of the development of Christian thought, and the idea of God as over against the created order came to have more and more prominence. The identity of God and creation that the Incarnation represents was eclipsed. The struggle between these philosophies has continued throughout the history of Christian thought, and at various times the "incarnational" view has emerged from its eclipse. But since the Renaissance, the "God out there" tradition has completely overshadowed that of God Incarnate. This has been paralleled—and perhaps is explained in part—by the alienation of the Church from the forces promoting the humanization of modern life. (The evolution through which the Roman Catholic mass has passed is symptomatic of this trend toward idealism: what used to be a communal meal, where the bread and the wine were treated as symbols of the unity of the sacred and the material in those things that give men life, has become a ritual in which individuals, in comparative isolation from one another, treat the elements as though they had been stripped of their materiality.)

Enough remained of the earlier interpretation of the Incarnation to make some Christians uncomfortable during the rise of capitalism. But Christianity itself could not summon the resources to transform this discomfort into revolt. That task was left to Marxism. (Whether Christianity still has the resources necessary to accomplish such a revolt remains to be seen; there are some encouraging signs in this regard in post–Vatican II Catholicism.)

The dialectical materialism of Marx had the effect that an Incarnational Christian theology might have had. It rejected the idealist absolutes. It reasserted the value of the material world. And it turned attention to the "social question"—to the human condition and the ways in which social processes develop. Marx debunked the "God out there" of idealist theology, asserting that a theology that diverted attention from the problems of this world was not worthy of belief. Even more important was his attack on the static social vision that tended to accompany such theology. It was through this attack that Marxism came to have its appeal for the poverty-stricken masses. "Workers of the world unite; you have nothing to lose but your chains" was much more than a slogan for fomenting rebellion. It carried within it a philosophical alternative to fatalism. The age-old enemy of the poor and friend of the rich, Fate—or Providence, as idealist theology characterized it—was presented with a frontal challenge. This challenge can be considered in some respects as a social application of the "good news" of the Incarnation.

MARXISM AND CHINESE SPIRITUALITY

Among the "wretched of the earth" who saw Marxism as a liberating philosophy were the Chinese. Critics of communism have gone to great lengths to prove that China made a tragic mistake in rejecting the capitalist-Christian formula that the West offered her. Yet it does not take much knowledge of Chinese history to see why China would be more attracted by a materialist philosophy than an idealist alternative.

For one thing, the Chinese are peasants. Eighty per cent of them till the soil for their living. They know, therefore, that the source of their life is in *things,* that they are linked inseparably to their material environment. They believe in matter in a way that few Westerners (perhaps only the minority of peasants that remain) can fully understand. Their philosophy and religion—in ancient times as well as under communism—spring from and never wander far from the material ground of their existence.

The Chinese have always been more concerned with the study of man in his world than with transcendental speculation. China took the otherworldly Buddhism of India and transformed it into what is perhaps the most pragmatic of all the great world religions. Chinese Buddhism, in its Ch'an or Zen form, declared that the world of matter, which Indians had mistrusted as illusion and the source of suffering, was in fact synonymous with the "mind-blown" world of nirvana. Heaven and Earth were one. Religious life was a process of realization of this truth, culminating in a dramatic but enduring awareness of the marriage of spirit and matter.

When Mao insists on the unity of theory and practice, he is echoing this old Chinese vision. The Zen master who answered the novice's abstract question, "How deep is this ravine?", by trying to throw him off the edge of the cliff is in the same philosophical tradition as Mao, who has said, "If you want to know the taste of a pear, you must sink your teeth into it and change it." Knowledge, both assert, is inseparable from experience. Idea and matter are one.

Many features of Chinese culture reflect this pragmatism. The ideographic script, for example, draws the reader directly into the world, visibly and concretely manifested in the barbed little characters. The pentatonic musical scale represents a voluntary repression of man's least plastic art form. The relationship between painting and calligraphy has prevented the abstraction of either art.

China is also the country that elaborated the world's most durable system of government. The Confucian scholar-officials, who so impressed the philosophers of the French Enlightenment and the planners of the British Civil Service, were social scientists rather than philosophers. Chinese philosophy, even at its most religious, never moved far from the question, "What is good government?" Philosophy and theology never developed in isolation from sociology. Chinese intellectuals were rarely sidetracked into such brainteasers as whether angels have bodies or how many people make up the number of the elect.

This link between philosophical and religious thought, on the one hand, and social thought, on the other, was paralleled by a similarly close link between intellectuals and government. Even the famous Taoist hermits who went off to meditate in the mountains were often retired or disgraced scholars from the bureaucracy. Given a change of government, they might pack up their meditation kits, leave the hills, and take office again. The St. Benedict model, of a great man leaving society altogether, is unknown in China. Monasticism in the Western sense was never in the mainstream of Chinese history. Great minds, even the most maverick, were convinced that man and society are perfectible, and they spent their energy seeking this *social* perfection.

This approach persisted into the nineteenth and twentieth centuries. Although traditional China was shattered by the impact of Western civilization, the search began immediately for a philosophy that would allow the Chinese to absorb the shock of European technological superiority without sacrificing the essential qualities of Chinese culture.

THE FAILURE OF "GOD OUT THERE"

Christianity was seriously considered more than once. It was believed at first to be the dynamic of Western history and ways were sought to adapt it to Chinese conditions. It took several decades for the Chinese to realize that Christianity, though it had certainly once provided Europe with spiritual energy, was no longer the motor-force behind capitalism. The real secret of Europe's success lay in its scientific method and its economic system.

The Russian Revolution of 1917 initiated a new chapter in this modernization formula. Many Chinese were persuaded by the victory of the Russian proletariat over a decadent ruling class that this was the model for China to follow. If we are going to borrow from the West, the argument ran, we might as well take the most advanced theories. Marx's prediction that capitalism bred its own executioners seemed to have been proven true in Russia, and many Chinese intellectuals turned toward Bolshevism.

The bitterness of subsequent Chinese anti-Christianity can in large part be explained by a sense of disillusionment, a feeling that the Church had somehow betrayed China by appearing to be something it was not. Ironically, the missionaries contributed to this process; they spoke eloquently of love, justice, and truth, but their words hung in the air, abstracted from the actual situation. They worked tirelessly for the good of China, but their charitable institutions and their medical, educational, and religious activities were divorced from the harsh political realities of the time. China desperately needed a political solution, some means to catapult her out of the confusion and disgrace of the past and into a more promising future. Schools, hospitals, and churches were superficial answers; these served only to convince the Chinese of the impotence of Christianity. When their revolution happened *despite* "religion," they then turned on the missions and accused them of "cultural aggression."

Christianity failed in China—a case could be made out that it has also failed in Europe—because it allowed itself to become and with the "vindication" of history. It was to be a world where disembodied from material and political reality. It preached a "God out there," who rewarded and punished individuals for their personal behavior, when what China (and Europe) needed was a whole theology of "God in man," "God with and among us," which would not simply *say* that the Kingdom would belong to the poor, but would act on that assumption immediately and start to *build* just such a kingdom of justice.

Marxism offered a way to *construct* a new world, scientifically, Christ's basic message would be incarnated, not suspended in the air as a mere ideal. Faced with a choice between words and deeds, China chose as her history had conditioned her to choose: for action; for truth-in-motion; for the incarnation of theory in practice; for ideals incorporated in things, people, and communities.

The final irony was that Christianity, a religion based on the Incarnation, was rejected by the Chinese as an extreme form of *alienation*. This has been interpreted as an unqualified "No!" to the Gospel, but if we look closer we see that it was really a rejection of a particular kind of theology, of a theology that represented nineteenth century Christianity's massive denial of its own theological roots and its profound compromise with the philosophical underpinnings of capitalism.

Marxism was a natural choice for the Chinese. Perhaps an Incarnational brand of Christianity would also have been natural. But the conversion of China *en masse* to any brand of post-Renaissance Christianity would have been a cultural reversal of the first magnitude. It would probably have also failed to meet China's real needs. Chinese progress under Marxist leadership has been rapid and rational; under capitalism, which a Christian conversion would certainly have entailed, China might possibly have developed with equal speed, but the social fabric and culture that capitalism produces would eventually have destroyed her.

THE "SPIRITUAL ECONOMY"

We should consider the question of technology, where we see exposed not simply a facet of modern Western civilization, but the core of its economic and spiritual thrust. We in the West have become so accustomed to the mechanized, urbanized, and computerized vision of the future that we find it hard to conceive of alternatives to it. We therefore easily assume that China and the countries of the Third World will follow the Western pattern of industrialization, evolving the same kind of society and the same kind of "technological man." But China has already made radical departures from this stereotype. Her approach to industry has been cautious and experimental, reflecting an obvious reluctance to subvert agriculture as the base of her economy.

Urbanization, too, has been discouraged, as if the Communists were instinctively apprehensive at the prospect of peasants moving in droves to the cities. At present the trend is toward decentralization. Industry is now being cultivated *in the countryside*. Schools and colleges, hospitals, technicians, and administrators are being shifted from urban centers to the villages where they are needed. Technological development is being managed so as to make sideline and cottage industry at the production team level (100–150 people) the order of the day.

The Communists claim, in fact, that it is their intention to destroy the distinctions between mental labor and manual labor, industry and agriculture, city and countryside. In China this will not be done by stripping the countryside of people and turning it into a mechanized "agrobusiness," as has happened in parts of the United States. On the contrary, people will continue to live in the villages and will continue to farm the land, while learning the techniques of industry in order to make their communes more productive.

Such a trend is in direct opposition to the way in which the West is developing (and encouraging Third World countries to develop). It has already produced remarkable results in China, particularly in the attitudes and behavior of the people.

It is this "spiritual economy" that is the most remarkable and difficult phenomenon in China for the modern Western mind to fathom. By rejecting capitalism and its philosophy of antimaterialism, the Chinese have been set free to experiment with discoveries made through the capitalist system while at the same time holding on to a traditionally Chinese framework.

This has enabled them to adopt industry, for example, without adopting the principles of *waste* that go with modern capitalist industrialization. Still peasants at heart, the Chinese hate waste as much as European peasants once hated it. Unlike those Europeans, however, they *know* what happens when capitalism is allowed free use of the world's materials. They know that not only matter, but people, too, will be wasted. Goods will be produced to wear out quickly because it is "good for business"; people will be left without work because "business goes better" with some unemployment. They also know the connection between war and an economy of waste.

These things the Chinese have so far been able to avoid, and the chances are that they will continue to avoid them. Waste is about the worst word in the Chinese language these days, as it was in China's (and Europe's) past. Waste represents a misuse of matter—what amounts in materialist terms to a perversion of the basis of life. Shanghai, an industrial city of ten million inhabitants, a city which cut its teeth on foreign capitalism and learned the economy of waste before any other part of China, has no garbage collection! Householders convert everything into something useful. Even the family's dung is a part of the economy; a "honey cart" pulled by a bicycle calls each morning and pays a few cents a bucket for the precious fertilizer!

In the cities of the West frugality has become an obsolete virtue. The mention of the term conjures up an image of grandmother darning socks that we would throw out. We have also forgotten the *theology* that underlies frugality, a theology of respect for matter because God made it.

In turn we have learned that if man makes a practice of abusing *things,* he sooner or later comes to abuse *people* also. Our behavior has a wholeness; there is no dividing line between animate and inanimate matter. We see this dramatically illustrated in the recent history of the ethics of warfare. The plane that drops bombs on bridges, dams, and railway tracks (World War I) soon is blitzing cities (World War II). The air force which defoliates and poisons forests and crops soon is dropping skin-searing napalm on children. The attitudes bound up with Western capitalism and materialism seem to lead inevitably from the rape of the land and plunder of its minerals to the annihilation of whole populations in nuclear or bacteriological war. Such is its inner logic, a logic which goes hand in hand with a philosophical and theological error, namely, that ideas are primary and material things derivative, and that ideas bear the stamp of divinity in the created order, while matter carries with it evil.

"LIFE IN ABUNDANCE"

We call China these days an "irreligious" or "antireligious" society, with the assumption that the "free world" countries at least protect religion and at best are in fact religious. This is a rather superficial judgment, based on the continuing toleration of the mainline churches in the West. If religion is Gothic churches, the Legion of Mary, and charity to the poor, then China is certainly antireligious; but if religion begins with *taking the substance of the world seriously,* then China has much to teach us.

St. John captured the whole spirit of Christ's life when he said, "How can you love God if you don't love people?" We might extend the logic of this—in a way not at all out of keeping with St. John's thought—to "How can you love people if you don't love the world, of which people are an inextricable part?" A society that undermines the world's ecological balance and makes life less possible for human beings can hardly be called religious; in the same way, a society striving to give people life in abundance, whether or not it adheres to any traditional religious doctrine, code of ethics, or behavior, is already essentially religious.

Let me be precise: I believe there is enormous *religious* significance in the fact that China has eradicated capitalism as a system and is trying to wipe out the profit motivation that goes with it. So many books on China ignore this fact and go on to describe in detail the Chinese political or military system. Few analysts have paused to consider the quality of the *spiritual* energy released by the Chinese revolution, or what happens to a nation of peasants that decides not to postpone any longer the kingdom of justice, or to buy salvation on the never-never of hire purchase.

Westerners who go to China are often shocked by what this produces. They are totally unprepared for the appalling *purity* of the people. It is like being thrown back into the innocence of one's childhood or into the cultural infancy of the human race. The initial reaction of many is to reject what they see; they dismiss it as "all right for peasants, but. . . ." Others feel unaccountably guilty, as though they were personally responsible for the history of Europeans in China. A very few respond with open enthusiasm. One thing is clear: it is not a country to tour. It cannot arrange itself, as the tourist industry does to whole societies, into something for the pleasure and edification of affluent Americans. It is an experience that hurts.

For Christians, particularly, China can be excruciating. It is not unlike confronting Christos Pantocrator, as he appears in those sunrise-shaped frescoes in medieval Catalan cathedrals: the stern face and jet-black hair, eyes wide with the evil of the world yet still somehow full of light and hope. The giant-sized portraits of Chinese workers and soldiers that stare down from the billboards over a sign reading "Down with U.S. Imperialism!" have eyes like that.

A Christian in China is inevitably reminded of passages in the Gospel that he may have read once and forgotten, pieces that modern Western Christianity has chosen not to emphasize:

> What was the spectacle that drew you to the wilderness? A reed-bed swept by the wind? No? Then what did you go out to see? A man dressed in silks and satins? Surely you must look in palaces for grand clothes and luxury. But what did you go out to see? A prophet? Yes indeed, and far more than a prophet . . . (Luke 7:24–27).

> I know all your ways; you are neither hot nor cold. How I wish you were either hot or cold! But because you are luke-warm, neither hot nor cold, I will spit you out of my mouth. You say, "How rich I am! And how well I have done! I have everything I want in the world." In fact, though you do not know it, you are the most pitiful wretch, poor, blind and naked. So I advise you to buy from me gold refined in the fire, to make you truly rich, and white clothes to put on to hide the shame of your nakedness, and ointment for your eyes that you may see. All whom I love I reprove and discipline. Be on your mettle therefore and repent . . . (Revelation 3:15–19).

This is the tone of modern China's religion. It is not a comfortable creed, for it amounts to deep commitment to the cause of the poor and *against* the cause of the rich. In the religious equation, money and God cancel out. The Chinese would say with Mao, "Our God is none other than the masses of the Chinese people." Money and people cancel out also. Yet it is not money itself which is to blame. The rich are damned—in the Gospel and in the little red book alike—not for the quantity of their wealth, but for the damage they have done to the world, to other people, and to themselves in the process of acquiring wealth. "You cannot serve God and money." The Red Guards would say that is exactly what modern Western Christians have done. They have "followed the capitalist road" and are so much the less Christian for having compromised.

We in the West, who desperately need to escape from "god-less capitalism" and the alienating philosophy that goes with it, should study the Chinese experience very closely. We could well find clues in China's incarnate religion to guide us in our own struggle for human existence.

The long march and the exodus:
"The Thought of Mao Tse-tung" and the contemporary significance of "emissary prophecy" *

KAZUHIKO SUMIYA

The Long March

The Red Army fears no hardships on the Long March
    Thousands of mountains and ten thousands of rivers are
      as nothing.
Though the five mountain ranges curve and ripple as the
      waves of the sea
    And the endless dusky peaks roll on;
The waters of the Gold Sand River strike the warm cliffs
    And the bridges across the Broad Span are suspended
      On slender iron ropes;
Though the Min Mountains are snow covered for a thousand
      leagues
    The Three Armies lift their spirits,
      Look for a passage
        And laugh!

                —Mao Tse-tung

The Exodus from Egypt

I will sing to the LORD, for he has triumphed gloriously;
    the horse and his rider he has thrown into the sea.
The Lord is my strength and my song, and he has become
    my salvation;

* Translation from the Japanese by Pharis Harvey, Hiroshi Shinmi, and Tadashi Miyabe. Slightly abridged, for stylistic purposes, by the editors.

189

This is my God, and I will praise him,
  My father's God, and I will exalt him.

. . . .

"Thou hast led in thy steadfast love the people whom thou
    hast redeemed,
Thou hast guided them by the strength of thy holy abode.
The peoples have heard, they tremble;
  Pangs have seized the inhabitants of Philistia.
Now are the chiefs of Edom dismayed;
  The leaders of Moab, trembling seizes them;
  All the inhabitants of Canaan have melted away.

. . . .

Thou wilt bring them in, and plant them on thy own
    mountain,
  The place, O Lord, which thou hast made for thy abode,
  The sanctuary, O Lord, which thy hands have established.
The LORD will reign for ever and ever.
                                        —*Exodus,* Ch. 15 (RSV)

"THE PRESENT AGE" FROM THE VIEWPOINT OF SOCIOLOGY OF RELIGION

I would like to examine, from the standpoint of Max Weber's sociology of religion, some questions posed by Mao Tse-tung's Thought, what Lin Piao calls "Marx-Leninism in the age of the total collapse of imperialism and the advance toward the world-wide victory of socialism."

The uniqueness of Mao Tse-tung's Thought became known throughout the world at the time of the "Sino-Soviet Dispute," which occasioned a terrible conflict and discord between the Communist parties of China and the Soviet Union. This ideological and political opposition originated in a different understanding of how to interpret in depth the present moment in world history as a process of shifting from capitalism to socialism. Also, the shock waves of the "Proletarian Great Cultural Revolution," that has been led and developed by Mao Tse-tung's Thought, should cause us also to be strongly and increasingly concerned with understanding the present age. Regardless of our ideological stance, it is impossible to ignore socialism; we stand in a point of time when the very meaning of the present age can be apprehended only within some relationship to socialism.

The fact that Max Weber, the giant of late nineteenth and early twentieth century German intellectual history, devoted his un-flagging intellectual passion continually to the question of social-ism makes his thought of utmost contemporary significance for our time. It is obvious that one aspect of his intellectual concern for socialism derived from the various peculiar political, eco-nomic, and intellectual conditions of his homeland, Germany. However, another aspect is related deeply to the universal his-torical concerns that characterize his sociology of religion, that is, the consciousness of the problem of salvation—from where does human salvation derive and where does it lead us—the so-called "from where to where" problem. In *The Protestant Ethic and the Spirit of Capitalism,* in which Weber analyzed the spirit of modern capitalism, he takes careful note of what happens when the "solid fuel" that runs this "gigantic machine" burns out. There are three possibilities in such a situation:

> No one knows who will live in this cage in the future, or whether at the end of this tremendous development entirely new prophets will arise, or there will be a great rebirth of old ideas and ideals, or, if neither, mechanized petrification, embellished with a sort of convulsive self-importance. For the last stage of this cultural development, it might well be truly said: "Specialists without spirit, sensualists without heart; this nullity imagines that it has attained a level of civilization never before achieved." [1]

Just how he perceived these three possibilities concretely we do not know. However, if we may dare to guess his intention, in the first instance it was socialism; and in the second, the five world religions that he treated in his *Sociology of Re-ligion* (particularly Christianity); and in the third, we could imagine a thought type which is exemplified by Robert Mc-Namara, who has been nicknamed "the Computer."

However that may be, the unique phenomenon of "the separa-tion of laborers from the means of labor" in modern capitalism, which was examined and emphasized throughout Marx's *Das Kapital* should, in Weber's view, be understood as a "partial

phenomenon of the rationalization of life." It is carried out in all
the various spheres of culture, such as politics, the military, and
the academic disciplines. To take the realm of academic disciplines, researchers working at institutes are separated from the
means of research in the same way as factory workers. Soldiers
and officers in the modern military are no longer the owners of
the means of managing warfare as were the knights or samurai
in medieval times. In the sphere of politics, the staff of the administrative structure is apparently separated from the means of
administration. In the places where the modernization process de-
velops in this way, and in each cultural sphere where human relations are organized solely in bureaucratic forms, there appears
a tendency toward the concentration of the means of administration in the hands of those people who run this "machine." However, Weber states that modern socialism begins to grow only on a
foundation of *bureaucratic organization,* which symbolizes the total process of the "rationalization of life," and the *discipline* which
provides its internal support.

> From this life situation and from within its factory dis-
cipline, modern socialism was born. Various types of socialism have
existed in all ages and nations. But the special characteristic of
modern socialism is that it is possible only on this basis.[2]

It seems to me, after having examined very carefully *Sociology
of Religion,* vol. III, and numerous other studies dealing with
various theoretical and historical problems relating to the formation of modern capitalism, that Weber's intellectual concern
focuses with increasing intensity on problems of socialism, particularly toward the end of his life. His research into clarifying the
starting point of modern capitalism may have also implicitly included his intention of ascertaining its *ending point* as well. If
so, this brings us to consider the contemporary aspect of the
problem, which is "Max Weber and Socialism."

MAX WEBER AND SOCIALISM: SETTLING THE CATEGORY OF "EMISSARY PROPHECY"

Weber took the *Manifesto of the Communist Party* as the *norm*
for his criticism of German Marxism. According to Weber, the

Manifesto of the Communist Party is not only a first-rate academic work—a fact which nobody denies—but is also to be valued as a *prophetic* writing. That is, this manifesto prophesies the collapse of capitalist society and asserts the formation of a new society by means of the dictatorship of the proletariat as a transitional step. Furthermore, this prophecy is expressed out of a background of a particular eschatological desire and expectation that unless the rule of man over man is dissolved, the proletarians cannot liberate themselves from the yoke of subordination. That this is an *eschatological* pattern of thinking is shown clearly by the fact that nothing is said about the tangible structure of society that comes into existence when the rule of man over man is dissolved. There is nothing more stated than that the present society is fated to destruction; that this is inevitable according to the law of nature; that it will be totally destroyed by the dictatorship of the proletariat; and that what will come after—other than an absence of rule of man over man—cannot be predicted by anyone.

In Weber's view, the prophetic character of the *Manifesto* is shown at the point of its assertion that the collapse of capitalism is *determined* by the development of history as a law of nature. Weber pointed to the paradoxical situation that this prophecy (just like the Calvinist doctrine of predestination) in spite of its deterministic character—no, *because of it*—did not fall into simple fatalism but rather "gave an enthusiastic faith to the masses."

Although Weber did not touch on it here, it seems apparent from his comparison with Calvinism that he understood the prophetic character of the *Manifesto* within the category of "emissary prophecy," a term in his sociology of religion.[3]

Now the prophecy of Marx and Engels had three theoretical pillars: the theory of the "destitution of the masses"; the "class theory"; and the theory of "panic"—the idea that the capitalist order would be catastrophically destroyed by a world panic. What attracted Weber's concern here is the problem of how, in the process of its incarnation in the revolutionary movement of German Marxism, the "emissary prophecy" held by the founders of Marxism underwent a change of character.

Weber says that it was an ideological peculiarity of German

Marxism that all three pillars supporting this prophecy were either abandoned or revised. As for the first pillar, even Kautsky of the mainstream of the party called explicitly for abandoning it on the basis of the "bourgeoisification" phenomenon among the proletariat of the various Western European countries. The second pillar itself was not abandoned but revised greatly, particularly when its irrelevance became clear in reference to agricultural theory. And, even while the cyclical nature of panic was being spoken of, the theory of catastrophic collapse was in fact abandoned.

Thus, the *evolutionistic* pattern of thinking of German Marxism presumed that as production became gradually "socialized," socialism would be accomplished as a natural consequence of social development:

> Society and its economic order develop strictly according to the laws of nature, namely through periodic steps; accordingly, it can never happen that before bourgeois society has fully ripened, a socialist society can come into existence.[4]

According to this doctrine, if its thrust were thoroughly carried out, the consequence would be no more than the following:

> Because of the immaturity of the proletarian social order, they all, no matter how radical, anticipate the establishment of a bourgeois social order as the only possible result of the present revolution.[5]

There is *nothing more* implied here than the *single point* that one step has been taken in the direction of the formation of a proletarian social order. The hope that the prophecy embodied remains as before, and the question of when a real socialist society should be realized in the future becomes nothing but a totally vague desire. The socialist revolution actually cannot help but become a problem that is pushed farther and farther away from the hands of the present laborers. Having seen this, it *appears* that Weber recognized in general that speaking of the formation of a socialist society was a complete illusion and accordingly accepted fatalistically the contemporary capitalistic society as an inevitable destiny. But is this really so?

I am not yet fully convinced, for various reasons, of this picture of Max Weber, which has so often been portrayed. For example, it seems at first glance that Weber made a negative evaluation of socialism, but when we examine his views carefully, we must reconsider this judgment. What he strongly criticized was *German* Marxism with its evolutionistic interpretation of socialism. His understanding of socialism *as an ideology* recognized the only *meaningful* situation to be that in which the "emissary prophetic" character, as seen in the *Manifesto,* is tightly maintained. By having removed the three pillars which supported the prophecy, the Germans

> have taken away from the masses a faith in a happy future which would come suddenly, which had been proclaimed in the same way as Jesus' words, "Tonight may salvation come!" [6]

And in doing so, they performed a fatal operation on that prophecy. According to Weber's view, this replacement of the prophecy of an inevitable panic that would bring a catastrophic collapse of capitalism, with something else, even if it were possible, could not be easily accomplished.

If this is so, does it not inevitably mean that socialism has already lost the various subjective and objective conditions necessary for preserving its "emissary prophetic" character? It seems that Weber did not think in that way. Rather, he appeared to anticipate that the prophetic character of socialism had certainly degenerated in adjusting to the bourgeoisification of society in Germany, and that only when *prophecy* stands on an ideological foundation that is thoroughly disassociated from such evolutionistic conceptions can it blossom fully.

Here he turned his attention to Russia. The reason was that Russian Marxism itself was the only revolutionary movement at that time that gave birth "autogenetically" to a *sect* (using this term in Weber's sense) that did not stand on an evolutionist doctrine. That is to say:

It is this progressive evolution (as an ideology) that has been the doctrine of pure socialism until now, and that has been refused *solely* by the indigenous sect in Russia. This sect (the Bolsheviks—Sumiya) believed that Russia could leap over such a developmental stage.[7]

According to Weber:

This was a wholly justifiable procedure, and the only effective or possible way of acting. The reason is that there is no way, I believe, to destroy Socialist conviction or hope.[8]

What is worth noting in this context is Weber's understanding of the Lenin-led Bolsheviks as a so-called "sect." The famous concept of the "avant garde" in Lenin's theory of the party organization coincides precisely with Weber's theory of the "sect"—at this point.

Now, upon reconsidering *The Protestant Ethic and the Spirit of Capitalism* from this perspective, I conclude that one cannot necessarily claim that Weber had a positive view (as is often claimed by his critics) toward the spirit of capitalism that comes into existence in the disintegration of both extremes of the petit bourgeoisie. What he says of the "spirit of capitalism" is that it *can* "serve both God and Mammon"; that religiously speaking, it is an ethos that is structured on the *perversion of value* and that it is the *adaptation* of the ascetic ethos of the early Protestantism that had attracted the petit bourgeoisie, the "womb" of the "spirit of capitalism." In addition, Weber sharply criticizes, quoting Wesley, the fact that whereas early Protestantism was absolutely negative toward the old profitmaking impulse, later it was unable to summon a resistance of sufficient strength.

In short, the ethic of the old Protestantism, as a result of producing a vocational ethic particularly suitable to the inner psychological interests of the upper stratum of the petit bourgeoisie (which was caught in the net of a money economy), happens to have cut itself off from the possibility of creating ideas that could represent and attract the lower stratum of the petit bourgeoisie and the lower class, who were being deprived and "pariah-ized," and resisted the development of the new profitizing. (In order to reestablish such capacity, Protestantism had to wait until the appearance of the so-called "dialectical" theology of Barth, Brunner, Bultmann, and others of the twentieth century.)

Accordingly, from the perspective of Weber's sociology of religion, any ideas or ideals that can mobilize the lower petit bourgeoisie and the poor against the development of bourgeois profitmaking as the active core group for the renewal of society must possess the *character* of such an *ascetic ethos*.

It is common knowledge today that it was Lenin who first succeeded in comprehending ideologically this problematic aspect. Is it not for this reason that Weber paid particular attention to the Russian "sect"? And would it be mistaken to insist in this context that it was actually Mao Tse-tung—to advance the understanding of Weber one step further—who by means of consistently adhering closely to this aspect accomplished the full realization of this thought?

I do not think it necessarily mistaken. Since Western Europe, the great center of culture, produced a situation in which even the proletariat, who should have been the bearers of the revolution, became as conservative as the privileged social stratum, there no longer existed a soil appropriate for the blossoming of "emissary prophecy." Looking thus, from the perspective of Weber's sociology of religion, one can say that from the latter part of the nineteenth century to the beginning of the twentieth century the frontier of Western Europe, the great cultural center of the world, was Asia, including Russia.

Furthermore, in China, which suffered incessantly from the capitalistic culture of Western Europe in the form of semicolonialism, one could see to a great extent the formation of the pariah-proletarian unprivileged social stratum whose situation was aggravated by both internal and external pressures.

Also, from the standpoint of the history of religions, since the masses were bound by a "magic garden" (*Zaubergarten*) that could truly be called ancient, one could see that there was a "thought situation" similar to the Orient of the time of "Ancient Judaism" that Weber analyzed.

Finally, one could say that a historical situation adequate to the coming of "emissary prophecy" was being created. The Russian Revolution, in this account, served as a breakthrough by sending the "emissary prophecy" of Marx to China. As Mao Tse-tung has appropriately stated, "The Russian Revolution sent Marxism-Leninism to us."

Accordingly, I would like to pursue the significance of the sociology of religion that is embodied in "the Thought of Mao Tse-tung" viewed from the above perspective.

THE SUPERIORITY OF "THOUGHT" IN THE THOUGHT OF MAO TSE-TUNG: THE STRUCTURE OF HIS PERSPECTIVE ON HUMAN REVOLUTION

The basic stratum of the so-called "Thought of Mao Tse-tung" is that which appeals to the internal-external, or the idealistic-materialistic interests of the Chinese agrarian class.[9] Two of his writings, *Report on an Investigation of the Peasant Movement in Hunan* (1927) and *The Struggle in the Ching-Kang Mountains* (1928) are especially important.

The *Report* contains fundamental criticism of the fact that at that time the mainstream of the Chinese Communist Party, headed by Ch'en Tu-hsiu, did not support the peasants' revolutionary struggle as a chief ally of the revolution, but adhered to the line of attaching more importance to the cities than the villages.

Here there is a reversal of the common opinion concerning the prospects for the Chinese Revolution on the issue of which class or social stratum should become the main bearers of that revolution. To exaggerate somewhat, the historical understanding expressed here is that it was the poor peasants and the lower stratum of the middle class peasants of the Chinese *countryside* rather than the *urban* proletariat who would be the *nucleus* of the revolution.

They will smash all the trammels that bind them and rush forward along the road to liberation. They will sweep all the imperialists, warlords, corrupt officials, local tyrants and evil gentry into their graves. Every revolutionary and every revolutionary comrade will be put to the test, to be accepted or rejected as they decide.[10]

There rises vividly to the surface here the unique view in the Thought of Mao Tse-tung that even the revolutionary party and the revolutionary comrades who stand on Marxism-Leninism will be judged ultimately by the peasant masses. It is undeniable that his *experience* of making an on-the-spot survey of the peasant movement in Hunan Province, which was the source of the *Report,* was decisive in placing this view in the forefront of his thought. Mao Tse-tung "closely examined all their activities . . . what they [had] actually done," [11] summarizing them in fourteen points.

Mao took a serious look at the situation of the inner psychological interests of the Chinese peasant class. He says:

> A man in China is usually subjected to the domination of three systems of authority: (1) the state system (political authority), ranging from the national, provincial and country government down to that of the township; (2) the clan system (clan authority), ranging from the central ancestral temple and its branch temples down to the head of the household; and (3) the supernatural system (religious authority), ranging from the King of Hell down to the town and village gods belonging to the nether world, and from the Emperor of Heaven down to all the various gods and spirits belonging to the celestial world. As for women, in addition to being dominated by these three systems of authority, they are also dominated by the men (the authority of the husband). These four authorities— political, clan, religious and masculine—are the embodiment of the whole feudal-patriarchal system and ideology, and are the four thick ropes binding the Chinese people, particularly the peasants.[12]

Mao did not forget to add that "the political authority of the landlords is the backbone of all the other systems of authority." [13] However, among these four power systems, the three systems of clan, religion, and male-female relationships have different structures from that of the landlords, and it is the individual functions that they perform to which he pays particular attention.

There can be no thorough overthrow of all three until the peasants have won complete victory in the economic struggle. . . . As for the clan system, superstition, and inequality between men and women, their abolition will follow *as a natural consequence* of victory in the political and economic struggles (italics Sumiya's).[14]

That is, in the first place, these three power systems cannot be eradicated by force. This is because the "peasants . . . made the idols, and when the time comes they will cast the idols aside with their own hands; there is no need for anyone else to do it for them prematurely."[15] A clear consciousness pervades here concerning the problems in the area of faith or value systems. To attack them by force or from the outside is unreasonable; rather, there is no other way than that based on *internal, voluntary* reform. What can be done in order to make such reform possible?

Mao emphasizes the *political* aspect; the goal is as follows:

. . . to pull down landlord authority and build up peasant authority in rural society. This is a most serious and vital struggle. . . . Without victory in this struggle, no victory is possible in the economic struggle to reduce rent and interest, to secure land and other means of production, and so on.[16]

The most important aspect for our concern here is the fact that he laid particular stress on destroying the *influence* of the landlord class, particularly the oppressive landlords. This indicates that his ideological position—destroying the privileged *status* of the landlord class, eradicating the inferiority complex that resulted from the pariah-like status of the peasant class, and thus stimulating their political consciousness—was directed toward utilizing the peculiar dynamics of what Weber called a "status situation."[17] These dynamics have recently been theoretically categorized by Mao as "The Four Firsts":

When treating the relationship between weapons and men, the human factor is to be given first priority; when dealing with political maneuvers in relation to other types of stratagems, the political are placed first; within a political maneuver, when dealing with the relationship between bureaucratic affairs and ideological matters, the ideological comes first; and in ideological matters, when relating living thought and thought from written sources, the living thought is primary.[18]

A "status situation" functions as a "resonating apparatus" in a situation determined by subjective interests, and this results in an attitude toward life directed toward social *honor* as a goal. To the extent this situation is set in motion or stimulated by contact with ideology, it will "resound" all the stronger. The perspective that gives a special color to Mao Tse-tung's Thought (his allotment of a "superior status to ideology" utilizing the dynamics of the "status situation" of the poor peasants and lower middle class peasants of that time, whom he considered to constitute the core group of the Chinese Revolution, as a sounding board or *resonator*) was based on his own experience in the peasant uprising in Hunan Province. This perspective was made more concrete in the process of building up a base of operations in the Chingkang Mountains.

As Mao interpreted it, the situation in Hunan Provincial District in 1928 was extremely tense:

> Since the struggle in the border area is exclusively military, both the Party and the masses have to be placed on a war footing. How to deal with the enemy, how to fight, has become the central problem in our daily life. . . . As the struggle is getting fiercer every day, our problems have become extremely complex and serious.[19]

He built up his stronghold in the Chingkang Mountains not only in this tense situation, but also at a time when, as he said, "Having fought for the past year in various places, we have felt deeply the ebb-tide of the revolution all over the country." With only a handful of followers, he acted decisively to construct this difficult base. The majority of the soldiers of the Red Army who had come with him were from mercenary units, consisting partly of workers and peasants, and partly of *lumpen proletarians*. Of course it is inadvisable to have too many of the latter . . . but in these circumstances, the *only solution is to intensify political training* (italics Sumiya's).[20]

Even though many of the soldiers of that time had been mercenaries, it was said that "once in the Red Army, their character changes." What was the cause for this change? According to Mao Tse-tung, this *human change* was the *result* of *political education*. He began by saying:

The Red Army has abolished the mercenary system, making the men feel they are fighting for themselves and for the people, and not for somebody else.[21]

Then, through political education based on his thought, he brought about this consciousness:

The Red Army soldiers have become class-conscious, learned the essentials of distributing land, setting up political power, arming the workers and peasants, etc., and they know they are fighting for themselves, for the working class and for the peasantry.[22]

Then, finally, *in their daily life, training in an ascetic attitude toward life* was carried out:

Apart from the role played by the Party, the reason why the Red Army has been able to carry on in spite of such poor material conditions and such frequent engagements is its practice of democracy. The officers do not beat the men; officers and men receive equal treatment; soldiers are free to hold meetings and to speak out; trivial formalities have been done away with; and the accounts are open for all to inspect. . . .[23]

Mao Tse-tung writes somewhat proudly about the process of changing human nature which developed in this spiritual atmosphere:

The newly captured soldiers in particular feel that our army and the Kuomintang army are worlds apart. They feel *spiritually liberated,* even though material conditions in the Red Army are not equal to those in the White Army. . . . The Red Army is like a *furnace* in which all captured soldiers are transmuted the moment they come over (italics Sumiya's).[24]

Truly, they experienced for the first time in the Red Army an inversion of their values much like that spoken of in Revelation 21:1: "Behold, I saw a New Heaven and a New Earth." Ultimately, this was summarized in the famous "Three Main Rules of Discipline" and the "Eight Points for Attention." [25]

In this manner, Mao Tse-tung made "Human Revolution" the point of departure for the construction of a base of operations. But, precisely at this point, he ran head-on into the thick wall of the *land problem,* the issue of the revolution. He somehow had to cope with the situation of the inner-psychological interests of the *middle* class.

When the Revolution is at a low ebb in the country as a whole, the most difficult problem in our areas is to keep a firm hold on the intermediate class,[26]

who:

exploited their traditional social position and clan authority to intimidate the poor peasants for the purpose of delaying the distribution of land.[27]

In turning his gaze steadfastly on the peculiar ideological and material interests of the middle class, Mao Tse-tung deepened his realization of the important role this class played in the solution of China's land problem. At the same time, he came to know the severity of the problems presented by their deeply rooted tribalism and the structure and provincialism of the rural villages and behavior patterns that were deeply intertwined with this familism.

As the feudal family system prevails in every county, and as all the families in a village or group of villages belong to a single clan, it will be quite a long time before people become conscious of their class and clan sentiment is overcome in the villages.[28]

He came to realize this situation in the process of training the revolutionary cadres, especially in connection with the problem of strengthening the party organization.

This problem was summarized by Mao Tse-tung in two points:

1. *Localism.* The economy in the border area is agricultural with some places still in the age of the hand-pestle. . . . The unit of social organization everywhere is the clan, consisting of people having the same family name. In the Party organizations in the villages, it often happens that a branch meeting virtually becomes a clan meeting, since branches consist of members bearing the same family name and living close together. In these circumstances it is very hard indeed to build a "militant Bolshevik Party." . . . Localism exists to a serious extent in the relations between counties and even between districts and townships within the same county.

2. *The question of the native inhabitants and the settlers.* There is another peculiar feature of the border counties, namely, the rift between the native inhabitants and the settlers. A very wide rift has long existed between the native inhabitants and the settlers whose forefathers came from the north several hundred years ago; their traditional feuds are deep-seated and they sometimes erupt in violent clashes. The settlers [number] several millions. . . . In theory this rift between the native inhabitants and the settlers ought not to extend *into* the exploited classes of workers and peasants, much less into the Communist Party. But *it does, and it persists by force of long tradition* (italics Sumiya's).[29]

The problems of provincialism and conflict between the indigenous and immigrant populations that Mao Tse-tung points to are, as we know, phenomena which occur not simply in China but wherever the basis of production is organized communally. But what is so noticeable here is that in China this agricultural community consisting of a "familistic structure with one clan per unit" *was so entrenched* that "a party cell meeting was at the same time a family council." When clan organization is this universal, it ought to be easy to comprehend why outsiders could not enter easily. Not only that, but the outsiders would inevitably remain perpetually in the status which Weber termed that of a "guest tribe." [30]

Mao Tse-tung, therefore, in the process of building his base of operations in the Chingkang Mountains, came to know the comparative importance occupied by the middle class in the solution of the land problem, and in pursuing the dynamics of their particular interests he came to comprehend the peculiarly Chinese aspects of the problem. However, this itself was a point at issue in the problem area that Weber had persistently attempted to pursue in his analysis of Chinese society from the standpoint of sociology of religion. So we next must touch on that subject.

MAX WEBER'S THEORY OF CHINESE SOCIETY: GROPING TOWARD THE RE-CREATION OF AN ASCETIC ETHOS

Among the special investigations of the economic ethic of various world religions that make up Max Weber's study of the sociology of religion, his analysis of Chinese society is a particularly important point for the problems we are confronting here.

Weber's view was this. In the first place, Chinese cities, like those of the Occident, frequently originated as fortresses and princely residences. Like the European cities, they were also centers of trade and craft production, with the various separate quarters under the control of guild organizations. But the Chinese cities can be distinguished from those in Europe in that they never acquired political autonomy. They never won charters such as those that stipulated the political privileges of the medieval cities. Rather than constituting legally independent districts, Chinese cities consisted of several "village districts," or blocks, so that what functioned as an autonomous self-governing body was not the city but the rural village.[31]

Why did the Chinese city fail to develop political autonomy

along the lines of the European example? Weber's conclusion was that it was because the "fetters of the kinship group were never shattered." [32] Whenever men moved from rural villages into the city, in addition to establishing residence in the city, they retained their ties to the native places of their families by preserving all ritually and personally important relationships in the ancestral lands. One is reminded here of that custom in ancient Egypt.

However, Weber points out that in the case of China this bond among bloodline relatives is deeply intertwined and coterminous with the *custom of ancestor worship*. The "fetters of the kinship group," by tightly binding each town resident to his native village, that is, to the place where the worship of his family's ancestors was carried out, effectively prevented the development of the political solidarity of the urban citizenry or the growth of independent communities based on mutual interest. The basis for mutual help in the urban merchant or craftsmen guild organizations was located exclusively in the kinship groups, and thus the internal motivating force pointing toward the development of an independent "citizen" *status,* having an autonomous jurisdiction involving distinct privileges and obligations as in Western Europe, did not develop.

Weber recognized that in China the city was at all times a mere semblance while the real social substance persisted in the villages themselves. This has a deep relationship to the question of where the starting point of social revolution in China ought to be located. It bears a relationship to the major religio-sociological significance that Mao Tse-tung's "Base of Operations" theory possesses.

The religion of China is particularly noteworthy *in the lack of a prophetic or priestly class*. The Chinese Emperor not only held the ultimate sovereign political power, he was the religious high priest as well. The Emperor's religious authority was absolute. Unlike ancient Israel's situation, he never received any purely religious prophetic challenge. The Emperor who controlled both the political and religious affairs of this world was supported by a political bureaucratic class steeped in Confucian learning, who also for their own advantage strongly opposed the formation of a separate priestly class with autonomous political power.

It can be said that China's religion, therefore, consisted of three aspects: a patrimonial-bureaucratic state cult with the Emperor functioning as the high priest; the worship of the ancestral spirits of the regional kinship groups with the support of the state; and various popular magical religious beliefs among the common masses which had the tacit support of the government. These phenomena of the unity of cult and state and the separation of state cult and popular faith represent quite a contrast with Europe; Confucianism and Taoism, in a sense, brought about the "locking up" of the general masses in a "garden of magic." This has an extremely important meaning for the present; that is, as Weber has analyzed and shown in various ways, when the masses remain locked up in a "garden of magic," to overturn this *without the development of emissary prophetism* is extremely difficult.

Historically it can be stated that it was first accomplished by the prophets of ancient Israel.

Considering the strong interest that Weber had in socialism, I have more and more come to think that the approach of his sociology of religion was an attempt to see if he could discover, by means of the investigation of the subjective and objective conditions necessary for the appearance of "emissary prophetism," the objective possibility of a *rebirth* in the contemporary world of "emissary prophetism."

When we view it this way we can understand fully why Weber showed such great interest in the T'ai-P'ing Rebellion (or as it was called, the Great Peaceful Heavenly Kingdom) of 1850–64, as a foreshadowing of that course in China. The Great Peaceful Heavenly Kingdom, with its peculiar form of the Eucharist and the Lord's Prayer and its revision of the Mosaic Ten Commandments into the so-called "Ten Heavenly Articles," was an "indigenous religion" produced on Chinese soil, which was nevertheless "inwardly relatively close to Christianity." [33] It appears that Weber considered this development as a *preview* of the possibility of "emissary prophetism" in modern times. He states:

It was not an insurmountable "natural disposition" that hindered the Chinese from producing religious structures comparable to those of the Occident. In recent times this has been proved by the impressive success of Hung Hsiu-ch'uan's iconoclastic and anti-magical prophecy of the *T'ien Wang* ("Heavenly King") of the *T'ai P'ing T'ien Kuo* (Heavenly Kingdom of Peace; from 1850–64).[34]

Certainly the T'ai-P'ing Movement, in the sense of being "simply an ethics which teaches primarily an inner-worldly lay morality," [35] aimed at the realization of an "ethical righteousness" that was closer to Protestantism than to the "ritual righteousness" of a Confucianism that stood on the borderline between ethics and religion. The T'ai-P'ings themselves, "differentiating man from animal," believed not in the Confucian "Principle of Heaven" but in a "personally benign and universal god of the world, freed of national barriers," who "would otherwise have remained entirely alien to Chinese religion." They adhered to the concept that man's true character was such that he was "incapable of really fulfilling all the commandments." That is, man is a sinner—a concept close to the Christian concept of original sin. For redemption from sin they looked to "repentance and prayer." (In this connection it is interesting to note that Mao Tse-tung attached importance to "self-criticism," emphasizing that one should adopt the attitude of a doctor dealing with a sick person.)

By modifying the fatalistic faith of Confucianism toward a Christian vocational ethic; through the existence of a "Christian Chiliastic-type" utopian ideology; and with the concept of the equality of all men before God, the T'ai-P'ings had "opportunity [that was] incomparably greater than that offered by the hopeless missionary experiments of the Occidental denominations." At any rate, in this movement, the strength of the ascetic element "was outstanding and was unsurpassed anywhere else in China. Moreover, the magical and idolatrous fetters were broken and this was unknown elsewhere in China." Because it was a departure from the long span of orthodox Chinese thought, Weber evaluated the T'ai-P'ing Rebellion as "by far the most powerful and thoroughly hierocratic, politico-ethical rebellion against the Confucian administration and ethic which China has ever experienced."

It is a matter of deep significance that Weber saw in the T'ai-P'ing Rebellion *alone* a *reborn ethical prophetism*, which accounts for his high evaluation of it. But it does not necessarily follow that he favored the possibility of T'ai-P'ing success. (It is significant at this point to compare his evaluation of the T'ai-P'ing Rebellion with that of Marx and Engels.) That is to say, in comparison with the inner-worldly asceticism of Puritanism, this movement produced a peculiarly Chinese *deviation*. The notion of God got confused with the Confucian "Principle of Heaven." Moreover, the consciousness of sin became ambiguous: "happiness is easily obtainable." [36] The law was to be kept in the sense of a ritualistic Confucian optimism. And although such observation of the law touches on "repentance," "prayer," the "Ten Commandments," and so forth, Confucian and Taoist interpretations became so intertwined with it that finally "memorial services before the tombs of the dead" and "memorial services at the tombs of one's ancestors" were introduced. Weber predicted that, had the T'ai-P'ing Rebellion been victorious, "the selection of officials according to charismatic or moral qualifications," which was in operation in its administrative districts for a time, would gradually have been perverted from this "sect-type" principle in a formalistic direction. Thus, a "church-type" principle of "institutional grace" would have come to predominate.

When we look at the T'ai-P'ing Movement from the perspective of the sociology of religion, we can say that it had within it an *internal limitation* to prevent it from accomplishing an ethos that could destroy the "garden of magic" in which the Chinese masses had been locked since time immemorial. Although Weber anticipated from afar the quickening movements of China's modernization within the T'ai-P'ing Rebellion, when he saw the deepseatedness of its entanglement with Confucian and Taoist thought, it must have been a gloomy thought for him indeed! *

* Just for the record, allow me to add that Weber did not overlook the fact that the T'ai-P'ing Rebellion was put down by the military power of various foreign countries, in particular, England. He emphasized that the T'ai P'ing Rebellion was *both* a rebellion against the tyranny of the Manchu Dynasty *and* a resistance movement against the trend toward the colonization of China by the several European powers. However, our subject here is Weber's constant facing of issues from the viewpoint of searching for the creation of a revolutionary force capable of succeeding from within.

Accordingly, when Weber wrote, "It may well have been the last opportunity for such a religion in China," [37] it is possible that he had already discerned that the objective situation of China was such that its modernization could not take the form of Europeanization (i.e., capitalization). Nevertheless, when we investigate the T'ai-P'ing Movement that Weber saw as the foetal quickening of the formation of the first modern ascetic ethos in China, and examine further the various factors that were inescapably enmeshed within it as indigenous Chinese deviations—the major element of which was the "family piety" mentality,* the ethos of the traditional "five moral duties"—we can only conclude that it would have been extremely difficult, so long as this persisted, to reform the thought structure of the pariah-like proletarian classes who would constitute the "Archimedean point" of the Chinese Revolution. In other words, this was above all a Chinese ethic of sentiment (*shinjo rinri*). Now the thought that was applied to the formation of the nucleus of the Chinese social revolution, the ideology that itself was most vividly conscious of its revolutionary significance for digging up this "deeply buried stone," was the Thought of Mao Tse-tung, specifically his *Base of Operations* theory mentioned above. His aim of overthrowing "political authority, family authority, religious authority, and marital authority" accurately located the "Archimedean point" from which to attempt the overthrow of the total structure of China's premodern traditionalistic society. It corresponds exactly with Weber's sense of the problem in analyzing Chinese society.

The most characteristic aspect of Mao Tse-tung's Thought (his perception of the latent energy of the peasant class as the revolutionary nucleus for China's Revolution, and his drawing out of this energy) was itself equal to a "rebirth" of that ascetic ethos, which during the two thousand year "rationalization"

---

* Expressed in the hymn from the T'ai P'ing Movement:

> To serve one's parent with filial piety
> And to repay one's Lord with fidelity
> Is to unite with the Will of Heaven
> To receive the Blessing of Heaven. [38]

process in Europe had been squeezed to the limit and finally exhausted.

However, in order for this kind of ideological quality of Mao Tse-tung's Thought to take root in Chinese soil, the construction of a base of operations in the Chingkang Mountains was not enough; it was also necessary for one purely historical event to intervene.

This was, of course, the so-called "Long March," extending some 6,000 miles, which was the "incarnation" of Mao Tse-tung's Thought among the Chinese masses. It seems to me impossible to grasp the surpassing contemporary significance of Maoism's challenges to the present age without making clear the religio-sociological significance of this event.

"THE LONG MARCH" AND THE "EXODUS": MAO TSE-TUNG'S THOUGHT AS A SWITCH LEVER OF HISTORY

In today's China, "Long March" has already become a symbolic term. Robert Payne[39] recorded that, when he talked with Mao Tse-tung about the Long March, the Chairman remarked, "There will be many more Long Marches." In 1960 Edgar Snow revisited China and had an interview with Prime Minister Chou En-lai. The two discussed the difficult situation of the newly born state of China, caused by the Sino-Russian dispute that had then become a sort of open secret, and also by the greatest drought since the last century. Chou En-lai said, "as though he were reminded of the hardships of the Long March, 'China has started on a second Long March. We have just taken the first step. Yes, this is only the first step.' " [40]

It is to be specially noted that both Mao and Chou En-lai, who are in the very core of the leadership of the Chinese Revolution, define the meaning of the Long March as a "symbol." A glance at the well-written works of Ryuzo Okamoto (*The Long March* and *The Long March Continued*) is sufficient to indicate the scale of the measure they are using in patterning the future of China after the Long March. The Long March served as an occasion—first conceived at the Chingkang Mountains base—to *fix the idea* of the Chinese Revolution realistically into China's historical process. Mao Tse-tung stated:

> Speaking of the Long March, one may ask, "What is its significance? We answer that the Long March is the first of its kind in the annals of history, that it is a *manifesto,* a *propaganda force,* a *seeding-machine* [italics Sumiya's].[41]

Now what kind of a campaign was the Long March? To quote from Mr. Okamoto:

> In short, the Long March was a large-scale strategic move made by the Chinese Workers and Peasants' Red Army between 1934 and 1936, from the several bases along the Yangtze River to the Shensi-Kansu border region.

> From October, 1934, for a full two years, being pursued persistently by the Kuomintang Army and facing the constant threat of annihilation, they carried out a massive long march from the various bases along the lower reaches of the Yangtze River, along the mountain ridges of the Southwestern region, through heavy snows over the Tibetan highland. This we call "the Long March."

> During the early period of the Long March, the main body of the Red Army suffered a great loss due to the wrong directives given by the Moscow faction of leadership, their numbers being reduced from 100,000 to only 30,000 while crossing the Kiang River. Again, toward the end of the march, due to the schism of Chiang Kuo-tao, only 8,000 soldiers were left in Mao Tse-tung's hand. In addition to these military tribulations, there were the so-called "Three Greatest Geographical Barriers"—the Great River Crossing, the Great Snow Mountains, and the Great Steppe. The Red Army was visited by hunger, bitter cold weather, and all kinds of diseases, and a great many starved, froze to death or succumbed to disease, while some disappeared in the bottomless moors of the Tibetan plateau. Young girl soldiers deserted the Army, unable to endure the incredible

hardships. Nevertheless, the Red Army emerged from these trials as the world's strongest army, unwavering in its revolutionary zeal.[42]

These soldiers, after having endured such a historical trial, became the core group of the reconstructed Red Army, putting into practice the Reform Movement of Mao Tse-tung, and eventually forming the leadership of the "Proletariat Great Cultural Revolution" under the guidance of Lin Piao, who is looked on as the incarnation of the "Yenan Spirit."

I would like to emphasize the nature of the Long March in the terms that Mao Tse-tung used, as a "Manifesto," "Propaganda force," and "Seeding-Machine." The Long March was not merely a military campaign. Mao boasted:

> Since Pan Ku divided the heavens from the earth and the Three Sovereigns and Five Emperors reigned, has history ever witnessed a long march such as ours? . . . Let us ask, has history ever known a long march equal to ours? No, never.[43]

He declares that the "Long March" was nothing but a "missionary campaign" to bear witness to the *miracle* of the *birth and formation of Chinese communism*.

Let us take only one example from Okamoto's *Long March*. In the course of the Long March, the Red Army had to pass through the area occupied by the Lo Lo tribe, which held a traditional hatred against the Han race and especially against the Chinese army. Among the many stories that are told are tales about numerous Lo Lo tribesmen (great lovers of drink), who in the process of joining the Red Army underwent great changes.

> The Red Army put the Lo Lo soldiers under very strict discipline. When a drink-happy Lo Lo passed by a liquor shop which had been sacked by the Kuo-min-tang Army, he could not resist the nice smell of wine. But when he tried to steal a sip, he was severely scolded. Later, during the daily group session, the Lo Lo heard the same superior criticizing himself for his insufficient effort at educating the soldiers in their attitude toward the people. This

made the Lo Lo ashamed of himself. . . . In the same evening, the Lo Lo was astonished to see the group chief hanging three yards of cloth securely to the back of the door of a deserted house together with an I.O.U. The cloth was meant to be the price for the three bundles of fuel used by the troops. Such an event during the rainy days in Hai-Tang greatly moved the Lo Lo soldier.[44]

In this way, the heterogeneous tribe of the Lo Lo, by being put into the spiritual *melting pot* of the Red Army ("the Saints of the Revolution") were able to overcome their foreignness and become a part of the Chinese people; were awakened to become individual men. This event also symbolically related how Mao Tse-tung was able to solve, in theory and practice, the well-known "question of the native inhabitants and the settlers" to which he referred in his "Struggle in the Chingkang Mountains."

There is another side to this story. The main body of the Red Army that took part in the Long March was composed of three Regional Armies: the First Army Group (in southern Kiangsi and western Fukien) under Mao Tse-tung and Chu Teh; the Second Army Group (in Hunan, Hupeh, Szechuan, and Kweichow) under Hu Lung and Kuan Hsiang Ying; and the Fourth Army Group (Szechuan and Shensi) under Chang Kuo-tao and Hsu Hsiang Chien. This means that the whole Army was composed of many different groups of varied geographical, cultural, and linguistic background. It also means that the Long March was a process of human revolutions (or reform of humanity), which by putting the souls of people of such diverse localities and cultures into the melting pot of the Red Army and burning them by the fire of Marxism-Leninism, thus transformed them into comrades serving the common cause of achieving the Chinese Revolution, as well as the communization of the world. The thick wall of regionalism, of which Mao Tse-tung was acutely conscious, was thus torn down.

Finally, it is worthy of note that the Red Army was *not* an ordinary army composed only of male soldiers.

Among the central corps, a strange troop drew people's attention; they included old men with canes, women and even children carried on the shoulders of young soldiers. . . . The so-called "General Staff First Company" was made up only of those who could not walk fast, such as old men, women, and the be-spectacled "men of culture." On the shoulders of young soldiers who accompanied this strange-looking troop were seen "child-soldiers"; they certainly startled the people wherever they went. . . . To mention another strange-looking troop, there was one called the Fifteenth Battalion, which carried with it all kinds of money, gold and silver coins, bank notes, etc. This was the "Central Workers' and Peasants' Government National Bank Corps," which was responsible for financial matters of the whole army, including the arrangement of accommodation and the provision of food.

Speaking of the "strange look," everything was more or less strange with the Long March. Some soldiers wore huge straw hats, or student's uniforms, some put Hunan-type umbrellas in their rucksacks, others carried washing-bowls, cups and glasses, or chopsticks stuck in their leggings, or needle and thread in the rims of their hats, etc., etc. It was as colorful a scene *as if hundreds of villages had picked up and started moving* [italics Sumiya's].[45]

As is clearly described here, the Long March included this phase of "housemoving," as it were, of *one big family clan.* This aspect of the Long March should not be overlooked when we consider the historical significance of this event; but what is its meaning?

Here I would like to summarize the special characteristics of the Long March. *The Long March was more than a mere military expedition. Its significance lies in the realm of politics, economics, and ideology. It was a purely historical event which testified in the land of China to the "emissary prophecy" of Marx. The Long March was a "missionary expedition" through which people of different cultures and languages were reformed to become men dedicated to a common purpose. It was a "seed-sowing machine" to produce new converts. It united the people of various customs and languages by means of comradely affection, in order to form one "Covenant Community"* (Eidgenossenschaft).

The Red Army achieved, with iron discipline and solidarity, the difficult "Great River Crossing," which even the prominent General Shih Ta-k'ai of the Taiping Rebellion had been unable to do. Thus the Communist Revolution supersedes the T'ai-P'ing Movement, on the historical as well as the ideological level. In this sense, we could agree with Mao Tse-tung when he says: "Since Pan Ku divided the heavens from the earth and the Three Sovereigns and Five Emperors reigned, has history ever witnessed a long march such as ours?" Even so, could we accept his conclusion that follows, that "In history, there has *never* been a long march equal to ours"?

When we examine the broad history of the world, we would say that there was only *one* expedition—with some differences of scale, to be sure—comparable to the Long March in terms of its *cultural-historical significance*. It is the Exodus from Egypt under the leadership of Moses. The people of Israel who had been suffering as slaves under the patrimonial-bureaucratic, *Leiturgie* state of ancient Egypt were led out of that country by the order of Yahweh, and in the process the twelve tribes of differing culture, customs, and languages became united as an "Amphictionie," and eventually formed a nation-state in the land of Canaan.

This *purely historical event,* the Exodus under Moses, occupies the same important place in the history of Israel as the Long March does in the history of the Chinese people. Politically and religiously, the Exodus was the point of reference to which the people of Israel went back whenever they were confronted by some hardship; it was the point of departure of the faith of the great prophets, such as Amos, Hosea, Isaiah, and Jeremiah, who had a unique place in the general history of thought. It is worth emphasizing that the Exodus, like the Long March, was a purely *historical (historisch) event*. In his book, *Ancient Judaism,* Max Weber emphasizes repeatedly how profound was the influence of the Exodus on the history of Israel. The Covenant (*Bund*), which Yahweh made with Israel promising salvation, was:

> clearly the product of that concrete, historical event. The event which all the prophets took as a true sign of the absolute dependability of God's power and His covenant, and which the prophets

thought of as the sign for Israel's obligation to acknowledge thanks to God eternally, was the event of the miraculous defeat of the Egyptian Army at the Red Sea and the emancipation from the forced labor in Egypt. The unique character of this event is that the miracle was wrought by a God hitherto unknown to Israel, and that the same God was accepted through the solemn "*Berith*" as the God of the amphictiony when Moses instituted the cult of Yahweh. This *acceptance* was established on the basis of a mutual covenant between God and the people mediated by the prophet Moses. The covenant, on the part of the people, laid the foundation for the special obligations over a long period of time, whereas God's promise, revealed as grace, made this God the God of the Covenant for Israel in a sense so unique that it has not been found anywhere else in the history of the world. This is clearly the viewpoint of the tradition. But it is also clear that this view produced the concept of "rebellion" as the gravest of all sins. This concept has never been found in any other part of the world, but in Israel it was already pre-supposed in the Song of Deborah. In particular, this view served as the indispensable foundation on which the prophecy or blessing-prophecy played its most important, unique, role in Israel.[46]

Having said this, Weber added the following comment, "There is no reason to have doubts about the historicity of Moses. The only question to be discussed is what the special quality of his work was." At any rate it is obvious that wherever Israel faced a crisis, especially in the exilic period, this ancient law of the Covenant, and the significance of the observance of Yahweh's commandments as the condition of His grace, came back with full force to give the people a clear mark of hope for the future.

When Marx's "emissary prophecy" reached China by way of the Russian Revolution, what was the reaction of the Chinese people (and especially of Mao Tse-tung), who were suffering under the tyrannical rule of the Manchu Dynasty and of the colonializing tendencies of the Western powers? Mao himself has only a few words to say, "Ever since I accepted Marxism as the correct interpretation of history, I have had no hesitation about it." [47] And we know from the book just cited above, how, during the Long March, people welcomed enthusiastically the

Red Army that had been trained both politically and ethically by Mao and his comrades.

No exact dates for the Exodus are known to us, but the prevailing theory among historians puts it around 1230 B.C. Nor is the number of people led by Moses out of Egypt known, but according to the biblical accounts (Exodus 12:37; Numbers 1:46) the number of males alone was 600,000, which would become much larger when we add old men, women, and children. Some historians interpret the figure as meaning 600 families (the word translated "thousand" can also be read "family"); that is, somewhere between five and ten thousand people. At any rate, the parallel between the Exodus and the Long March is striking in that each was an expedition of a huge group of people including old men, women, and children, and of a mixture of tribes of different cultures and dialects. Each one was also a process in which the group was gradually trained by charismatic leaders such as Moses and his faithful successor, Joshua.

The parallel does not stop there. Both leaders, Moses and Mao Tse-tung, had not only a prophetic element based on charismatic authority, but had also the aspect of a law-giver (what Weber calls "aisymnete," to distinguish it from the promulgator of specific laws); of one who *actually* created a new order. It is also important to mention the problem of the so-called "routinization of charisma"; that is, when a charismatic leader succeeds in revolution and seizes power, there always arises this question of "routinization," including the question of the succession of leadership. In the case of Moses, this problem is clearly seen in the fact that the Ten Commandments, revealed by God at Mt. Sinai (Exodus 20, Deuteronomy 5) was generally called the *Law*. This Decalogue begins with the words: "I am the Lord your God, who brought you up out of the land of Egypt. You shall have no other Gods besides me." Here it is already clear that the spirit of the whole commandment points to the relationship between the Covenant and the Law. The relation to God is consciously understood as *Covenant,* and the loyalty promised to God is, at the same time, the *Law*. It was the declaration of the basic principle of the life and faith of the nation, the culmination of the great event of Exodus. Needless to say, the Law was given after God's saving act was done, on the basis of the Covenant. It is in this sense that the Book of the Law was called the Book of the Covenant. In Moses' case, his function as transmitter of the "emissary prophecy" *preceded* that as law-giver. Theoretically this order must not be reversed. However, we are all aware that in history there have been many such cases of the phenomenon Weber called "routinization of the charisma." Can we not say that the dynamic of correlation, tension, and mutual supplementation between "the Gospel" and "Law" runs through beneath the surface of history? When the prophet is also law-giver, this aspect of the problem cannot help but stand out in particularly bold relief. The Old Testament itself speaks most eloquently of how much energy has been expended by the people of Israel on this problem. No, rather, the whole history of Christianity, which is symbolized in St. Paul's words as the fulfillment of the Old Testament law, is the history of a life and death struggle centered around this problem of Law and Gospel.

Mao Tse-tung has a thesis: "In a cultural fight, fight culturally; in an armed struggle, fight with arms"; and again he says:

> There is only one way to eliminate [war], and that is to oppose war with war, to oppose counter-revolutionary war with revolutionary war, to oppose national counter-revolutionary war with national revolutionary war, and to oppose counter-revolutionary class war with revolutionary class war.[48]

If this thesis is the *Law,* in the sense of having the same *logical structure* as the Old Testament Law, "an eye for an eye and a tooth for a tooth," the parallel here is too close to be taken merely as accidental. Rather, it is because both events have common elements regarding the nature and the historical setting of "emissary prophecy" viewed from the standpoint of the sociology of religion. Particularly, when the ideas of Mao Tse-tung begin to settle down in Chinese society as "Mao Tse-tung-ism," there is a real possibility of a shift in the relationship between "the Gospel" and "the Law," just as in the seventeenth century Calvinism was condemned by the Lutherans as legalistic for developing the doctrine of "the Assurance of Salvation."

It may, therefore, be rather easy, in a sense, for those who have already tasted the Gospel of Christ to criticize the Thought of Mao Tse-tung for its legalistic character. But at the same time it does not help to resolve the overwhelming power of law that is still at work in history if we simply fold our arms and do nothing about it. St. Paul knew this better than anyone; he says:

> Do you not know that in a race all runners compete, but only one receives the prize? So run that you may obtain it. Every athlete exercises self-control in all things. They do it to receive a perishable wreath, but we an imperishable. Well, I do not run aimlessly, I do not box as one beating the air; but I pommel my body and subdue it, lest after preaching to others I myself should be disqualified (I Corinthians 9:24–27).

Today it is well known that the *spirit* of Paul was succeeded by the constant efforts of the monastic orders (*Ora et Labora*) that swarmed in Western Europe through the Middle Ages, and by the Reformers who transformed this "other-worldly ascetic ethos" of the monastery into an "inner-worldly asceticism."

This ascetic ethos has pushed forward the process of "total rationalization of life" through two thousand years of Western European history, and finally, having achieved the task of "emancipating the world from magic," it has vanished. Max Weber touched upon this point in his work cited at the beginning of this essay:

> Since asceticism undertook to remodel the world and to work out its ideals in the world, material goods have gained an increasing and finally an inexorable power over the lives of men as at no previous period in history. Today the spirit of religious asceticism—whether finally, who knows?—has escaped from the cage. But victorious capitalism, since it rests on mechanical foundations, needs its support no longer. The rosy blush of its laughing heir, the Enlightenment, seems also to be irretrievably fading, and the idea of duty in one's calling prowls about in our lives like the ghost of dead religious beliefs.[49]

We have already noted that Weber turned his sharp eye to Russia and Asia in search for the objective possibility of the *revival* of the ascetic ethos which had disappeared from modern Western Europe.

What image should we be able to imagine when, from the viewpoint of Weber's sociology of religion, we superimpose the Exodus and the Long March on each other? The track of the gigantic dynamism of world history may now, once more, be "switched over" by the Long March and the Thought of Mao Tse-tung in the same way that the Exodus of Moses was the takeoff point that set the direction of cultural development in ancient Israel and on down through two thousand years of European history. It seems that a totally new *Law,* in the form of "the East wind prevailing over the West wind," and its new process of the "total rationalization of life," are spreading from one corner of China all over the world.

What will happen in history when Mao Tse-tung's Thought that took roots in China through the Long March has completed successfully its task as a *switch lever of history,* just like the Yahweh-faith of Moses of the Exodus has done? Perhaps the time will come for us to say of Mao what Weber said of Moses: there is no question as to his accomplishment; the only question to discuss is its special character.

NOTES

1. Max Weber, *The Protestant Ethic and the Spirit of Capitalism* (New York, Scribner, 1948), p. 182.

2. From Weber's lecture on "Socialism," 1918 (in *Gesammelte Aufsatze zur Soziologie und Sozialpolitik,* 1924); translated from the Japanese translation. (*Kenryoku to Shihai,* 1969), p. 199. Cf. *Protestant Ethic, op. cit.,* p. 23.

3. Translator's note: Weber's term *missions-prophezie* has been variously translated into English as "ethical prophecy" (*Sociology of Religion,* trans. by Ephraim Fischoff, cf. pp. 55ff.) and "emissary prophecy" (Hans H. Gerth and C. Wright Mills, *From Max Weber: Essays in Sociology,* (N.Y.: Peter Smith, p. 291). The Japanese equivalent is *Shimei-yogen,* the nuance of which is closer to mission than to ethics; therefore we have adopted the latter term, "emissary," as appropriate to this essay, in

spite of its rather awkward sound. For a discussion of this categorization of prophecy, cf. *Sociology of Religion,* pp. 46–54.

4. Weber's lecture on "Socialism," *op. cit.,* pp. 214–15.

5. *Ibid.,* p. 215.

6. *Ibid.,* p. 209.

7. *Ibid.,* p. 217.

8. *Ibid.,* p. 217.

9. What I should like to deal with is the "Thought of Mao Tse-tung," which has suddenly come to the world's attention because of the present "Proletarian Great Cultural Revolution," but in order to do this it is necessary to examine the predisposition of the Thought of Mao Tse-tung. Specifically, this requires that one hold firmly to a methodological perspective which makes the same distinctions and similarities that Weber made between the "Thought of Calvin" and "Calvinism" in *Protestant Ethic.* . . .

10. "Report on an Investigation of the Peasant Movement in Hunan" (1927). *Selected Works of Mao Tse-tung* (Peking: Foreign Languages Press, 1965), vol. I, pp. 23–24.

11. *Ibid.,* p. 34.

12. *Ibid.,* p. 44.

13. *Ibid.,* pp. 44–45.

14. *Ibid.,* p. 46.

15. *Ibid.*

16. *Ibid.,* p. 35.

17. Cf. Gerth and Mills, *op. cit.,* pp. 186–88.

18. Quoted from *Peking News,* 1967.

19. "The Struggle in the Chingkang Mountains" (1928), in *Selected Works,* vol. I, p. 80.

20. *Ibid.,* p. 81.

21. *Ibid.*

22. *Ibid.*

23. *Ibid.,* p. 83.

24. *Ibid.*

25. Cf. *Quotations of Chairman Mao Tse-tung,* p. 145.

26. "The Struggle . . . ," *op. cit.,* p. 88.

27. *Ibid.,* p. 87.

28. *Ibid.,* p. 88.

29. *Ibid.,* pp. 93–94.

30. Cf. Gerth and Mills, *op. cit.,* pp. 398–99.

31. Reinhard Bendix, *Max Weber: An Intellectual Portrait* (Garden City, Doubleday Anchor, 1962), p. 99.

32. *Ibid.,* p. 100.

33. Weber: *The Religion of China* (New York: Macmillan & Co., 1951), *op. cit.,* p. 222.

34. *Ibid.,* p. 219.

35. All quotations in this and the following paragraph are from *Religion in China,* pp. 221, 222, 219, 223.

36. *Ibid.,* p. 221.

37. *Ibid.,* p. 223.

38. From "The Tai P'ing Salvation Songs," in *Tai P'ing Heavenly Kingdom,* from "Recent Chinese Historical Source Material Series" (in Japanese).

39. Cited in Ryuzo Okamoto, *Chosei-Chugoku Kakumei Shiren no Kiroku* (*Long March—A Record of the Trial of the Chinese Revolution*), 7th printing (1965), p. 2.

40. *China Today* (1960), quoted from the Japanese translation by Yoko Matsuoka. An English version may be found in Edgar Snow: *The Other Side of the River* (New York: Random House, 1961).

41. "On Tactics Against Japanese Imperialism," *Selected Works,* I, p. 160.

42. Okamoto, *op. cit.,* p. 2; Preface, pp. 1, 5.

43. "On Tactics Against . . . ," *op. cit.,* p. 160. ("Pan Ku, according to Chinese mythology, was the creator of the world and the first ruler of mankind. The Three Sovereigns and Five Emperors were legendary rulers in ancient China." [Note on p. 176].)

44. Okamoto, p. 69.

45. Okamoto, p. 10.

46. *Ancient Judaism,* pp. 190–91, 201 (from the Japanese translation, 1967).

47. *Mo Taku To, Sono Shi to Jinsei* ("Mao Tse-tung, His Poetry and Life"), 4th printing (1967), p. 44.

48. "Strategy in China's Revolutionary War" (December 1936), *Selected Works,* I, pp. 182–83.

49. *Protestant Ethic* . . . , pp. 181–82.

The socialist tradition
and China's new socialism

BRUCE DOUGLASS

> In history it is always the newcomers who outstrip the old.
> —Chinese Communist Party, 1958

How to be in but not of industrial civilization? This was the question that prompted the modern idea of socialism. In the first blush of industrialization in the early nineteenth century in Western Europe, the figures who were to become known as the early or "utopian" socialists—Robert Owen in England, Charles Fourier in France—in fact found themselves reacting to the new phenomenon with intense yet mixed feelings. They were both attracted and repulsed by it. They were certain that it promised a better life than that of earlier periods, yet they were also certain that in the form in which it was appearing it did away with worthwhile features of the old order. The quest that led them to dream socialist dreams was for an order that would combine the best of both worlds.

The question with which the early socialists began has never really found a satisfactory answer. That is to say, it has never found an answer fully relevant for industrial society. On the one hand, the early socialists failed to relate their vision to a realistic strategy of social change, so industrialization in its capitalist form followed its own logic of development without being seriously affected. On the other hand, by midcentury, a new type of socialist idea emerged with a realistic strategy of social change, and that idea eventually came to have a definite impact on the shape of industrialization. But the price of the realism was a shrinkage of the original vision. Socialism fell prey to the spirit of capitalism even as it denied its substance.

The quest for a satisfactory answer to the original question goes on today. Even in advanced industrial societies, where men have long since lost any living relationship with preindustrial society, sensitive spirits continue to try to regain community and meaningful work and personal wholeness. The quest is even more keenly pursued, perhaps, in less advanced nations, where the memory of the preindustrial order is still fresh. Everywhere the quest is pursued with a new, distinctively twentieth century realism. Thoughtful men no longer can believe, as many once did, that industrialization in itself brings heaven on earth.

The loss of innocence has led many to believe that the original vision itself was a mistake. Even some socialists tell us today that the problem is not in the first instance that society has been ordered wrongly, but rather that too much has been expected from social organization. The future of socialism, they say, rests in putting away the dreams of its childhood and facing up realistically and pragmatically to the limits imposed by the logic of industrialism. The problem with the Marxist-Leninist tradition, they further argue, is that its shrinkage of the socialist idea did not go far enough.[1] This view is appealing to men in societies that have come to reap the material fruits advanced industrialism brings and who have come to appreciate the complexities of the social problems confronting advanced industrial societies. It is less appealing to men whose societies do not yet enjoy the industrial cornucopia. Those who come later, they often feel, must do better.

The China of Mao Tse-tung is one place where the aspiration for a higher order of industrial society lives on. It is also one of the few places where such an aspiration plays a major role in determining public policy. Chinese socialism, say the Chinese Communists, will be a distinctive socialism, and the implicit meaning is clear: they will make of this huge country a socialist society superior not only to the industrially advanced capitalist societies, but to the socialist ones as well.

In this Chinese quest for a higher socialism one can discern, I believe, a return to the original aspirations behind the original socialist idea—this in spite of the fact that the leadership is Communist and thus identifies with that socialist tradition that is responsible for the shrinkage of the socialist vision; and in spite of the fact that the Chinese Communists have learned their

Marxism from the Russians, and demonstrate little or no positive awareness of pre-Marxist Western socialism.

The Chinese experiment is, to be sure, just that—an experiment. It raises as many questions as it answers. Because of its dependence on the Marxist-Leninist-Stalinist tradition it is wrought with ambiguities. Still, we find in this experiment a serious attempt to grapple with the problem of a humane social order under modern conditions. Its significance can be more fully appreciated by looking back into the history of the development of the socialist idea.

THE ORIGINAL VISION

Like the conservative romantics with whom they shared many assumptions, the early socialists used an idealized picture of the preindustrial past in their criticism of capitalist industrialization. The idealization lay primarily in omission. They simply did not choose to remember what was dehumanizing in village life. In what they did remember there was a definite element of truth. They knew that in some respects preindustrial life was clearly superior to that of industrial society. They knew, for example, that there was a solidarity in the communal existence of the village that compared favorably with the atomization and class polarization which industrialization brought. They knew that however arduous labor had been in the village, it still had a meaningfulness which labor in a mill did not have. They knew that however undemocratic the politics of the village had been, people did not feel the burden of the state as an apparatus in the way that they did in industrial society.

There were, naturally, economic dimensions as well to the problem of industrial society as the early socialists defined it. They saw that the power of the machine afforded new possibilities of material abundance and physical security for man; but they were also aware that those possibilities were not being utilized to improve the lot of the majority of men. A few prospered while the majority suffered (what could be construed as) a decline in well-being. A socialist society would alter this; the possibilities of the machine would be harnessed for the *common* good. But the economic factor was not the whole of their concern. Their understanding of the problem of industrial society and their vision of the alternative were complex. Certainly it was important to feed and clothe and house the workers adequately, but these measures would hardly solve the problem of industrial society. The remedy could not stop there. Somehow, industrial society had to be reconstructed to provide not only economic justice, but community, meaningful work, and a more humane politics as well. The problem of industrial society was preeminently a *social* problem, and the remedy had to be a social one.

Was it really possible, however, to create an industrial order that preserved the virtues of village life? The uncertainty of the answer provides much of the explanation for the fiddling with blueprints that characterizes this period of socialist thought. Owen and Fourier and the disciples of Saint-Simon were sure, and yet they were not.

The dominant tendency was to answer this question in terms of decentralization, spontaneity, and the commune. Fourier and Owen elaborated detailed plans for the reorganization of society from within through the free creation of limited, self-contained "societies" of producers and their families. Only an "association communale sur le terrain de la production et de la consummation" would make possible, Fourier felt, the integration of collectivism and individualism.

Marxists have tended to say that these early socialists had no strategy for the achievement of their ideals or that their strategies were silly. The first is certainly not true and the second dubious. They had a strategy, but it was not the Marxist strategy. Nor was it silly. It was naive in its psychology perhaps, but there was realism at precisely those points where Marxists have tended to be naive. As Martin Buber has pointed out in *Paths in Utopia*,[2] one of the reasons why the early socialists were led to adopt the strategy they did was that they doubted that the socialist ideal in its wholeness could be realized in any way other than social renewal from the ground up.

This was not the only reason, of course. They lived in a time when the labor movement was in its infancy, and it was hard to think of a political force capturing state power on behalf of the socialist idea. Also, they had inherited from the Enlightenment an exaggerated sense of the power of reason. Owen traveled widely in Europe and North America to spread the gospel, especially among men of means, and Fourier announced to the public that he would be available at his home every day at noontime to discuss socialist experiments with prospective backers. (The fact that no one ever appeared seems not to have daunted him; he continued this practice for a decade.) For all of their naivete, there was an important kernel of truth in their thinking. They believed that existing industrial society was dehumanizing not simply to laborers, but to managers as well. Socialism at this stage was not a sectarian creed. Social transformation was to be accomplished by and on behalf of the *whole* people.

This catholicity of the early socialist vision was related to the complexity of the understanding of the social problem that went with it. The problem with existing industrial society was not simply that it made a few rich and the majority destitute. The rich man suffered in his own way as well as the poor man. Socialism had something positive to offer to all.

Discussion of revolution in the writings of Fourier and Owen is scant, but the little there is tells us a great deal. They rejected this strategy because it was not really effective. Fourier argued that "in themselves and by reason of the measures which they provoke, revolutions are incapable of creating anything which lasts." [3] Equally important, they viewed revolution as capitulation to the spirit of capitalist industrialism in the sense that it perpetuated (and even aggravated) the polarization of group against group. Later socialist revolutionaries were of course to deny this, saying that revolution is an act of the "people" and that its objective is to create a new social solidarity; and there is a certain truth in the proposition that the act of revolution, like that of war, creates solidarity. But it is a half truth. Revolution is preeminently a sectarian act. The early socialists doubted that genuine community could come of such a divisive gesture.*

---

* We get some indication of how the early socialists responded to the Marxist challenge on the question of revolution in Proudhon's reply to Marx's invitation to join in correspondence among socialists. "Perhaps you still hold the opinion that no reform is actually possible without a *coup de main,* without what used to be called a revolution. . . . I believe

THE MARXIST ALTERNATIVE

The next chapter in the history of socialist thought belongs principally to Karl Marx and his collaborator Friedrich Engels. Marxism's relation to earlier socialist doctrines is an enormously complex question. Obviously there are debts and continuities, some of which Marx and Engels recognized in spite of their dismissal of their predecessors. But the break was what they emphasized. Socialism, they believed, was entering a new era with the development of a "scientific" theory, and this was bound to be an improvement over its antecedents.

The disjuncture is most apparent in the reorientation that socialist thought undergoes. The socialist idea itself recedes into the background; the primary concern is analysis of the dynamics of industrial development. The goal remains, to be sure, but it is taken for granted. What matters is knowing how to realize it. Marx harbored a positive contempt for systematic thought about the ideal. The nature of the new society could not possibly be discovered prior to the end of capitalism. As a result, Marx had little that was concrete to say about the meaning of socialism. When his disciples were later to confront the task of putting together the nuts and bolts of socialism, they found that the most his writings offered was a few fragments. Those fragments were confusing, moreover, in that they did not distinguish carefully between socialism and communism.*

---

that we have no need of that for success. . . . This so-called means would be simply an appeal to force, an appeal to the arbitrary—in a word, a contradiction. . . . The problem as I see it is . . . to turn the economists' theory against Property in such way as not to endanger what your German socialists called *community* and what I confine myself for the moment to calling *liberty* and *equality*."

* The fragments suggest, however, that Marx probably carried around in his head a much more complete conception of socialism than what he committed to the printed page. They also suggest that this conception was not altogether unlike to the idea of socialism of his "utopian" predecessors. In spite of his dedicated urbanism and his contempt for rural life, we find him caught in the same attraction-repulsion relationship to industrial society, and we find him looking forward to a time when ideals derived from a preindustrial setting can be realized anew in an industrial setting.

Yet even as the socialist idea is set aside, its meaning is chang-ing. On the one hand Marx sees how apparently everything in society is reshaped by the power of the burgeoning industrialism, and is led to the conclusion that it is economic organization that really determines what happens to man in society. On the other hand he aspires to alliance with the emerging labor movement, whose primary concerns are economic. So Marx moves toward an emphasis on the economic factor in his conception of socialism. The problem of industrial society is presented in the first instance as a problem of economic organization, and socialism is presented as an answer to *this* problem. Solve this problem, Marx teaches, and the rest will follow quite naturally. State ownership of the means of production becomes the defining feature of socialism.

The way to the achievement of socialism is through seizure of the power of the state by labor. Here Marx breaks decisively with his predecessors. The time of monkeying with communal experiments is past. Socialism as a form of economic organization for industrial society can be realized only through state initiatives that span the whole of society.

"To conquer political power has become the great duty of the working classes," he declared in his *Inaugural Address* to the First International. Did he think of this conquest as a revolution-ary act? Under certain circumstances (not always clear). Under others—such as those which Britain afforded—he was quite ready to think in terms of parliamentary politics. The particularities of strategy were not the main issue to him; his principal concern was to establish that the way to socialism lay through seizure of state power.

Marx was able to define his strategy for socialists the way he did because of his emphasis on the economic factor in his con-ception of socialism. The doubts of his predecessors about the possibilities of constructing socialism through state initiative could be swept aside because of his conviction that social relations and cultural phenomena were determined by economic organiza-tion. He never really developed a strategy for socialist construction in the sense in which the early socialists understood that. His sub-stitute is a strategy for the elimination of capitalism.

The direct identification of the prospects of socialism with the labor movement, moreover, introduces the sectarian motif into socialist thought. Marx himself is too subtle and complex a thinker to identify socialism neatly with a proletarian paradise, but the turn away from catholicity begins with his argument.

THE BOLSHEVIK REVISION

After Marx's death, his legacy was claimed by two competing brands of socialists. Both Social Democrats and Communists could claim to be picking up the mantle because "there were contradictions latent in his outlook . . . fused into a doctrine which Janus-like confronted the beholder whatever his angle of vision." [4] It is the Communist side of the story that interests us here.

The Bolsheviks were capable of playing loose with some elements of doctrine when it suited their needs, but their theory of socialism bears a distinct Marxist imprint. They learned what socialism meant from Marx, without needing or desiring to go behind him to his predecessors, and as a result the important changes that Marx effected in socialist theory are carried over into Bolshevism.[5] We find in Lenin, Stalin, and the others the same skepticism about socialist blueprints, the same conviction about the priority of the economic factor in defining and constructing socialism, the same equation of socialism with industrialism, and the same conviction that only through seizure of state power can socialism be achieved. The theory of permanent revolution, moreover, that was to turn out to be the core of the *lasting* theoretical justification for the October Revolution, was derived from Marx.

Unlike Marx, however, the Bolsheviks were forced by their own achievement in the October Revolution to confront the tasks of socialist construction—and in an economically backward country. As they grappled with this task, problems that had been swept under the rug in Marx's reorientation of socialist thought came quickly to the fore once again. That their solutions to these problems were often less than satisfactory was due in no small part to the fact that they tried to provide solutions on the terms provided by Marx.

From the start, then, they were at a disadvantage. When the

revolution came they had few concrete ideas of what socialism meant, and many they did have quickly proved to be illusory. We see this clearly in Lenin's pamphlet *State and Revolution,* written in the months between the February and October Revolutions, and whose prescriptions correspond loosely to the course of Bolshevik policy in the first few months following the seizure of power. Drawing directly and entirely from Marx's scattered notes on Communist society, the pamphlet proposes that the social and political evils of the old order will almost automatically disappear in the aftermath of the revolution. The state apparatus will "wither away," with its functions devolving "upon the people generally." "The transition from capitalism to Socialism is impossible without a 'return,' in a measure, to 'primitive democracy,'" he writes.

"Primitive democracy" on the basis of capitalism and capitalist culture is not the same primitive democracy as in prehistoric or precapitalist times. Capitalist culture has created large-scale production, factories, railways, the postal service, telephones, etc., and on this basis the great majority of the old functions of the old "state power" have become so simplified and can be reduced to such simple operations of registration, filing and checking that they will be quite within the reach of every literate person, and it will be possible to perform them for "workingmen's wages," which circumstances can (and must) strip those functions of every shadow of privilege. . . . All officials, without exception, elected and subject to recall at any time, their salaries reduced to "workingmen's wages" —these simple and "self-evident" democratic measures, which, completely uniting the interests of the workers and the majority of peasants, at the same time serve as a bridge leading from capitalism to Socialism.[6]

Lenin and his comrades quickly learned that the problem of socialist construction was not quite so simple—especially under backward conditions where there was no capitalist culture to build upon—and quickly reversed their field. In quick order, the talk of primitive democracy was replaced by an emphasis on dictatorship (a term that Marx used, but with a very peculiar meaning), and Lenin was saying that it was "fantasy" to think that Russian workers and peasants could take over the administration of state affairs.

So there was a good deal of experimentation in the first decade of Bolshevik rule in order to adjust the Marxist inheritance to Russian conditions. The task was further complicated by a critical contradiction in the theory they inherited from Marx. In one sense the contradiction was of their own making, since they tried to take over the theory of Marx the Communist Leaguer while ignoring much of what Marx the Social Democrat had said in later years. But Marx himself never gave up the earlier position entirely. However that may be, when the Bolsheviks turned to socialist construction, they found themselves with a theory that held on the one hand that a socialist revolution was possible in a backward country, but on the other hand that socialism presupposes advanced industrialization.

The way out of this dilemma was the equation of the building of socialism with the building of industrial society. Thus the doctrine of "socialism in one country," that represents one of the few important original Bolshevik contributions to socialist thought.

Of course it was not simply Marx's obsession with industrialism which prompted "socialism in one country." The socialist revolution in backward Russia took a turn that the theory of permanent revolution did not anticipate. It appears that Marx envisioned socialist construction in such a country going forward with assistance from more industrialized countries, and the Bolsheviks shared this expectation in the beginning. The other half of the theoretical justification for the October Revolution—the half that did not endure—suggested that this Russian event was to function as a "spark" for proletarian revolt in Western Europe. When it became clear that events in the West were not going to turn out this way, and that the Bolsheviks were going to have to go it alone if at all, industrialization became a necessity. As Stalin put it in 1930, if industrialization were not set in motion quickly and efficiently, socialist Russia would be overcome by its enemies in less than a decade.[7]

This siege mentality (it was hardly unjustified with the memory of a bitter civil war less than a decade old and fascism on the rise in Germany) made socialism in one country mean something more than simply industrialization under conditions of state ownership. It meant fast, lock-step industrialization as well. Socialist Russia had to catch up to her advanced capitalist opponents quickly; she had to do in a few decades what had taken them over a century. The effect of this—reflected more clearly in policy than in theory—was to make socialism the servant of industrialism.

This submission of socialism to industrialism is evident in the cultivation of materialist attitudes among industrial personnel at all levels, in the repudiation of equality as a "petty bourgeois" ideal, in the cultivation of a Puritan work ethic, in the heavy stress on science and technology in the reorganization of education, in the utilization of the farms as servants of industry, in the denial of consumer goods and social services in order to accumulate capital and invest in heavy industry, and in the expansion of the state apparatus as a means of controlling and rationalizing the economy. Although formally the Russian leaders continued to subscribe to the larger vision with which Marxism had been identified (and probably with more sincerity than their critics usually grant them), in practice most of the concerns represented by that vision were sacrificed on the altar of productivity. In a distant tomorrow they might be realized; for the immediate future they had to be set aside because they were not compatible with rapid industrialization. As Lenin recognized as early as 1920, the practical doctrine of the Bolsheviks had to be that "Socialism is nothing else but a monopoly of state capitalism, initiated for the benefit of the whole nation, and by virtue of that ceasing to be a capitalist monopoly." [8]

But it was not quite so simple as Lenin's formula suggests. Socialism in one country in fact turned out to be state capitalism, but the tradition the Bolsheviks inherited from Marx as well as their political situation made it impossible for them to stop there. They knew that socialism meant something more than a simple reorganization of state and economy; they knew that socialism as Marx had understood it had a wholeness that implied more sweeping changes. Education and the arts and scientific inquiry and public morality—in short, the whole superstructure—had to be remade as well. Yet the demands of industrialization limited their options in this area. So, by an ironic twist of fate, there was indeed an attempt at total transformation of Russian society, but *in the service of industrialization.* Socialist morality, socialist art, socialist science—in every area of cultural life an effort was made to create something new; the primary criterion of worth in each case, however, was fidelity to the ends prescribed by the emerging industrial state capitalism.

What made this so anomalous, moreover, was that at the same time that, in practice, socialism was operating as state capitalism, in theory it was often seen in terms of Marx's ultimate vision. We find Stalin declaring, in the late thirties, that the social contradictions in the Soviet Union have all been resolved in principle, and that socialist construction is on the verge of completion. We find onerous labor, characteristic of the early phases of industrialization, being presented to Russian peasants and proletarians as the fulfillment of Marx's vision of meaningful work. We find the dictatorial political system interpreted as a realization of communal democracy.

THE CHINESE DEBT TO BOLSHEVISM

The ambiguities of Stalin's attempt to build socialism in one country have led many socialists to despair of the Russian experiment. Even the Russian Communists themselves have made gestures at repudiating this period in their history, and the majority of Communists around the world have joined in this "de-Stalinization." But the Chinese Communists are an exception. Far from repudiating Stalin, they present themselves as inheritors of his line. They also present themselves as innovators—as agents of the "Sinification" of Marxism and the builders of a distinctive brand of socialist society. They are in fact both of these things—and more as well.

The respect of the Chinese Communists for the Russian example is a natural outgrowth of their history. Chinese communism took shape in the shadow of the attempt to build socialism in Russia, and by the Chinese own self-understanding, their movement and revolution is a child of the Russian Revolution. The seizure of power by the Bolsheviks sparked the emergence of communism as a living political force in China, and the ideology of the Chinese Communist Party was heavily influenced by Bolshevik thought. It was not original Marxism, but rather Marxism-*Leninism,* that was the ideological ground of the party formed in Shanghai in 1921. Moreover, despite the great ambiguities of the support that the Soviet Union provided the Chinese Communists during their long struggle with the Kuomintang, that support compared very favorably with the responses to Chinese communism of the major non-Communist nations. When Mao's party finally came to power, the Russians alone assisted China.

Yet even if the Chinese had endorsed Stalin's idea of socialism unequivocally, the building of socialism in China was not likely to be a simple repetition of the Russian example. Their experience and situation were too different. The moment of October 1917 in Russia, for example, has all the marks of a palace coup. This may not have been contrary to the will of the broad masses of Russian proletarians and peasants, but it did not depend directly on their initiative. (Indirectly it depended heavily on their initiative, since it was the political confusion created by the mass uprisings of the preceding months that made possible the Bolshevik triumph.) Consequently, the Bolsheviks came to power with no real experience of government and few ties with the masses whose interests they claimed to represent. Insofar as they had any mass base at all it was in the proletariat in the cities, which represented a small part of the total population. Mao's party, by contrast, experienced revolution as a long protracted process, spanning decades, during which time power was built up slowly through a gradual extension of the territory they governed. In that process, moreover, they depended heavily on a mass peasant base—in a country that, like Russia, was predominantly agrarian. Thus by 1949 they had already had long years of experience in government, and they had firmly established confidence and roots in the peasant population of a large part of China.

Equally important, they had the Russian experience from which to learn. Not only did Stalin's experiment provide them with blueprints to follow and mistakes to avoid, but they were not burdened with the illusions that the Bolsheviks brought to the business of building socialism. No visions of mature communism just around the corner danced in their heads as they carried out the revolution. They knew well—in those days, at least—that mature communism was a long way off, and that in the meantime the building of socialism would be an arduous business. In some respects they seemed to have grasped more realistically than the Russian leaders what the lessons of the Russian experience were.

Chinese socialism was likely to be different from Russian socialism, moreover, because of the nature of Chinese civilization. As early as 1938 Mao was speaking of the "Sinification" of Marxism (at a time when the notion of "separate roads" was heretical). We must respect China's uniqueness, he said. Its history and civilization will produce a socialism unique to China, just as Russian history and civilization have produced a socialism unique to that country. "We are Marxist historicists; we must not mutilate history. From Confucius to Sun Yat-sen we must sum it up critically, and we must constitute ourselves the heirs of all that is precious in the past. . . ." [9]

The Chinese Communists thus aspired to be faithful to the Russian example, to transcend its errors and limitations, and at the same time to develop a distinctively Chinese brand of socialism.

The ideological debt to Bolshevism is obvious at two fundamental points: the terms that the Chinese Communists use to explain the development of the Chinese Revolution and the terms that they use to define the contours of their socialist project. Their theory of the Chinese Revolution, for all of its distinctive features—such as the emphasis on imperialism[10] and the reliance on the peasantry[11]—bears a Bolshevik imprint. Like the Bolshevik theory of the Russian Revolution, it relies on Lenin's version of the theory of permanent revolution—which is to say, the view that in industrially backward countries in the age of imperialism, the bourgeois and proletarian revolutions can and must be telescoped into one continuous process, with the proletariat (read: *party* of the proletariat) taking the initiative in both because of the incapacity of the native bourgeoisie to play out its role. The Chinese

Communists, like the Bolsheviks, see themselves as executing both the proletarian and the bourgeois revolutions in straight succession. Likewise the Chinese Communists have taken over Stalin's terms for the outline of the definition of the socialist project in their country. They, too, see themselves as building socialism in one country (without any of the Bolshevik qualms about this "nationalization" of the idea of socialism). They also believe that socialist construction can be successful without a long prior period of capitalist development. Likewise they believe that socialism can and must be created by state initiative. Likewise they accept in principle the Bolshevik identification of socialism with industrialism, and move to industrialize their country as quickly as possible.

However the identification of socialism with industrialism is not so complete or wooden in Chinese Communist thought—or at least in the Maoist variant—as it is in Stalin's thought, and here the distinctiveness of their position begins to emerge. It would be wrong to say that Stalin so completely identified socialism with industrial society that he was willing to accept anything in order to industrialize Russia, but he was willing to accept much more deviation from the rest of the socialist idea than the Maoists. With the advantage of hindsight, they know that the commitment to industrialization must be held in balance with other commitments, and that if this is not done, the result can very well be a society similar to those of the capitalist world.

THE "SINIFICATION" OF SOCIALISM

The likelihood of a simple commitment to industrialization by the Chinese Communists would not have been great, however, even if there had not been Russian mistakes from which to learn. Both the distinctively Chinese preoccupation with social relations and the Chinese Communists' roots in the countryside militate against this.

The stream of modern Chinese intellectual life that the Chinese Communists represent did, of course, embrace the industrialism of the West, and define the problem of China's renewal in terms of industrialization. But as inheritors of the thought of Confucius, they never could make that embrace quite so complete as men formed by Western civilization. They did not derive proper social relations simply from the demands of industrialization, as has been the tendency in the West. As committed as the Chinese Communists have been to bringing the natural environment under man's control and making China into a modern industrial society, they have not cut themselves off from the traditional Chinese concern with social relations as ends in themselves.[12]

Their conception, in turn, of what constitutes proper social relations has been influenced by their roots in China's agrarian society during the long years of civil war. In the early years of Chinese communism, many of the cadres, including Mao himself, adopted the standard Marxist-Leninist love of the city and contempt of the village. As Mao confessed in 1942,

> I began as a student and acquired the habits of a student; surrounded by students who could neither fetch nor carry for themselves, I used to consider it undignified to do any manual labor, such as shouldering my own luggage. At that time it seemed to me that the intellectuals were the only clean persons in the world; next to them, the workers and peasants seemed rather dirty.

China's salvation, he thought at that time, lay in overcoming the agrarian character of its popular culture. But then he became a revolutionary, went among the peasants, and discovered that

> it was those unreconstructed intellectuals who were unclean as compared with the workers and peasants, while the workers and peasants are after all the cleanest persons, cleaner than both the bourgeois and the petty-bourgeois, even though their hands are soiled and their feet smeared with cow-dung. . . .[13]

There remained, to be sure, many distasteful features of agrarian life—in that same speech in 1942 Mao characterized the workers and peasants as "illiterate, ignorant, and uncultured"—but they had that greatest of all virtues, the purity of heart that makes for social solidarity. Thus, unlike the Bolsheviks, the Chinese Communists came to power with an appreciation of the social experience of the village. By a strange twist of fate created by the circumstances of the Chinese Revolution, the Chinese Communists have been able to go behind Marxism-Leninism to those experiences out of which the modern socialist idea first emerged, in spite of the fact that they learned their formal ideology largely from the Russians.

As a result of these various influences on their thought, Mao and his comrades have a conception of socialism that tends toward a revival of the original socialist ideal. Their struggle against the simple equation of socialism with industrialism is seen on many fronts. By the late fifties they were aware that adoption of the Russian model was not going to produce the kind of socialist society they wanted; and as the dispute with the Soviet Union forced the issue, they made open departures. They rejected Stalin's idea of making agriculture the servant of industry and the farmlands the servant of the cities. The two had to develop side by side, they insisted, with equal weight in the allocation of resources. The socialist transformation of the countryside had to proceed apace with that of the cities. They rejected, moreover, the urbanism of Stalin's formula. Rather than creating large cities, toward which the bulk of the population would eventually gravitate, leaving the countryside sparsely populated (as has happened in the Soviet Union), they cultivated a decentralized form of social and economic organization through the commune system. The communes were to combine industry and agriculture; they were to be self-sufficient units, each with its own education, housing, and recreational facilities. The Chinese people were not to create sprawling metropolises.

Like Stalin, the Maoists have emphasized that their brand of socialism is to be understood as a transitional stage to communism, and have tried to read Marx's vision of mature communism into socialism. But unlike Stalin, they have done so with some realization of the distance separating them from mature communism and have made consistent efforts to harmonize their policies with their rhetoric. Thus, ever since the thirties, they have made recurring efforts to proletarianize intellectuals. Consonant with Marx's vision of communist man as Renaissance man, every Chinese must be made into an effective jack-of-all-trades. The division of labor and the distinction between manual and mental labor must be overcome in People's China. Likewise material incentives and their byproducts, materialist values and class inequalities, must be overcome. Chinese workers of all kinds must be shaped to the vision that they produce for the love of work and society, not for more rice than the next fellow. Likewise Chinese workers and peasants must be drawn fully into the political process. They must develop a mature political consciousness, and the political system of China must be made responsive to their needs and aspirations. As the rhetoric of the Cultural Revolution has re-emphasized, China must become a kind of giant Paris Commune —or federation of communes—with full democracy, integration of legislation and administration, and immediate recall of way-ward officials. Finally, China must become one huge community: "650 million united as a single man." Not only must China have the same unity that other nations enjoy (and which it has so often lacked)—common language, system of government, economy, culture—it must also have *spiritual* unity, an equality and unity of mind so complete that there are no significant breaks in the social solidarity. This quest for community explains the severity of the Maoist strictures against individualism, which go farther than anything that has appeared in European communism.*

"CREEPING REVISIONISM"

It is difficult, however, to look into the eye of utopia and keep one's balance. The Maoists have had moments of dizziness, such as the period of the Great Leap Forward in the late fifties when they dared to think that mature communism could be realized in China in a generation or less. But for the most part they have kept their balance, holding soberly to the conviction that the building

* In an article that ostensibly attacks the European Marxist revisionists (which is to say, those who characterize themselves as "socialist human-ists"), Chou Yang goes to a point which implicitly attacks Marx himself: "In advocating the return of Man to himself they are actually advocating absolute individual freedom and asking the people who live under Socialism to return to the human nature of bourgeois individualism and to restore the capitalism by which it is fostered" ("Fighting Tasks of Workers in Philosophy and Social Science," *Peking Review*, January 3, 1964).

of socialism will be a long, difficult process spanning many generations. "We have taken the first step in a journey of ten thousand *li*," declared Mao in 1949, and the same theme is struck again in the Cultural Revolution.[14]

One reason why socialist construction, as the Maoists understand it, is so difficult is the scope of their idea of socialism. The magnitude of the goal increases the distance to its realization; a genuine utopia is not realized in a day. Another reason is the danger of revisionism and capitalist restoration. Trying to make sense of what has happened in the Soviet Union, the Maoists have elaborated in the last decade a full-blown theory of the reversal of socialist construction from within. In a nutshell, their argument is this: Because socialism is a total social system, with a distinctive culture and morality as well as a distinctive form of political and economic organization, a society that is formally socialist can be twisted into neo-capitalism if the ideological remnants of bourgeois society are not rooted out. This must be done again and again. Socialist construction is consistently threatened because there are always neo-capitalist tendencies in the minds of citizens; they persist until socialism is superseded by a higher form of society.

It is this theory that provides much of the explanation for the Cultural Revolution.[15] A revolution is not complete with seizure of state power and transfer of ownership of the means of production. It is not even complete when the patterns of social organization have been rearranged. There must also be cultural revolutions to complement what has been done in political and economic affairs. Because socialist construction takes as long as it does, socialist revolution can be carried through to completion only as there are *several* cultural revolutions to keep hearts and minds pure. Revisionism appeared in Khrushchev's Russia, according to this theory, because there was no cultural revolution.

Although the danger of revisionist attitudes is universal, it is especially great among those in positions of power. Because of the temptations that their power and authority create, they are more likely to fall prey to bourgeois thinking. This, the Chinese believe, lies behind the "capitalist restoration" which the Soviet Union has suffered under Khrushchev and his successors. A privileged stratum arose which sacrificed socialism for personal and class interests. Here we touch upon a distinctive feature of Maoist thought: an awareness of the ambiguities of social power and, by implication, of the dangers involved in the use of state power in socialist construction. As good Marxist-Leninists, the Maoists insist that politics must take command and the party of the proletariat must enjoy a monopoly of state power if socialism is to be realized. "The dictatorship of the proletariat is the basic guarantee for the consolidation and development of socialism," they say. Yet at the same time they are aware, to a degree unique among Communist parties, of the tendencies toward "elitism" and "commandism" and "bureaucratism" that this strategy involves, and over the years they have devised one tactic after another to root out these tendencies. The Cultural Revolution and its frontal attack on the Party—something unprecedented in the history of communism—is but the latest example. There will always be contradictions between the leaders and the led throughout socialist construction, Mao declares, and great care must be taken lest these contradictions deepen to the point where the socialist project itself is thwarted. Socialism, he insists, implies democracy. The masses cannot simply be led; they must be drawn fully into the political process. Good cadres will listen to their views; such solidarity is the surest safeguard against the emergence of a self-serving elite.

This theory is not a recent development; it has been a central part of Maoist thought from the beginning. As early as the thirties Mao was stressing the elitist tendencies in political and other forms of leadership. It bears, moreover, a distinctively Chinese imprint, reflective of the pre-Marxist radical traditions in China. It is reminiscent of the antibureaucratic populism of groups such as the T'ai-p'ings, who cried *ta-kuan*—"Smash the Officials." European Marxists have recognized the ambiguities of leadership, too, but they have tended to explain "bureaucratism" and "commandism" in terms of the personal immorality and limitations of individuals. The Maoists in contrast have traced the problem to the nature of leadership. Their answer in turn is not simply to create new men but to create new forms of social organization as well. As Franz Schurmann has pointed out, the Chinese hope to create a non-Weberian form of social organization, one that has built-in deterrents against bureaucratization.[16]

THE OUTCOME IN DOUBT

Thus, in terms of political and other key issues in the history of socialist thought, the Chinese Communist quest for a new socialism can be interpreted as a return to the original concerns from which the socialist idea first emerged in the West. The outcome remains in doubt, however, for two principal reasons.

For one thing, Chinese industrialization has not proceeded very far. One of the reasons why the Maoists have been able so far to get around the demands of industrialization as experienced by other nations is that they have not had to face mature industrialism. Their politics and social organization can be what they have been because most of the population remain peasants. As industrialization proceeds, as the economy becomes more sophisticated, and as proletarians and professionals become a majority, they are certain to confront many of those problems which have burdened other advanced industrial nations. It would be the height of presumption to say, as so many Western commentators do, that the Chinese will necessarily fail where those who have gone before have failed: Mao is certainly right when he stresses the importance of China's distinctive history and civilization in shaping its development. But at the same time it is no more probable that the Chinese will succeed. The Chinese are unique, but they are also men; and it just could be that what finally militates against the original socialist vision is human nature itself.

The other reason why the future of Chinese socialism remains in doubt is the effect of the twin factors of the Stalinist legacy and the siege mentality. Because of both fidelity to Stalin's example and the harsh measures that military encirclement by hostile powers has necessitated (the two are not unrelated), socialist construction in China is beset with internal contradictions, so that even the most sublime aspirations often have perverse effects. Enormous faith in the masses, for example, goes hand in hand with an equally large paternalism toward them. The masses can do anything, Mao says, even move mountains, yet they must be watched over carefully lest they be led astray by revisionist notions and schemes. Demands for intellectual independence and initiative go hand in hand with cultivation of the cult of Mao. One of the main political objectives of the Chinese Communists is evidently to produce the kind of participatory politics that depends on mature consciousness and judgment on the part of the masses; the effect of biblicization of the Thought of Mao, however, is certain to be political fundamentalism. Socialist culture is trumpeted as a superior culture, yet at the same time it is interpreted as proletarian culture. This can only mean, from what the Chinese say, a vulgarized culture fit for those whom Mao himself has characterized as ignorant.[17] The Maoists manifest, as we have noted, an awareness of the dangers involved in building socialism through the power of the state, yet they do not go to the core of the problem. Elitism is attacked, yet the notion of the vanguard, which is its ultimate source, remains sacrosanct. Socialism is presented as a catholic ideal (the populism in Maoism is another of its distinctive features in the Communist world), yet the Chinese Communists return again and again to celebration of certain classes over others and cultivation of class struggle as a means to the extermination of some classes.

THE TWO REALISMS

It is not the Stalinist legacy and the siege mentality alone that account for the contradictions in Chinese socialism. When Maoism is seen in the light of the development of the socialist idea, we can see that the sources of these contradictions lie even further back, and that they reflect conceptual problems which have troubled socialism from the beginning.

The significance of the Chinese experiment lies in the attempt to hold big dreams analogous to those of the early (Western) socialists together with realism about strategy. Ever since Marx this problem has troubled socialists, and the Chinese approach to it is obviously a distinctive one. Yet is their realism sufficiently deep? Few things are more Marxist-Leninist than the notion that politics takes command in socialist construction, and it was this assumption, along with one or two others, that led to the shrinkage of the original socialist vision. One moral that could be drawn from the history of socialism is that state power is simply not adequate to the full scope of the original vision, and that attempts to rely solely on state power lead to shrinkage of the vision and often to its perversion as well. On this point the early socialists appear to have been more realistic than the "realists" who followed them.

The Marxists have been right, on the other hand, in insisting that there are some features of the socialist vision that can only be achieved through politics, given the conditions imposed by industrial society. The future of socialism depends to a considerable extent on the combination of these two types of realism: using politics as fully and effectively as possible where it is capable of yielding positive results and at the same time knowing its limits and shifting to other strategies where it is not appropriate.

The Chinese could make an important contribution in this regard *if* their socialist project continues its present trend away from Marx, Lenin, and Stalin and back toward aspects of the Chinese tradition, and *if* the external pressure upon them reduces.

The larger question—which will get still another test as Chinese industrialization matures—is the one with which we began. Are the social and spiritual ideals of the original vision really compatible with industrialism? Like the early socialists, the Chinese Communists simply assert that they are. But it remains assertion, not yet explained or demonstrated. So the question lingers on.

NOTES

1. Cf., for example, the recent article by Stanley Moore, "Utopian Themes in Marx and Mao: A Critique for Modern Revisionists," *The Monthly Review,* vol. 21, no. 2, June 1969. Discussing the status of the inheritance from original Marxism in humanist revisionism in Europe on the one hand, and Maoism on the other, Moore concludes that "viewing socialism as a prelude to communism has proved a serious hindrance to facing, rationally and empirically, the problems of improving existing socialist societies." His recommendation is that socialism be viewed simply as a form of economic organization.

2. Martin Buber, *Paths in Utopia* (Boston: Beacon Press, 1949), chapters 1, 2, and 8.

3. Hubert Bourgin, *Fourier: Contributions à l'étude du socialisme français* (Paris, 1905), p. 237.

4. George Lichtheim, *Marxism: An Historical and Critical Study* (New York: Praeger, 1961), pp. 122–23.

5. Because of the limitations of space, I use the term "Bolshevism" as a shorthand formula to refer primarily to the doctrine of the Bolsheviks *while in power* and not to the many other theories (often contradicting the later ones) to which figures like Lenin and Trotsky subscribed in the twists and turns of the earlier years.

6. Nikolai Lenin, *State and Revolution* (New York: International Publishers, 1932), pp. 38–39.

7. Cf. *Problems of Leninism* (New York: International Publishers), p. 356. "We are fifty or a hundred years behind the advanced countries. We must make good this lag in ten years. Either we do it or they crush us."

8. *Works*, vol. 26, p. 261.

9. "On the New Stage," Stuart Schram translation, *The Political Thought of Mao Tse-tung* (New York, Praeger, 1963), p. 113.

10. As my co-editor has pointed out to me, the fact of imperialism has played a major role in Mao's theory of the Chinese Revolution ever since the 1920s. The Bolsheviks, on the other hand, came to stress imperialism *after* 1917, and this difference is reflected in their theory of the Russian Revolution.

11. The distinctiveness of Mao's emphasis on the peasantry can be stressed too much. As Karl Wittfogel has pointed out, particularly in "The Legend of 'Maoism,'" *The China Quarterly*, no. 1, 1960, it is an oversimplification to say that the notion of a revolutionary role for the peasantry is not anticipated in Marx and Lenin. But Mao's emphasis is so different as to constitute a genuine doctrinal innovation. As Stuart Schram points out, "one must distinguish between the idea that the peasantry must constitute the chief *force* of the Asian revolution, and the idea that the Communist Party, which directs the revolution, can issue from the peasantry. The first notion is indeed of Leninist origin. The second most emphatically is not." And here Mao's originality comes in. (*op. cit.*, p. 31.)

12. I do not mean to suggest that the substance of traditional Chinese social thought is being reproduced in the socialism of the Chinese Communists. There are obvious continuities, to be sure, but there are equally obvious discontinuities, such as those that Arthur Wright has emphasized in "Struggle vs. Harmony: Symbols of Competing Values in Modern China," *World Politics*, vol. VI, no. I, October 1955.

13. Mao Tse-tung, "On Literature and Art," *Selected Works*, vol. 4, p. 72.

14. "On People's Democratic Dictatorship," *Selected Works*, vol. 4, p. 422.

15. The term "cultural revolution" has long been a part of the Communist lexicon. Throughout the thirties and forties in the Soviet Union there were appeals for cultural revolution in the name of many of the same objectives that the Chinese have in 1965–69. The cultural transformation that such revolution was supposed to produce was usually construed, however, primarily in quantitative terms—elimination of illiteracy, raising the level of formal education of the masses, and so on. The Chinese themselves used the term that way until recently. In the late fifties they were speaking of cultural revolution largely as a war against peasant backwardness. The theory that has developed since 1965 is distinctive in at least two respects: the emphasis on struggle as a means of change and the linking of cultural change to the larger theory of revisionism.

16. Franz Schurmann, *Ideology and Organization in Communist China* (Berkeley: University of California Press, 1966), p. xlv.

17. Few things are more Stalinist than the notion of "proletarian culture." The Chinese usage appears to be burdened with those same conceptual ambiguities that Trotsky pointed out in *Literature and Revolution* (Ann Arbor: University of Michigan Press, Ann Arbor Books, 1960).

Notes on contributors

FELICIANO CARINO's essay reflects his Filipino citizenship. A graduate of Philippine Christian College and Union Theological Seminary in Manila, he later began a doctorate at Princeton Theological Seminary. While completing his dissertation, Mr. Carino works on Student Affairs for the United Presbyterian Church of the U.S.A.

BRUCE DOUGLASS was staff secretary, in Geneva, of the Political Commission of the World Student Christian Federation, 1965–68. A U.S. citizen, he graduated from the College of William and Mary and Yale Divinity School and is now a graduate student in political science at Duke University. He edited *Reflections on Protest* (John Knox Press, 1967) and his essays have appeared in *Student World* and *Union Seminary Quarterly*.

TOM ENGELHARDT, a New Yorker, is an activist in the Committee of Concerned Asian Scholars, an organization of dissenting Americans formed in 1968. Mr. Engelhardt has a B.A. from Yale and an M.A. in Far Eastern Studies from Harvard. He assisted Jonathan Spence with *To Change China* (Little, Brown & Co., 1969).

STEPHEN FITZGERALD, a graduate of the University of Tasmania and the University of Hong Kong (in Chinese), finished a Ph.D. at the Australian National University on China's policies toward the overseas Chinese. For six years he was a Foreign Service Officer of the Australian government. He visited China in 1968, and is presently a research fellow in Far Eastern History at the A.N.U. His articles on China, Taiwan, and the overseas Chinese have appeared in *The China Quarterly, Far Eastern Economic Review,* and Australian publications.

EDWARD FRIEDMAN is assistant professor of political science at the University of Wisconsin. He received his B.A. from Brandeis

University, his M.A. and Ph.D. from Harvard, and spent two years in Formosa, 1964–66. Mr. Friedman's articles have appeared in *Asian Survey, Journal of Asian Studies, Journal of Asian & African Studies, Comparative Studies in Society & History,* and *Dissent.* He is co-editor of a book to be titled *America's Asia* (Pantheon, 1970) and has a forthcoming book on "The Chinese Revolutionary Party" as well as a work in progress on Chinese foreign policy.

NEALE HUNTER is an Australian who taught at the Foreign Languages Institute in Shanghai from 1965 to 1967. After graduating in French Literature from the University of Melbourne, he pursued Chinese and Japanese studies at Canberra. Since returning from China, Mr. Hunter has written (with Colin MacKerras) *China Observed* (Praeger, 1968) and *Shanghai Journal* (Praeger, 1969).

JON SAARI graduated from Yale and is a doctoral candidate in modern Chinese and American History at Harvard. He taught for two years at New Asia College with the Yale-in-China Program, and spent 1969 in Hong Kong and Taiwan doing research for his dissertation, which deals with the experiences of Chinese students in the United States.

KAZUHIKO SUMIYA, a Japanese, did graduate study in Vienna, and is now professor of economics at Rikkyo University in Tokyo. His writings include *Max Weber Kenyu* ("Studies in Max Weber") and *Kyodotai no Dhiheki Kozo Ron* ("The Theory of Historical Structure of Community"). The present essay appeared in the Japanese review, *Tenbo.*

ROSS TERRILL is an Australian teaching at Harvard University. A graduate of Melbourne University, he visited China in 1964, and has published articles on China and other issues in Asian and Communist politics in *The New Republic, The Atlantic Monthly, Problems of Communism, The China Quarterly, Politics,* and *Crosscurrents.* He edited *China Profile* (Friendship Press, 1969) and is at work on a book about the U.S. and China (to be published by Atheneum). He is a contributing editor of *The Atlantic Monthly*.

RAY WYLIE, born in Belfast but now a Canadian, has an M.A. in history from the University of Toronto. From 1965 to 1967 he taught at the Foreign Languages Institute in Shanghai, and since then has published articles on China in the *Bulletin of the Atomic Scientists* and other journals. He is a doctoral candidate in Chinese Politics at the School of African and Oriental Studies of the University of London.

based on scholarship. Here is a cornucopia edited *The Apple*

... was ... born in Belfast but now a Christian, ... A.C. in history from the University of Toronto. From 1950 to 1970 he taught in the Foreign Languages Institute of Shanghai, and since then has published ... ... this book, and is the author of several ... and other journals. He is now the general consultant for Chinese Studies for the School of African and Oriental Studies of the University of London.

Index